The CIS, the EU and Russia

Studies in Central and Eastern Europe

Edited for the International Council for Central and East European Studies by
Roger E. Kanet, University of Miami, USA

Titles include:

Graeme Gill (*editor*)
POLITICS IN THE RUSSIAN REGIONS

Katlijn Malfliet, Lien Verpoest and Evgeny Vinokurov (*editors*)
THE CIS, THE EU AND RUSSIA
The Challenges of Integration

Forthcoming titles include:

Thomas Bremer (*editor*)
RELIGION AND THE CONCEPTUAL BOUNDARY IN CENTRAL AND EASTERN EUROPE

Joan DeBardeleben (*editor*)
THE BOUNDARIES OF EU ENLARGEMENT
Finding a Place for Neighbours

Stephen Hutchings (*editor*)
RUSSIA AND ITS OTHER(S) ON FILM
Screening Intercultural Dialogue

Roger E. Kanet (*editor*)
RUSSIA
Emerging Great Power

Rebecca Kay (*editor*)
GENDER, EQUALITY AND DIFFERENCE DURING AND AFTER STATE SOCIALISM

Stanislav J. Kirschbaum (*editor*)
THE MEANING OF EUROPE, CENTRAL EUROPE AND THE EU

John Pickles and Robert M. Jenkins (*editors*)
GLOBALIZATION AND REGIONALIZATION IN POST-SOCIALIST ECONOMIES
Common Economic Spaces of Europe

John Pickles and Robert M. Jenkins (*editors*)
STATE AND SOCIETY IN POST-SOCIALIST ECONOMIES

Stephen Velychenko (*editor*)
UKRAINE, THE EU AND RUSSIA
History, Culture, International Relations

Stephen White (*editor*)
MEDIA, CULTURE AND SOCIETY IN PUTIN'S RUSSIA

Stephen White (*editor*)
POLITICS AND THE RULING GROUP IN PUTIN'S RUSSIA

Studies in Central and Eastern Europe
Series Standing Order ISBN 0–230–51682–3
(*outside North America only*)

You can receive future titles in this series as they are published by placing a standing order.
Please contact your bookseller or, in case of difficulty, write to us at the address below with
your name and address, the title of the series and the ISBN quoted above.

Customer Services Department, Macmillan Distribution Ltd, Houndmills, Basingstoke,
Hampshire RG21 6XS, England

The CIS, the EU and Russia

The Challenges of Integration

Edited by

Katlijn Malfliet
Institute for International and European Policy
Catholic University of Leuven, Belgium

Lien Verpoest
Institute for International and European Policy
Catholic University of Leuven, Belgium

and

Evgeny Vinokurov
Institute for World Economy and International Relations (IMEMO)
Russian Academy of Sciences, Moscow, Russia

First published 2007 by
PALGRAVE MACMILLAN
Houndmills, Basingstoke, Hampshire RG21 6XS and
175 Fifth Avenue, New York, N.Y. 10010
Companies and representatives throughout the world.

PALGRAVE MACMILLAN is the global academic imprint of the Palgrave
Macmillan division of St. Martin's Press, LLC and of Palgrave Macmillan Ltd.
Macmillan® is a registered trademark in the United States, United Kingdom
and other countries. Palgrave is a registered trademark in the European
Union and other countries.

ISBN-13: 978–0–230–52106–3
ISBN-10: 0–230–52106–1

This book is printed on paper suitable for recycling and made from fully
managed and sustained forest sources. Logging, pulping and manufacturing
processes are expected to conform to the environmental regulations of the
country of origin.

A catalogue record for this book is available from the British Library.

Library of Congress Cataloging-in-Publication Data
    The CIS, the EU and Russia : the challenges of integration / edited by
Katlijn Malfliet, Lien Verpoest and Evgeny Vinokurov.
        p. cm.
    Includes bibliographical references and index.
    ISBN-10: 0–230–52106–1 (cloth)
    ISBN-13: 978–0–230–52106–3 (cloth)
        1. European Union – Former Soviet republics. 2. European
Union – Russia (Federation) 3. Former Soviet republics – Economic
conditions. 4. Russia (Federation) – Economic conditions – 1991–.
    I. Malfliet, Katlijn. II. Verpoest, Lien, 1977– III. Vinokurov, Evgeny.
HC240.25.F6C57 2007   2006052963
337.1'420947—dc22

10 9 8 7 6 5 4 3 2
16 15 14 13 12 11 10 09 08

Printed and bound in Great Britain by
Antony Rowe Ltd, Chippenham and Eastbourne

Contents

List of Figures, Tables and Annex

Figures

Tables

Annex

Notes on the Contributors

Mikhail A. Beznosov is a PhD candidate in political science at the University of Arizona, Tucson, and an affiliate of Kharkov State University (where he earned a PhD in sociology). He is the author of articles and chapters that have appeared in a number of Ukrainian journals and books. His current research focuses on relations among FSU (former Soviet Union) states, Russian and Ukrainian domestic politics, and post-communist political markets.

Tom Casier is Assistant Professor and Programme Director of the MA in European Studies at the University of Maastricht (The Netherlands). He holds an MA in International Relations from the Université Libre de Bruxelles (Belgium) and a PhD in Political Science from the University of Leuven (KU Leuven, 1995). He lectures and researches in the field of International Relations, Central and East European Studies and European integration. His current research focuses on Russia's foreign policy and the European Union's Neighbourhood Policy.

Antoaneta Dimitrova is Lecturer at the Department of Public Administration at the University of Leiden. She holds an MA in European Integration and a PhD, both from the University of Limerick. Her current research focuses on the development of institutionalist frameworks to account for processes of Europeanization in European Union member states, and problems with the transposition of directives. She continues to be engaged in comparative research on democratization in Central and Eastern Europe. In Leiden, she lectures on various aspects of European Union politics and policies, democratization and institutionalist theories. In addition to her courses at the Department of Public Administration in Leiden, she has lectured as visiting professor at numerous European studies programmes in Germany, Norway, Slovakia, Bulgaria and Turkey.

Rilka Dragneva graduated in law from the University of Sofia, Bulgaria, and holds a Master's and Doctorate degree from the University of Sussex, UK. In 1999, she joined the Institute of East European Law and Russian Studies, University of Leiden, The Netherlands. Her research interests cover the international and comparative aspects of company and commercial law, the law of (regional) economic integration, legal reform, legal institutions and development with a special reference to the countries of Central and Eastern Europe. Her teaching profile at Leiden included LLM courses on International/EU and Comparative Company and Commercial Law, Corporate Governance, and Private Law in Eastern Europe. She is currently completing a post-doctoral research project on legal harmonization and economic integration in the CIS.

Irina Kobrinskaya graduated from Moscow State University. She received her PhD from the US and Canada Studies Institute in Moscow in 1983. Since 2002, she has worked as Executive Director of the Foundation for Prospective Studies and Initiatives (Russian think-tank) and as a leading research fellow at the IMEMO of the Russian Academy of Science. She is the author of four and co-author of numerous 30 monographs and articles in periodicals on domestic and foreign policy, international security, published in Russia, USA, Sweden, Poland, Norway, France, Germany, Bulgaria and various other European Countries.

Gennadi Kurdiukov is Head of the Chair on Constitutional and International Law in Ul'ianov-Lenin Kazan' State University. He has published on the issues of Russian federalism and constitutional law.

Katlijn Malfliet studied Law and Philosophy at the Catholic University of Leuven (KU Leuven). She received an MA in East European Studies from the Universities of Ghent, Brussels and Leuven, and a PhD in Legal Science from KU Leuven. At this moment she is Research Director Central and Eastern Europe at the Institute for International and European Policy (at KU Leuven). She lectures on Political Institutions, Policies and Law of the Central and East European countries. Her research and publications are in the field of Russian and East European political institutions and law.

Holger Moroff has published academic articles on EU foreign policy, security theory, and political corruption. He was senior researcher at the Institut für Europäische Politik (IEP) in Berlin and is lecturer at the University of Jena. He holds Masters degrees in Political Science and European Studies from Washington University in St Louis and the University of Bonn. He is currently conducting research on the EU policies towards Russia as Fellow of the European Foreign and Security Studies Programme.

Marius Vahl is Research Fellow at the Centre for European Policy Studies (CEPS) in Brussels and a PhD candidate at the Catholic University of Leuven on a thesis on EU–Russia relations. He received an

MA in International Relations from Johns Hopkins University in 1999. At CEPS, he works in the European Neighbourhood Programme on relations between the expanding European Union (EU) and its neighbours, focusing on EU relations with Eastern neighbours and with EFTA. He has published extensively on EU neighbourhood policy, including on EU relations with Russia, Ukraine, Moldova and EFTA countries, as well as on the Northern Dimension initiative, Europeanization and conflict prevention, and regional cooperation in the Black Sea region.

Lien Verpoest studied Slavonic Languages and Eastern European Culture (KU Leuven and Saint Petersburg State University) and International Relations and Conflict Management (Lund University, Sweden and KU Leuven). She also obtained an MA in Eastern European Studies from the Universities of Ghent, Brussels and Leuven. Interested in the application of IR theories on Russia–EU Relations, and more particularly in studying the post-Soviet region from a neo-institutionalist vantage point, she is currently working as a Research Fellow at the Institute for International and European Policy (KU Leuven) on her PhD 'Institutional isomorphism in the Slavic Core of the Commonwealth of Independent States: a comparative analysis of institutional change during post-communist transition'. She has published articles and co-edited publications on the foreign policy of Russia, Ukraine and Belarus towards the EU.

Evgeny Vinokurov is post-doctoral researcher at the Institute for World Economy and International Relations (IMEMO) of the Russian Academy of Sciences in Moscow. He received his LLM from the University of Göttingen and a PhD from Kaliningrad State University. He has published on EU–Russian relations, Kaliningrad, and a theory of enclaves.

John P. Willerton is Associate Professor of Political Science at the University of Arizona, Tucson. He is the author of *Patronage and Politics in the USSR* (1991) and over three dozen articles and chapters dealing with various facets of Soviet and post-Soviet Russian domestic politics and foreign policy. His current research focuses on Russian foreign policy and relations with FSU (former Soviet Union) states, the CIS and the Russian presidency.

List of Abbreviations

ACP	African, Caribbean and Pacific group of states
AP	Action Plan
APEC	Asia–Pacific Economic Cooperation
BNF	Belarusian Popular Front (*Belaruski Narodny Front*)
CAC	Central Asian Cooperation Forum
CBC	cross-border cooperation
CEE(Cs)	Central and Eastern European (countries)
CES (CEES)	Common (European) Economic Space
CFDP	Council for Foreign and Defence Policy
CFSP	Common Foreign and Security Policy
CIS	Commonwealth of Independent States
CMEA	Council for Mutual Economic Assistance
CS	EU Common Strategy on Russia
CST(O)	Collective Security Treaty (Organization)
EBRD	European Bank for Reconstruction and Development
EC	European Communities
EEA	European Economic Area
EEC	European Economic Community
EFTA	European Free Trade Area
EIB	European Investment Bank
ENP	European Neighbourhood Policy
ESDP	European Security and Defence Policy
EU	European Union
EurAsEC	Eurasian Economic Community
FRG	Federal Republic of Germany
FTA	free trade agreement
FSU	former Soviet Union states
GATT	General Agreement on Tariffs and Trade
GDP	gross domestic product
GDR	German Democratic Republic
GSP	generalized system of preferences
GUUAM (GUAM)	Georgia, Ukraine, (Uzbekistan), Azerbaijan and Moldova group
JHA	Justice and Home Affairs

IMF	International Monetary Fund
IPA	Inter-Parliamentary Assembly of the CIS
MEDT	Ministry for Economic Development and Trade
MFA	Ministry of Foreign Affairs
MFN	most favoured nation
NAFTA	North American Free Trade Agreement
NATO	North Atlantic Treaty Organization
ND	Northern Dimension
NGO	non-governmental organization
NIS	Newly Independent States
OECD	Organisation for Economic Co-operation and Development
OSCE	Organization for Security and Cooperation in Europe
PCA	Partnership and Cooperation Agreement
PPC	Permanent Partnership Council
PSC	Political and Security Committee
RF	Russian Federation
SES	Single Economic Space
TACIS	Technical Assistance to the Commonwealth of Independent States
TCM	thousand cubic metres
UN	United Nations Organization
USSR	Union of Soviet Socialist Republics
VAT	value-added tax
WTO	World Trade Organization

Preface by the General Editor

When the International Council for Central and East European Studies (ICCEES) was founded at the first international and multidisciplinary conference of scholars working in this field, held in Banff, Alberta, Canada, on 4–7 September 1974, it was given the name International Committee for Soviet and East European Studies (ICSEES). Its major purpose was to provide for greater exchange between research centres and scholars around the world who were devoted to the study of the USSR and the communist states and societies of Eastern Europe. These developments were the main motivation for bringing together the very different national organizations in the field and for forming a permanent committee of their representatives, which would serve as an umbrella organization, as well as a promoter of closer cooperation. Four national scholarly associations launched ICSEES at the Banff conference: the American Association for the Advancement of Slavic Studies (AAASS), the National Association for Soviet and East European Studies in Great Britain (NASEES), the British Universities Association of Slavists (BUAS), and the Canadian Association of Slavists (CAS).

Over the past three decades six additional Congresses have been held: in Garmisch-Partenkirchen, Germany, 1980; Washington, USA, 1985; Harrogate, UK, 1990; Warsaw, Poland, 1995; Tampere, Finland, 2000; and Berlin, Germany, 2005. The next Congress is scheduled for 2010 in Stockholm, Sweden. The original four national associations that sponsored the first congress have been joined by an additional seventeen full and six associate member associations, with significantly more than a thousand scholars participating at each of the recent congresses.

It is now a little over three decades since scholars felt the need to coordinate the efforts in the 'free world' to describe and analyse the Communist political systems, their societies and economies, and East–West relations in particular. Halfway through this period, the Communist system collapsed, the region that was the object of study was reorganized, and many of the new states that emerged set out on a path of democratic development, economic growth, and, in many cases, inclusion in Western institutions. The process turned out to be complex, and there were setbacks. Yet, by 2004, the European Union as well as the North Atlantic Treaty Organization had welcomed those post-Communist states that had met all of the requirements for membership. Not all of the applicant states achieved this objective; but the process is ongoing. For this reason, perhaps even more than before, the region that encompassed the former Communist world demands study, explanation and analysis, as both centripetal and centrifugal forces are at work in each state and across the region. We are most fortunate that the community of scholars addressing these issues now includes many astute analysts from the region itself.

ROGER E. KANET

Introduction

The concept

This book tries to look with a fresh eye at the integration processes in Europe. The challenge of integration in post-Cold War Europe has been considered as a process driven by the European Union. It is beyond doubt that this successful integration structure became attractive to post-communist countries in their search for regime change and economic progress. The period of steadily progressing European integration and the accompanying movement of European enlargement towards new member states seems, however, to be at an end. In a field of rapidly developing international relations new alliances arise, challenging the European Union as the sole core of integration in Europe. Perhaps these new cooperation and integration mechanisms will be inspired by the well designed EU integration methods and techniques; and perhaps they will rely on the same four freedoms, as these represent a modern form of transnational cooperation between states. Although they might not copy the European Union altogether, they will take away the uniqueness of the European Union as the sole post-Cold War integration mechanism in European territory. Here, we have discussed the Commonwealth of Independent States and, within this loose international cooperation structure, other more focused integration mechanisms, such as the Single Economic Space, the Eurasian Economic Community, and the Tashkent Security Cooperation Treaty. The challenges of integration on the territory of the former Soviet Union are among the most thrilling stories in current international relations.

The various approaches to integration processes in the wider European continent, as presented in this book, do not start from an assumption of an ever widening European Union. Instead, we regard two major powers in the post-Soviet space: on the one hand, the enlarged European Union and, on the other, Russia, who now possesses not only the ambition to become a self-conscious nation with great power but who also has the means to do so. Russia, as repeated throughout the book, is willing to invest in further integration with its neighbours. The perception of the impact and role of these two powers in the European theatre becomes increasingly important.

Each of the chapters of the book intends to contribute to the discussion on future international developments in the post-Soviet space, and searches for an interdisciplinary approach to the challenges of integration for 12 independent states (15 republics of the former Soviet Union minus the three Baltic states, which from the very beginning firmly opted for EU integration). It focuses on Russia and the Western Newly Independent States; namely, Ukraine, Belarus and Moldova. In spite of the often pronounced scepticism on a possible future for the Commonwealth of Independent States (CIS), the contributors to this volume see several developments inducing new integration mechanisms in the post-Soviet territory. The loose cooperation structures between these states managed to survive and gain some strength, especially the regional initiatives for integration within the CIS territory. Apart from the CIS, this includes such frameworks as the Eurasian Economic Community (EurAsEC), the Single Economic Space (SES), the Shanghai Cooperation, the Russia–Belarus Union, the Tashkent Cooperation Treaty, and GUAM (Georgia, Ukraine, Armenia and Moldova). The present situation poses multiple challenges for all participants involved: to each and every individual state in the post-Soviet space and, of course, the European Union itself. Furthermore, we thought it interesting to analyse the link between various integration mechanisms, state policies and elite interests in the territory of the former Soviet Union.

(Re-)integration in the post-Soviet space is a very recent and not particularly advanced phenomenon. The CIS marks its fifteenth anniversary in 2006. It is still a youngster among international cooperation structures.

However modest the Commonwealth's achievements might be so far, it cannot be ruled out as a failure. The CIS and several other integration frameworks have shown resilience throughout the 1990s and 2000s. They have not only managed to survive but have also advanced considerably with regard to regulatory convergence and mutual recognition arrangements.

One might be tempted to conclude that the CIS should both look at the European Union as *the* successful integration project and learn from its experience. This thesis should, however, not be taken for granted. Integration within the post-Soviet space cannot be a mere analogy of the EU integration process since it is unfolding in its specific conditions of economic and political transformation combined with the persisting, unavoidable and specific gravity of Russia.

The political, economic and military prevalence of Russia is, indeed, a major factor for integration in the post-Soviet space. Russia takes the lead in nearly all multilateral agreements. It has also developed an extensive web of bilateral agreements with its neighbours. Russia considers the whole of the post-Soviet space to be its natural sphere of interest – particularly regarding security and economics – and it acts accordingly. This is well reflected in the content of this book: seven of the ten chapters focus explicitly or implicitly on aspects of Russia's various integration arrangements with the countries of the former Soviet Union as well as the EU.

Undoubtedly, another major gravitational force for the post-Soviet states is the European Union. In May 2004, the EU launched its European Neighbourhood Policy (ENP) as a new approach to further enlargement strategies. That policy is not without ambition, as it exceeds the borders of Europe as a continent. The European Union is, however, not the only actor worrying about friendly relations with its neighbours. Russia is also very active in redefining its state concept and building its ties with neighbouring independent states, which happen to be former republics of the Soviet Union. Presumably, what we can call 'the New Neighbourhood Policy of Russia' finds its roots in 1991 with the declaration that the Soviet Union no longer existed (the Belavezha treaty).

How will the European Union and the Commonwealth of Independent States relate to each other within a decade? Perhaps the area in question will turn into a distinctive hub-and-spoke system with the EU as the sole hub. Another scenario is that the Newly Independent States will be divided in two groups: the ones that allied with, or even became, members of the European Union (although such a scenario is less optimistically envisioned after the negative referenda on the EU Constitution) and another group of pro-Russian countries who allied with Russia through various integration arrangements. Perhaps the Russia–Belarus Union state will then be headed by President Putin. Or perhaps Russia will by then have absorbed some states (such as Belarus) and regions with frozen conflicts (such as Transnistria and South Ossetia) within the borders of its own state.

Today it becomes apparent that the New Independent States are not immutable as political and legal entities. The former Union republics are going through a 'kaleidoscope stage', during which the New

Independent States form an assortment of new regional cooperation and integration structures. On the subnational level, we also see colours and structures changing; frozen conflicts are carefully watched by Russia, the European Union, and the USA. All three powers play major roles in designing this kaleidoscope process.

It is obvious that the situation in CIS territory is rapidly changing and the desire for stability will only increase. Soon we can expect a feeling of fatigue, and a longing for more stability. Our perspective is that we should look at this development in a pan-European framework. One reason for the rapid change is that the CIS is not hesitating to copy or, better, to utilize eclectically the legal texts as well as the political experiences of the European Union. But the European Union has lost its legitimacy as Europe's representative. Forced to change its profile and ambitions, the European Union is seriously thinking about a new design – for example, a core Europe surrounded by a loose confederal structure. Moreover, the European Union launched its far reaching European Neighbourhood Policy (ENP). While Russia is not a party to this, the majority of other post-Soviet states are.

How compatible are these (EU and CIS) integration processes? CIS integration mechanisms, and especially the rhetoric that was used, reminded us of EU phrases and procedures. Indeed, why reinvent the wheel if the European Union proves to be such a successful example of integration? However, with the move toward the four EU–Russia Common Spaces, on the one hand, and Russia taking the lead of the SES with Belarus, Ukraine and Kazakhstan, on the other, the question of compatibility arises regarding these so-called integration mechanisms. The compatibility of regulatory convergence and free trade arrangements, let alone the more developed forms of integration, such as a customs union, cannot be taken for granted.

In the field of human rights, the Venice Commission of the Council of Europe published its advice on the compatibility of the European and CIS treaties on human rights in the early stage of CIS development. Economically, there is a serious dilemma of the EU–Russia Common Economic Space, on the one hand, and the Single Economic Space within the CIS, on the other. In the field of security and defence, the Collective Security Treaty Organization (CSTO) seems to be developing a unified staff, after the CIS Military Coordination Staff was shut down. However, we again see that a number of countries are pursuing military-economic and geopolitical interests that differ from those of Russia.

Kto kogo? Will Russia be strong enough to renew and relegitimate its geopolitical influence, and what choices will the individual post-Soviet countries make?

The structure

This book comprises ten chapters written by researchers from Russia, Belgium, the Netherlands and the United States. It is divided into three interrelated parts. The first introductory part is entitled 'In Pursuit of Integration in the Post-Soviet Space'. It contains chapters which aim at providing a more general picture of the CIS to date. Chapter 1, written by Irina Kobrinskaya, 'The Post-Soviet Space: From the USSR to the Commonwealth of Independent States and Beyond', contains an analysis of the main factors (domestic political, socio-economic, security, institutional and foreign) and actors (political, business and so on) influencing the developments in the post-Soviet space since the demise of the USSR, and the changes in conceptual approaches to Russia and the New Independent States. Russia's policy in the post-Soviet space is assessed against a background of changing national and international priorities. Special attention is given to the changes in the decision-making process regarding the CIS and the legitimacy of the policy from the perspective of the elite and societal support in Russia.

From this point, we proceed to a discussion on the 'Russian Approaches to Integration in the Post-Soviet Space in the 2000s' by Evgeny Vinokurov. The author sets the general context of Russia's global and regional vectors of integration. Two vectors, the CIS and the EU, form the focus of this contribution. It is argued that Russian integration politics within the post-Soviet space in the 2000s can be divided into two periods that approximately coincide with the first and the beginning of the second of Putin's terms in power. The first period has shown the gradual move towards a greater role of economic considerations, which is based on the desire to defend national economic interests. The beginning of the second period of Putin's presidency has demonstrated the reassertion of the old paradigms. Considerations for reasserting the Russian zone of influence on the post-Soviet space are gaining ground at the expense of the pragmatic spirit of the benefit/cost calculations. It is argued further that Russia employs a wide variety of means to push the CIS states toward integration. Russia is ready to pay a high price while hoping that integration will pay off threefold – economically, in terms of security, and geopolitically – by asserting Russia's leading role in the post-Soviet space and increasing its weight in the global arena.

With the framework in place, we proceed to John P. Willerton and Mikhail A. Beznosov's chapter on 'Russia's Pursuit of its Eurasian Security Interests: Weighing the CIS and Alternative Bilateral–Multilateral Arrangements'. The study outlines the results of a project that entailed creating and analysing a database of all CIS security treaties from

1992–2004, with the goal of examining the dynamics of regional security and economic negotiations among the FSU states. Nearly a decade and a half of extensive negotiation has yielded a complex set of arrangements that represent varying levels of collective security for different groups of FSU–CIS states. The authors argue that FSU–CIS regional security interests have advanced by both multilateral and bilateral means. With no state seceding its sovereignty, and a resurgent Russia continuing to assert its 'natural' regional leadership role, any region-wide collective security arrangement will have to be sufficiently flexible to maintain all states' active engagement. The multi-tiered approach that FSU states have taken has a logic that permits engagement with unilateral discretion. In this regard, the CIS's past achievements and future promise should not be discounted. The analysis of the multilateral CIS security architecture in 1992–2004 reveals that a workable foundation of understandings and arrangements was laid.

At this point in the book, we take a look at the other side of the story. Part II delves into the complex relationship between the EU and the post-Soviet space. The three chapters of this part are closely interlinked, approaching the problem from different perspectives. While Tom Casier attaches more importance to the issue of norms and values in the EU's relations with third countries in the framework of the ENP and Russia, the institutionalist approach undergirds both Holger Moroff's and Marius Vahl's contributions. Moroff looks at the EU as an actor within the post-Soviet space, while Vahl gets to the heart of EU–Russian relations from a comparative perspective.

Chapter 4, 'The Clash of Integration Processes? The Shadow Effect of the Enlarged EU on its Eastern Neighbours' by Tom Casier, focuses on the ENP of the EU, which aims to establish privileged and differentiated relations with the states surrounding the enlarged Union. The objective of this policy is to create stability around the EU by offering the new neighbouring states the opportunity to share the benefits of European integration without offering them the prospect of accession. The paper analyses the ENP via some constructivist concepts that have already been applied to enlargement. The central question is whether the ENP will be characterized by a compelling 'logic of appropriateness' (Schimmelfennig),[1] similar to the one underlying the most recent enlargement wave. The political conditionality on which the ENP is based does not fundamentally differ from the conditionality on which enlargement was based. The crucial incentive, however, is absent: new neighbours can yield some of the fruits of European integration but lack the prospect of membership. The chapter investigates the hypothesis that the nature of enlargement is characterized by certain paradoxes (that is, it creates external effects that run against the Union's founding principles) that might force the EU into a logic of appropriateness. Casier elaborates on the clash of two integration processes. He remarks that, first, the strategies of Russia and the EU differ; second, the two regional forces have different interests in the area; and third, the overlapping integration processes in the CIS and EU are different in nature.

Holger Moroff, the author of Chapter 5, 'EU Policies Towards Russia: Secondary Integration by Association?', starts with the following question: Is the EU a collective actor or a loose network of actors in its foreign policy domain? He concludes that out of a foreign policy project of member states (EC/EU integration) grew a foreign policy actor in its own right, and with its own new policies. The EU policy towards Russia as its largest and arguably most important neighbour is a very telling test case for the functioning of EU policies against the backdrop of potential competition and cooperation within their overlapping 'near abroads'.

In Chapter 6, 'EU–Russia Relations in EU Neighbourhood Policies', Marius Vahl analyses EU–Russian relations from a comparative perspective. He also frames his subject in the context of the EU foreign policy. EU relations with neighbouring countries and regions were the main priorities of the Common Foreign and Security Policy at its inception in the early 1990s. While Russia and the other former Soviet republics were one of the stated priorities, it is argued that EU relations with the countries of the CIS have subsequently been least developed. In the course of the 1990s, Russia emerged as the EU's principal partner in the CIS. Vahl demonstrates that the EU may now be turning away from this 'Russia first' policy, focusing its efforts on developing relations with the other countries of the CIS. This is due to a confluence of factors, including EU enlargement, the accumulating EU competences in foreign policy, growing differences among the countries of the CIS with regard to their political and economic systems and policies, and their goals in relation to the EU. The most important reason for the absence of a real 'strategic partnership' is, however, that the two sides have different conceptions of what such a partnership entails in practice.

The third part of the book consists of four elaborate case studies. Lien Verpoest looks into the parallels of institutional integration in Ukraine and Belarus. Rilka Dragneva and Antoaneta Dimitrova provide a well-grounded case study of Ukraine torn between integration with Russia and the EU. Katlijn Malfliet and Gennadi Kurdiukov's chapter concerns the politically sensible question of 'integration by absorption'; that is, of

Russian–Belarusian relations but also of Russia swallowing up the regions of the currently frozen conflicts (such as South Ossetia and Transnistria). Finally, Evgeny Vinokurov analyses the EU–Russian Common Economic Space in the making.

The post-communist transition led to a significantly heterogeneous political landscape in the post-Soviet space. Lien Verpoest focuses on how geopolitical pluralism is reflected in the institutional changes of Ukraine and Belarus. Their disparate institutional development and apparent divergence in foreign policy preferences can lead to the question as to whether the institutions and state administrations in these countries have been (re)drafted to the liking of the EU or of the CIS cooperation structures. A particularly intriguing point of interest here are the institutional parallels between the CIS's and EU's organizational structures. A screening of CIS integration mechanisms in general and sub-regional initiatives in particular reveals interesting similarities with EU integration efforts. For example, the institutionalization of the Belarus–Russia Union State, as well as Putin's repeated statements that Belarusian–Russian integration should evolve in the line of EU integration appears to be an explicit case of institutional mirroring between organizational fields.

Interesting parallels can be drawn between Verpoest (Chapter 7), Vinokurov (Chapter 2), and Willerton and Beznosov (Chapter 3). Vinokurov comes to the conclusion that Russia's integration policy became more flexible and pragmatic in the 2000s. Willerton and Beznosov come to the same conclusion in their chapter on CIS security integration. Likewise, Verpoest confirms this observation in her analysis of Russian–Belarusian integration.

Debates in CIS countries have often revealed a perceived incompatibility between a Russian and pro-Western orientation. Recognizing their interest in participating in the CIS, many former USSR republics have been ambivalent in their CIS policies and have been reluctant to commit to hard law institutions within a Russian-led organization. Chapter 8 by Rilka Dragneva and Antoaneta Dimitrova, 'Patterns of Integration and Regime Compatibility: Ukraine between the CIS and the EU', studies an extremely important case. Seeking closer integration with the EU has become a realistic policy proposition since the Orange Revolution. The question arises, nonetheless, whether an essential incompatibility exists between membership in the EU and the CIS. In answering this question, the Chapter 8 examines the current commitments of Ukraine within the CIS in terms of legal arrangements, political ties, participation in decision-making or consultation structures, economic commitments, and expectations arising from the nature of the CIS as an international regime. This exploration is followed by a similar examination of the EU's current commitments to Ukraine and potential steps towards closer cooperation and membership. The authors come to the conclusion that at present there are few real incompatibilities between Ukraine's legal obligations, institutional arrangements and 'soft' rules in the context of the two regimes discussed here. Obligations under the CIS remain 'soft' and Ukraine remains able to pick and choose the institutions it participates in. Obligations under the Partnership and Cooperation Agreeement (PCA) with the EU take into account CIS obligations, so no real incompatibilities exist there.

In terms of both regimes, however, Ukraine is in a kind of halfway house. Both SES and the EU application lead to customs union arrangements, which are perceived as incompatible. There is also a certain incompatibility in governmental perceptions and statements. Furthermore, there are a number of developments that suggest potential changes to the middle of the road position Ukraine has held so far. The presence of the European Union as Ukraine's new neighbour and most important trade partner is one. The Orange Revolution of December 2004, with its drive not only to remove the previous corrupt leadership and hold free and fair elections, but also to join the West, the European Union, is another. Joining the EU has been reframed by President Yushchenko as Ukraine's civilizational choice. This gives Ukraine's bid to accede to the EU a new dimension – that of domestic mobilization for modernization and Europeanization – and may lead to changes that go beyond the mixed foreign policy messages which have maintained Ukraine's balancing act so far.

A distinctive facet of integration, absorption, is looked at by Katlijn Malfliet and Gennadi Kurdiukov in Chapter 9. The Russian Federation in its domestic law made possible the admission of states or parts of states as new subjects of the Russian Federation. In this way, the thesis of a potential absorption of newly independent states or parts of them into the Russian Federation lost its purely hypothetical character. The authors argue that the Russian federal constitutional law of 17 December 2001 did not appear by coincidence, as it opened avenues for Russia to profile itself as a multi-tier governance structure and as an actor of 'modernized Russification'.

Finally, Evgeny Vinokurov assesses the developments of the EU–Russian Common Economic Space (CES) in Chapter 10. The chapter delineates the phases and primary activities of the negotiation process in the CES. It argues that the CES Concept of 2003 and the CES Road Map of 2005 contain an original model of integration, combining elements of the EEA and 'Swiss' models, and uniting horizontal and sectoral approaches. However, there are multiple concerns in this respect. First of all, the documents are fuzzy and on the verge of being devoid of substance. Second, it is questionable whether the model envisaged by these documents would be capable of providing a satisfactory solution to the policy-taker challenge for Russia; that is, the obligation to converge unilaterally on EU legislation and to follow the changes in EU legislation while possessing only limited leverage in the EU's internal affairs. The policy-taker problem may represent a major hurdle to the EU–Russian economic integration in view of Russian multilateral foreign policy and its official goals.

Overall, the book intends to provide a comprehensive picture of integration processes in the post-Soviet space and the challenges to which the post-Soviet states and the European Union will have to provide proper responses. First of all, we look at the Russian integration challenge. Second, we delve into the specific challenges of integration facing other CIS states, particularly in its Western part, wherein our approach explicitly takes into account the predominant role of Russia as well as the major gravitational force exercised by the EU. Third, we regard the challenge to the EU in its European Neighbourhood Policy and in its relations with Russia. A large variety of integration scenarios are analysed in the book. Among them are the CIS as the oldest reintegration arrangement; the more recent initiatives, such as EurAsEC and SES; an important bilateral integration case of the Russia–Belarus Union; the opportunity for Russia directly to incorporate other states or parts of states; and the various integration schemes with the European Union.

Katlijn Malfliet

Lien Verpoest

Evgeny Vinokurov

Note

1 F. Schimmelfennig, 'The Community Trap: Liberal Norms, Rhetorical Action and the Eastern Enlargement of the European Union', *International Organization*, 1 January 2001, vol. 55, issue 1, p. 7.

Part I

In Pursuit of Integration in the Post-Soviet Area

1
The Post-Soviet Space: From the USSR to the Commonwealth of Independent States and Beyond

Irina Kobrinskaya

Introduction

December 2006 marks fifteen years since the demise of the USSR. The second world power turned into a 'post-soviet space', while its parts – former soviet republics – became independent sovereign states, a majority of which established a Commonwealth of Independent States (CIS).[1]

Each word in this sentence has a particular significance for explaining the past fifteen years and the current situation. First, the 'super-poweredness', or imperial syndrome, from these years has been and remains the main problem of Russia's self-identification as well as positioning itself both in global affairs and, more importantly, its relations with the other Newly Independent States (NIS). From this stem the controversial moods in society and the elite regarding the past and future of Russia in the post-Soviet space. In turn, the correspondence to or discrepancy of state policy from the dominating public mood demonstrates the legitimacy or deficit of the former and/or the manipulation by the latter.

Second, the most widely used and seemingly neutral definition, 'post-Soviet space', contains an allusion to the past that inhibits the region's deep transformation and development, and works against renewed integration. The main reason for this is 'Russia-centeredness', the direct dependence of a reintegration scenario upon (1) Russian economic potential (2) Russia's eagerness regarding integration, and (3) the political and socio-economic attractiveness of Russia as a centre for new integration. Other wide-spread functional definitions of the CIS, such as 'a formula for divorce', also presuppose an end to the previous period.

Third, the common deficits of the majority of NIS states – experience, social-economic and political prerequisites, and potential for the independent functioning of sovereign states – were aggravated by ethno-national controversies and conflicts, which broke out at the moment that the limits of the Soviet system loosened and were then destroyed. This resulted from different levels of development and different heterogeneous ethno-national, religious and geopolitical orientations.

Finally, all the processes in the post-Soviet space were, on the one hand, highly dependent on the domestic policy developments in Russia and the NIS and on the other hand, they were increasingly open to the impact of the processes of regional integration: European integration and globalization, first and foremost.

By 2006, the situation in the CIS and the orientation of Russian policy towards the post-Soviet space had gone through several stages. Its future is still unclear, however, and may develop according to a number of scenarios. While the integration process in the European Union undergoes a serious crisis, Russia is reformatting and upgrading its world stature.

The prospects of the CIS are defined by a traditional set of factors: economic-social, security, political and international. It is important to order these according to priority; for societies in transition, particularly Russia and the NIS, this order may be different from that of stable market democracies. The existing fifteen years of experience prove this thesis.

Expectations for the CIS

According to some experts, the volume and scale of economic ties have diminished because of the role of Russia and its economic policy.[2] Nevertheless, the CIS countries remain Russia's most important trade partners: they import 45 per cent of Russian oil and 19 per cent of construction equipment. Almost ten million people from the CIS countries work in Russia and send home up to four billion US dollars each year for their families.

In the meantime, even the top CIS officials admit that its institutions do not work – no more than ten per cent of the 1500 signed agreements and treaties are implemented. CIS summits have become routine. Many called the 2005 Summit in the city of Kazan the 'last CIS carnival'. The coming demise of the CIS is commonly held. In March 2005 in Yerevan, President Putin said:

> If anyone expected some special achievements from the CIS, for example regarding the economy or cooperation in political, military or other spheres, this indeed did not happen, nor could it have

happened. There were declared aims, but in reality the CIS was established so as to make the process of the USSR's dissolution the most civilized and smooth one, with the fewest losses in the economic and humanitarian spheres... The CIS has never had economic super-tasks, such as economic integration... This is a very useful club for mutual information and the clarification of general political, humanitarian and administrative problems.[3]

As mentioned above, the ambiguity grew as Putin occasionally expressed regrets regarding the dissolution of the Soviet Union. This opinion is supported by Russian public opinion and the political elite. Whether these are merely populist declarations or whether these sentiments provoke such feelings remains an open question. As public opinion polls show, the post-Soviet 'syndrome', and the 'phantom' nature of the moods regarding the CIS have resulted in a deeply controversial vision of the present and future of the CIS.

The opinion of the elite was expressed in the 1999 Council for Foreign and Defence Policy (CFDP) Report entitled 'Will the Soviet Union Revive?' The report stated that Russians have managed to adapt surprisingly quickly to the tragedy of the USSR's dissolution. The remaining nostalgia for the USSR is not accompanied by an aspiration to reconstruct the former state, and even less a desire to do so by force.[4]

Nevertheless, according to the April 2006 public opinion polls by the Levada Centre, the post-imperial syndrome is alive and well in the former Soviet population: only 34 per cent denied that they felt hurt by the former Soviet republics. More than 60 per cent explain that this feeling is due to: separation (19 per cent) or distance from Russia (17 per cent), violations against Russian speakers and the Russian language (28 per cent; here the misinformation is striking. The Baltic states scored highest regarding such violations, whereas Turkmenistan is perceived rather positively), and moving towards the West (13 per cent). Simultaneously, 20 per cent would prefer to reconstruct their states within the borders of the USSR: 17 per cent prefer the same assembly of states with the exception of the Baltic states, while 10 per cent want a Soviet Russia plus Belarus, Ukraine and Kazakhstan. *Only 29 per cent are satisfied with the present borders.*[5]

Earlier in 1996, Eurobarometer polls showed that 27 per cent of the European part of Russia connected the future of the country with the CIS, while another 27 per cent saw a future aligned with the United States and 13 per cent envisioned a connection with the EU. At the same time, in the CIS countries, 52 per cent saw a common future with Russia, 13 per cent with the United States and 12 per cent with the EU.[6] *Does this mean that Russia missed an opportunity to re-unite the state?*

Table 1.1 What future for the CIS?[7] (percentage of respondents)

	1998	1999	2000	2001	2002	2003	2004	2005
Integration, strengthening ties between republics	23	29	24	24	22	25	25	12
Long and difficult search for consent	33	31	38	34	36	32	33	37
Aggravated conflicts between republics	8	10	9	10	12	13	9	16
Dissolution of the CIS	13	12	11	16	14	9	16	18

Table 1.2 With which countries should Russia strengthen relations?[8] (percentage of respondents)

	2003	2004	2005
USA	13	13	12
China	9	9	7
The countries of Western Europe (such as France and Germany)	32	25	26
The CIS countries (such as Ukraine and Belarus)	27	34	40
Islamic countries	1	1	2

At least three conclusions can be reached from analysing this sociological data (see also Tables 1.1 and 1.2).

First, only a minority of the Russian population is satisfied with the situation, and their expectations regarding the CIS are only decreasing with time. The number of those expecting closer integration has *steadily* fallen from 23 per cent in 1998 to 12 per cent in 2005, while expectations of conflicts with and dissolution of the CIS have, respectively, doubled (from 8 to 16 per cent) and increased by one third (from 13 to 18 per cent).

Second, paradoxically, despite low expectations and feelings of being hurt, 40 per cent of respondents still believe that Russia should strengthen its relations with and orient itself more towards certain CIS countries (such as Ukraine and Belarus) in the future. This paradox both 'opens' the society up to manipulation and *legitimizes the Kremlin's policies, whatever tactics and strategies are chosen* (*integrationist or distancing*).

Third, *expectations regarding the CIS* (*at least its European core*) *are inversely proportional to the general opinion about the European Union and its leading members*. Meanwhile, it should be noted, the opinion about the United States and China remains more or less stable.

Pragmatism in Russia's CIS policy

Russian policy towards the CIS has apparently changed several times since the foundation of the CIS at the end of 1991. A comparison of the suggested strategies demonstrates a striking similarity between the logic, priorities and instruments of these policies.

Thus, in a 1992 report by the Centre for International Research of MGIMO, 'The CIS: Processes and Perspectives', experts concluded that the idea of transforming the CIS into a body of more closely integrated states was not only illusory, but also implied an unpleasant prospect of transforming the Commonwealth into a Russian–Central Asian union, which would certainly hinder reforms. The cooperation with post-Soviet states therefore 'should not lead to a regional integration or building of institutions, which would limit the freedom of action for Russia in its realisation of market and democratic reforms'. The development of bilateral relations with post-Soviet states was considered more desirable.[9]

In 1999, in comments to the CFDP report 'Will the Soviet Union Revive?', experts noted: 'We all deeply regret the dissolution of our former motherland. But this regret should not lead us to a course that will be unprofitable: either pseudo-integration at the expense of Russia or bureaucratic integration on paper.' The CFDP report is right in stressing that *the main vector of Russian policy towards the states of the former USSR should be bilateral relations with a tough defence of national economic interests*. Multilateral diplomacy in the CIS should add to, but not replace bilateral diplomacy. Taking into consideration the tendency towards reducing the level of integration in the CIS, it is expedient to reduce the number of their meetings in a timely manner.[10]

In the beginning of Vladimir Putin's presidency, 'economization' and pragmatism became key words in Russian foreign policy, including its position vis à vis the CIS.[11] Pragmatism and economization have particularly marked the period of 2001–03 (when Putin suggested that Lukashenko 'divide chops and flies' and when the first mini gas crisis took place). The tough line in the sphere of economy grew even stronger at the end of 2005 and in the first half of 2006, once again concerning gas prices for Ukraine (and planned price increases for Belarus). Simultaneously, Russia introduced trade sanctions against Georgia and Moldova on the grounds that the goods (wine) imported from these countries did not meet standards. To prove the validity of these claims, we note that Latvia did the same.

The political aspect of this policy is obvious. Nevertheless, as early as in 1996, scholar and supporter of reintegration N. Shmelev stressed that Russia could no longer afford to donate to other post-Soviet states.[12]

Moreover, even the strongest supporters of CIS integration admitted that selling energy to the NIS (particularly to the European part of the post-Soviet space) at low preferential prices supports these states' reforms and prepares them for European integration at Russia's cost. This has had an indirectly negative impact on Russia's relations with the European Union.

No matter what rhetoric and declarations were used, the guidelines of Russia's policy in the CIS have, from the beginning, demonstrated a strategy towards the post-Soviet space that can be characterized as rather pragmatic and oriented to developing bilateral relations with the aim of *creating an optimal economic system* in order to satisfy national economic interests.

What explains, therefore the deepening political tensions in Russia's relations with the NIS?

Causes of the current crisis

There are three main causes for the current crisis in the CIS:

- Recent regime changes in the NIS
- The strengthening of Russia's statehood and its position in world affairs
- Changes to the international environment.

The chain of 'coloured revolutions' in the NIS – in Georgia, Ukraine and Kyrgyzstan – and the policies of newly elected leaders in Moldova and Azerbaijan highlighted the natural change of the ruling regimes in the post-Soviet states. The new leaders, while maintaining strong ties with the old regimes, came to power with the agenda of building new *post*-post-Soviet statehoods in their countries. First and foremost, this means strengthening democratic procedures and institutions, the rule of law, a struggle against corruption, strengthening civil society and market- and socially-oriented reforms. In other words, these states are orienting themselves towards the future – not to the Soviet past.

Paradoxically, Russia was the first to move in this direction, proclaiming and (partly) implementing these goals in 2001–03. It is not surprising, therefore, that Putin's rating in the NIS was very high during this period. Nevertheless, the change of the elites in the NIS, and particularly the regime change in Ukraine, evoked traditional reservations in Moscow and temporarily coincided with a recoil in the process of democratic and liberal market reforms in Russia. Moscow could not

Table 1.3 Which policy should Russia realize in regard to CIS countries? (July 2005,[13] percentage of respondents)

Policy	Respondents (%)
Support democratic forces and progressive changes	23
Aim to maintain all present leaders who are loyal to Russia	14
Support their own economic and political interests and not interfere in neighbours' domestic matters	55
To be on guard against foreign states (the USA, China, Turkey and others) who might dangerously influence these countries	30

resist the temptation once again to turn to the practice of supporting 'pro-Russian' politicians in the NIS, this time by using its 'heavy artillery' (the high ratings of the Russian President). The failure in Ukraine is vividly expressed by the reaction of the Russian public in its opinion polls.

Neither the scale nor the depth of the reforms in the 'revolutionary' NIS can presently guarantee their irreversibility. The more extended the period of reform, the higher risk there is of recoil. In the new situation, the European NIS have proclaimed a pro-European orientation and have started along a path similar to that followed by the Central European states in the 1990s. GUAM and the newly formed Commonwealth of Democratic Choice repeat the purposes of the Visegrad group. Russia has turned into 'the Other'. Most of the new leaders base their identities on a contrast with the contemporary Russian polity (that is, corruption, a democratic deficit and so on). They position themselves as democrats, value-oriented, advanced, pro-European. At the same time, none of these leaders can afford to be 'anti-Russian', taking into account the economic, human and cultural interdependence with Russia and the heavy dependence of thousands of households on Russia for their incomes.

Another peculiarity of the new regimes is the understanding – if not in society, at least within the elite – of the fact that to implement reforms and modernize their countries, they need additional support, preferably from well-established integration structures such as the European Union. It is also understood that becoming part of these institutions means delegating some sovereign authorities to supranational bodies. The current stage of reforms has a greater chance of success if seen as a step to post-modern statehood. If the slogan 'Together in Europe' was discussed by the highest levels of Russian society in 2001–02, by 2005–06 the situation has changed. Russia is building *a modern national state*.

The great-power perspective and a concentration on national state building hinder Russia's experiment with integration formats in the CIS. Moscow traditionally understands only a paternalist type of integration, which presupposes preferential treatment in exchange for following Moscow's policy. Otherwise, these preferences work against Russia's interests, at least as seen by the Kremlin. The stronger Russia's statehood and economy (based respectively on a centralized model and sky-rocketing energy prices), the tougher its political stance toward the NIS.

Energy prices and energy transit are becoming an important lever for Russian policy. In a situation of guaranteed energy supplies and transit as a basic element of foreign policy making for the world powers and their institutions, it would be unreasonable not to use this instrument for Russian national interests. However, this lever is neither sufficient to build stable ties with Russia's closest partners nor for cooperation with the leading world actors.

Thus, Russian neo-pragmatism in the CIS is justified but insufficient because it cannot make up for a lack of long term strategy. The reorientation of the post-Soviet states towards Europe does not present a threat to the military or economic security of Russia, but it does present a serious modernization challenge to Moscow. An adequate response to this challenge lies in the European direction: strengthened and deepened cooperation and partnership with the European Union and NATO (and the West in general) is needed.

Conclusion

The transformation of the post-Soviet space can be interpreted according to either a concept of conflict of civilizations or a centre–periphery theory. But, in either case, Russia is not ready for integration with Europe and finds itself, additionally, beyond the borders of European civilization. Russia appears to be a loser in the competition of integrations – and this is what, in reality, takes place between the 'common neighbours' of the European Union and Russia, the latter's attractiveness now and in the foreseeable future is significantly weakened.

Though there is no direct proof in the official documents of Russia and the EU, presently both sides seem to be interested in 'freezing the situation'. For the EU, this is due to the crisis vividly demonstrated by the referenda on the European Constitution in France and the Netherlands, by the controversies between the 'old' and 'new' member states, the problem of Turkey, and so on.

Nevertheless, it is even more difficult to change the dominating algorithm: processes of globalization make participation in integration structures a *sine qua non* for the survival and stable development of the newly independent sovereign countries. After the dissolution of the USSR, the 'axis of dependence' has moved westward. Russia's leadership concentrated on strengthening its vertical power and seems realistically to estimate its chances in a competition with Europe, therefore preferring to maintain its status quo. Whether both sides will succeed depends on their constructive cooperation and further stable development in the NIS.

Notes

1 On 8 December 1991 in Viskuli, Belarus, the leaders of the Russian Federation, Belarus and Ukraine signed the Agreement on forming the Commonwealth of the Independent States. On 21 December in Almaty, it was signed by the leaders of eleven sovereign states (the Baltic states and Georgia not included).

2 P. Kandel, 'Russia – CID: the balance of centripetal and centrifugal tendencies', in *Post-Soviet States in 21st Century Europe*, Institute of Europe (Moscow: RAS, 1999): 53.

3 http://kremlin.ru/appears/2005/03/25/1735_type63377type63380_85912.shtml

4 'Russian Foreign Policy Facing the 21st Century Challenges', http://www.ieras.ru/journal2.2000/7.htm

5 www.levada.ru/press/2006050600.htm

6 Central and Eastern Eurobarometer, 7, Brussels, 1997.

7 *Public Opinion – 2005, Yearbook* (Moscow: Levada-Centre, 2005): 141.

8 *Public Opinion – 2005, Yearbook* (Moscow: Levada-Centre, 2005): 153.

9 'The Commonwealth of Independent States: Processes and Perspectives', Report, Centre for International Research, (Moscow: MGIMO, 1992): 17–18.

10 Russian Foreign Policy Facing the 21st Century Challenges, http://www.ieras.ru/journal2.2000/7.htm

11 http://kremlin.ru/eng/speeches/2005/05/10/1823_type70029type82912_105566.shtml

12 N. Shmelev, *Russia and the CIS/Europe and Russia. The Experience of Economic Transformation* (Moscow: Nauka, 1996): 208–9.

13 Public Opinion – 2005, Yearbook (Moscow: Levada-Centre, 2005): 141.

2
Russian Approaches to Integration in the Post-Soviet Space in the 2000s
Evgeny Vinokurov

Introduction

The issue of (re-)integration of the post-Soviet space arose simultaneously with the emergence of the new Russia. In the middle of the first decade of the twenty-first century, integration in the post-Soviet space remains a priority, and a field of constant concern for Russian foreign policy. The approaches to CIS integration are developing over time. There is a mix of continuity both in the underlying goals and in the means employed to achieve them. This chapter intends to identify the characteristics of the developing Russian integration strategy for the post-Soviet space in the 2000s.

There is a good deal of terminological confusion in the discourse on Russia's integration efforts. This requires clarification from the very beginning. For the sake of clarity and continuity, the term 'Single Economic Space' (SES) is used consistently throughout the chapter to refer to the ongoing process of creation of the Union of the 'Big Four' in the post-Soviet space (Belarus, Kazakhstan, Russia and Ukraine).[1] In EU–Russian relations, the idea initially launched was that of the Common European Economic Space (CEES). The same term has been used, for example, in the title of the CEES Concept. However, in 2004 the term 'Common Economic Space' (CES) asserted itself in the official discourse. Furthermore, another similar sounding term is the CIS, Commonwealth of Independent States. The latter term not only describes certain agreements and institutional structures, but is also often used to refer to the whole of the post-Soviet space, with the exception of the three Baltic States.

The chapter commences with a description of Russia's global and regional vectors of integration, emphasizing the priority of integration in the post-Soviet space. After introducing the CIS integration of the 1990s, the chapter goes on to argue that the Russian integration policy for the post-Soviet space in the 2000s can be divided into two periods that approximately coincide with Putin's first and the beginning of his second term in power. The first period witnessed a gradual move towards a greater role of economic considerations based on the desire to defend national economic interests. The beginning of Putin's second presidential term has demonstrated the reassertion of the old paradigms. The considerations of the reassertion of the Russian zone of influence in the post-Soviet space are gaining ground at the expense of the pragmatic spirit of the benefit/cost calculations. It is argued further that Russia employs a wide variety of means to push the CIS states toward integration. The chapter goes on to analyse the concept of multi-speed and multi-level integration. It comes to the conclusion that this concept underlies the CIS, EurAsEC and SES integration designs.

Integration in the post-Soviet space: other vectors of integration in Russian foreign policy

Various Russian legal documents and concepts delineate four global and regional vectors of integration (see Figure 2.1). The first integration vector is that of the global economy and multilateral agreements. The other three vectors are regional: integration with the EU, integration within the CIS, and integration with the Asia–Pacific region. There are certainly multiple links between global integration processes and all subcategories of regional integration.

The global integration vector is directed mainly towards international multilateral economic structures.[2] Having joined the EBRD and the IMF, Russia is now striving to accede to the WTO and the OECD. The G-8 can be included in this list as well. Integration into the global economy and active participation in the global multilateral institutions is combined with the pursuit of a deeper economic and political integration along the regional vectors. The CIS vector is of principal importance. This view is supported by the general documents directing and guiding Russian foreign policy. The Russian Foreign Policy Concept[3] delineates four regional priorities: the CIS, the EU, the USA and Asia. CIS regional integration is of primary importance. According to the Concept, emphasis will be put on the development of good neighbourly relations and strategic partnerships with all CIS member states. Practical relations with each of them should be structured with due regard for reciprocal openness to cooperation and readiness to take into account in a due manner the interests of

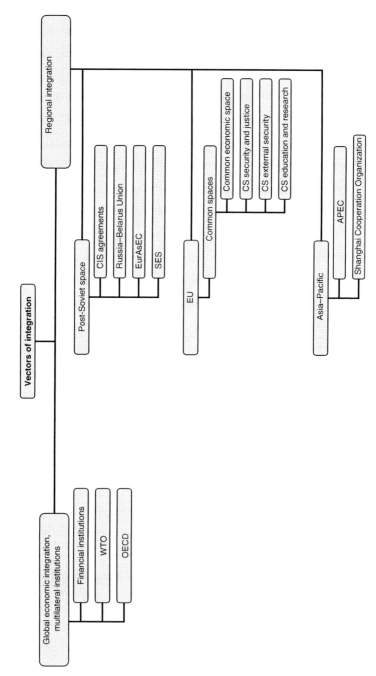

Figure 2.1 Vectors of Russia's integration and the most important organizational structures

the Russian Federation. At the same time, the Concept assigns clear priority to strengthening the Union of Belarus and Russia as the highest form of integration possible between two sovereign states. A priority importance is assigned to the two fields of cooperation: first, settling conflicts in the CIS member states and developing cooperation in the military-political area and in the sphere of security, particularly in combating international terrorism and extremism; second, the development of economic cooperation, including the joint rational use of natural resources and the creation of a free trade zone in the CIS.

The analysis of the major concepts and blueprints relevant to Russian foreign policy shows that the phenomenon of integration is assessed from two major points of view. First, there is the desirability and inevitability of Russia's integration into the world economy as a prerequisite for its economic growth and prosperity. Second, is national security and national security interests.

Upholding sovereignty is a constant concern, and the dogma of Russia's foreign policy. The National Security Concept[4] is echoed by the Foreign Policy Concept in that one of the principal objectives is 'to ensure reliable security of the country, to preserve and strengthen its sovereignty and territorial integrity, to achieve firm and prestigious positions in the world community, most fully consistent with the interests of the Russian Federation as a great power'.[5] Linked to this, the National Security Concept focuses on the growing risk of the economic system and information environment of the Russian Federation becoming dependent on external influences that could constitute a threat to Russian national interests. Thus, ensuring the sovereignty and territorial integrity of the Russian Federation is seen as one of the principal means of ensuring its national security. This would set limits to deep integration, which could be based on a functional understanding of sovereignty and a willingness to give up national sovereignty to a certain extent.

Furthermore, according to the National Security Concept, ensuring national interests and upholding the country's economic interests are, in the first place, closely connected to paving the way into a global economy; second, to expanding markets for Russian products; and, third, to creating a single economic domain with the members of the Commonwealth of Independent States. Russian foreign policy must be designed in order to develop integrative processes that can serve Russia's interests within the framework of the Commonwealth of Independent States and to ensure Russia's fully-fledged involvement in global and regional economic and political structures.

The CIS vector is also the oldest of the regional vectors of integration. As for the EU being one of the main political and economic partners, neither the Foreign Policy Concept nor the National Security Concept mentions the term 'integration' with regard to Russia's relations with the Union. This provides an argument in favour of the view that the idea of integration with the EU is a very recent vector. By contrast, the CIS vector has been in existence since the dismantling of the Soviet Union; that is, it became an inherent part of Russia's foreign policy agenda since its emergence. Despite the increasing relevance of the EU and (less so) of the Asia–Pacific region, the emphasis is being put on the post-Soviet space, even in the very recent speeches and documents of the 2000s. President Putin in his Address to the Federal Assembly in May 2004 stressed that the 'work on deepening integration in the Commonwealth of Independent States remains our priority, especially within the framework of the SES and the EurAsEC. This, without exaggeration, is one of the conditions of regional and international stability'.[6] Despite the growing importance of the European vector, integration in the post-Soviet space remains a priority and a field of constant concern for Russian foreign policy.

Russia's integration in the post-Soviet space in the 1990s

The agreements signed in December 1991 (Minsk) and January 1992 (Moscow) laid the legal grounds for the CIS. They were followed by the CIS Charter in January 1993 and the Agreement on the Creation of the Economic Union signed by the Heads of States in September 1993. The Economic Union was supposed to lead in stages to a common economic space, meaning the implementation of the free movement of goods, services, capital and labour. According to these agreements, integration along the four freedoms had to be accompanied by the concerted monetary, budget, tax, customs, and currency policies, as well as the harmonization of economic legislation. In other words, the CIS was supposed to move in stages toward a full scale EU-type common market.

In 1994, the CIS countries took measures aimed at transition to the multilateral regime of free trade on the basis of a corresponding 'Agreement on the establishment of a Free Trade Zone'. The CIS countries, however, have failed to agree on a multilateral list of exits from the free trade regime, as stipulated by the Agreement. There were further attempts to establish the free trade zone later on, which resulted in a long and impressive list of agreements signed by the parties in 1994–2000.[7] For example, the specification of measures on the establishment of a free trade zone can be found in (1) the 'Plan-Schedule of Implementation of Proposals on the Establishment and Functioning of the Free Trade Zone' adopted by the CIS Council of Heads of State on 21 June 2000, and (2) the 'Plan of Measures for the Realization of the Programme of Actions for the Development of the Commonwealth of Independent States for the Period up until 2005', adopted by the CIS Council of Heads of Government on 20 June 2000.[8] The first of these documents specifies the priority measures for the establishment of a free trade zone. These measures stipulate the implementation of internal state procedures regarding the entering into force of basic documents regulating: the functioning of the free trade zone; the elaboration of concrete proposals, including the elaboration of additional interstate legal acts on the functioning of the free trade zone; and information support for the establishment and functioning of the free trade zone. The second document, which is of a middle-term character, stipulates the preparation and signing of a number of intergovernmental agreements and documents that would facilitate the creation of conditions for the free movement of services, capital and workers, as well as other supplementary activities and measures. The stipulation was made that the movement of each of the countries towards fully-fledged free trade zone status would not be homogeneous due to existing differences in economic potentials, the degree of reformation of economies, and the internal and external conditions for economic development. A specific timetable for the establishment of the free trade zone for each of the CIS countries was envisaged along the lines of the conceptual decision to undertake multi-speed integration. These attempts were doomed to fail for similar reasons.

From the very beginning, the CIS and its objectives were ambiguous. The Russian left-wing opposition assumed that the CIS would be utilized as a tool for the restoration of the Soviet Union. For the liberal wing, the European Union served as a model for CIS integration. In addition, the CIS was understood and used as a means for implementing a 'civilized divorce' or leverage in relations with other post-Soviet states.[9]

On the whole, CIS integration activities throughout the 1990s and the beginning of the 2000s (understood broadly, as a complex of measures not only within the formal CIS framework but also through bilateral relations and other legal frameworks) cannot be simply dismissed as a failure. The record of successful integration is certainly inadequate.[10] However, there are positive aspects as well. First of all, the CIS worked with success as a 'civilized divorce' scheme, preventing the post-Soviet space from falling into a (potential) state of violent disorder, which could have effectively led to a degree of disintegration that would have made it impossible to achieve integration for decades. The CIS has never lived up to its expectations of creating an EU-type entity. However, as Olcott, Åslund and Garnett put it, 'the CIS is as much a failure as, for example, Russia is a failure'.[11] On the one hand, it is possible to argue that Russia has failed to transform its assumed technological and intellectual potential into a breakthrough and to become a model Western democracy. On the other hand, one might say that Russia has managed its transition into a 'normal country',[12] (that is, into a typical middle-income capitalist democracy comparable, for example, to Turkey or Brazil). Secondly, having so far failed to achieve significant successes in the field of free trade, the CIS has managed some smaller, but nevertheless important tasks (for example in the field of mutual recognition of various documents and licences). Another example is the preservation of the visa-free regime between CIS states due to the CIS 'Non-Visa Travel Agreement' to which the majority of the CIS states are parties.

One of the most important documents laying out the conceptual framework of Russia's official approach to CIS affairs is the Presidential Decree 'On Russia's Strategic Course in its Relations with the CIS States' of 14 September 1995.[13] The development of the CIS is viewed as corresponding to the vital interests of the Russian Federation. Relations with the CIS states are regarded as an important factor of Russia's inclusion in the world's political and economic structures. The priority of the relations with the CIS states is determined by the following factors: first, Russia's main vital interests in the fields of economy, security and defence are concentrated on CIS territory; second, effective cooperation with the CIS states counteracts centrifugal tendencies in Russia itself. The main goal of Russia's CIS politics is defined as the creation of an economically and politically integrated union of states able to claim a worthy place in the world community. Further, the Decree goes on to specify the principal goal in a series of main tasks:

- Providing for stability in political, military, economic, humanitarian and legal dimensions
- Assisting the formation of the CIS states as politically and economically stable entities enjoying friendly relations with Russia
- Strengthening Russia's role as a leading force in the formation of a new system of interstate relations in the post-Soviet space
- Building integration processes in the CIS.

The second half of the 1990s was marked by changes in the approach. Russia was increasingly working to design an economic integration arrangement with a limited number of participants. The first such arrangement was the Eurasian Economic Agreement in 1996 signed by Belarus, Kazakhstan, Kyrgyzstan and the Russian Federation (Tajikistan joined in 1999). The agreement was ratified by the Russian Duma in 2001 but has never been implemented. Another arrangement was the Agreement of Russia and Belarus on the Creation of the Union State. The Union came into existence after the signing in December 1999. The agreement specified the desire of the two states to move towards a common state with the interim customs union, a common currency and unified structural policies. While the Union has not resulted in a common currency so far, the customs union has been installed. However, the customs controls were restored in 2001. Thus, although the Russia–Belarus Customs Union was envisaged as a truly comprehensive economic integration arrangement, its factual scope is still limited.

Economic considerations during the first Putin presidency

The analysis of the Russian approaches to the integration of the post-Soviet space in the 2000s leads us to differentiate between two periods. The turning point between them falls in the first half of 2004, which was towards the end of the first presidency of Vladimir Putin and, more distinctively, in the beginning of the second term. The first period had witnessed the gradual move towards a more pragmatic policy based on the desire to defend national economic interests. The economic component was on the rise. Then, the beginning of the Putin's second term saw the reassertion of the old paradigms. The considerations of the power game and the defence of the traditional Russian zone of influence in the post-Soviet space have been gaining ground at the expense of the pragmatic spirit of the benefit/cost calculations.

While not pretending to give a comprehensive view, I outline several distinctive elements of Russia's approach to CIS integration showing dualistic dynamics combining continuity and change in the transition from the politics of the 1990s to the politics of the 2000s.

Foreign policy analysts widely concur that the new Russian foreign policy under Putin during his first term was characterized by the growing importance of underlying economic factors. Bobo Lo stresses this economization as one of the inherent elements of the new Russian foreign policy in formation.[14] According to Lo, this trend is being observed particularly in Russia–EU relations and in relation to the issue of WTO accession. The importance of economic priorities has been much enhanced. Is this also true for Russian policy on integration in the CIS?

In his article 'Making Headway to Integration',[15] Vice Minister Khristenko relates this argument to the issue of competitiveness as the precondition for a state to be salient in the world:

> There is no doubt that a country's high competitive capacity should be a critical goal for any state. Consolidation and integration processes are an important instrument for raising competitive abilities. Under conditions of globalization, regional and sub-regional integration tends to become a prevailing trend at all levels – from the corporate to the national. The choice of a particular niche for a nation or union to assume in the global division of functions is decisive. Our goal is to create a structure that is essential for the world – a structure in which the world would be unable to function without Russia and alliances involving it.[16]

Khristenko states goals of a dual nature: first, raising the country's global competitiveness; second, the geopolitical goal of creating a structure that will assert the country's salient place in the world – in other words, that will make Russia necessary for the world's functioning. The means to reach this goal are economic and political in nature; namely, economic growth and regional integration. Khristenko proceeds with arguments in favour of economic integration both within the CIS and with the EU on economic grounds. It is crucial for Russia to enable not only internal but also external sources of growth. While Russia's current growth is highly dependant on the extraction of energy carriers, oil and gas cannot be viewed as a basis for a long and sustainable growth. At the same time, processed goods produced in Russia have not yet reached a sufficiently high level of competitiveness on the international markets. Against this background, three possible approaches to foreign economic policy are outlined in the article. The first approach presupposes protectionism and saturation of the internal market by production that can eventually be exported. The second approach suggests a speedy liberalization and must be weighed against the risk of negative social consequences. The third approach is the widening of the accessible market. For Russia, this would mean the creation of the 'homogeneous space for Russian companies beyond the boundaries of the Russian Federation'.[17] If this scenario were to be accomplished, a greater internal market would have to stimulate investments, economies of scale would have to be achieved, and administrative costs would have to be lowered.

The latest integration attempt undertaken by Russia in the post-Soviet space is the Single Economic Space (SES) with Belarus, Kazakhstan and Ukraine. The process is ongoing. A number of documents establishing the SES were expected to be prepared for signature in 2005. As a preliminary step, the Concept of the SES was prepared and agreed to by the participating states in 2003.

The SES Concept[18] was agreed upon by the different parties in 2003. The States participants understand the SES to mean the economic space that unites the customs territories of the State participants. It is within this space that the mechanisms for regulating the economic function, which are based on common principles, secure the free movement of commodities, services, capital and the workforce. It is also within this space that common foreign trade policies and concerted custom, monetary credit and currency policies are pursued, to whatever degree and at what volumes are necessary for ensuring parity competition and for maintaining macroeconomic stability.

The SES is to be formed stage-by-stage, taking into account the likelihood of differences in the speeds and levels of integration (Art. II). This means that each state is free to decide when it enters into which international agreement, which entails the integration of participating states at differing stages in integration proceedings.

It is envisaged that the SES will be created in three stages. In the initial stage, the four countries will ensure a free trade regime. The first stage should accomplish a simplification of the customs procedures and the unification of legislation on the cross-border transfer of goods. In the second stage, a customs union will be created with single tariffs; exceptions regarding agricultural imports will be cancelled and protective and antidumping measures will be eliminated. A common competition policy will be pursued, and a single regulating organ will be set up. During the third stage customs controls will be abolished within the borders of the SES, and complete freedom of movement will be ensured for services, capital and the workforce. The single regulating organ will be further empowered to control natural monopolies.

In fact, despite the ratification of the Agreement by all participating states, there is still no consensus on what the SES should become or how it will develop. During the May 2004 Summit in Yalta, the leaders focused precisely on these topics in meetings that revealed considerable divergence of views. Putin proposed that the first package of agreements should include documents on foreign trade, customs tariffs and the business environment. While Kazakh President Nazarbaev recommended moving directly to the customs union, Ukraine was ardently persistent in restricting the initial stage to the formation of a free-trade zone. The Russian government expects Russia, Belarus and Kazakhstan to become the core of the SES. As regards Ukraine, it will continue to move towards integration at its own pace. The SES is based on the formula of multi-speed construction. The primary reason for this embedded flexibility, besides the lessons learned by the CIS, is the specific position of Ukraine.

The SES story shows, on the one hand, changes in Russia's official approaches to integration in the post-Soviet space during Putin's first presidency, with the integration policy becoming more pragmatic and more flexible. On the other hand, there has been a good deal of continuity. The approach has become more pragmatic and more flexible in two main respects: first, the policy is concentrated less on institution building and more on preparing a legal base for trade liberalization and economic expansion; second, it is concentrated on the creation of a union with fewer participants and with a built-in concept of multi-speed and multi-level integration.

Cutler, in his analysis of the fallacies often made in studying CIS affairs, notes that the assumption that integration necessarily takes place from above and that it by definition occurs through official supranational directives is one of the principal mistakes.[19] In fact, the Russian government was probably the first to make this mistake as it concentrated much of its efforts on institution building within the CIS. In the course of the last decade, this approach gradually changed. The underlying motivations of economic expansion in the CIS became more salient, while institution building took a position of secondary importance in the integration agenda. This is becoming apparent in the SES Concept. In contrast to previous integration attempts, the SES is focusing on substance rather than on institutional arrangements. No institutional body is envisaged in the first stage, except the Council of Heads of States with a 'One state, one vote' voting procedure and decisions taken on the basis of consensus. This is an omission that was hardly possible in the 1990s. A single regulatory body (or Commission, as it is conditionally named) will be created in the second stage, but only when the SES moves to the customs union stage. The Commission's decisions are to be made through weighted voting based on the economic potential of the participating states (Art. V). This modus operandi will automatically lead to the dominance of Russia.

The second, and probably more important, trend can be traced back to the end of the 1990s, when Russia started redirecting its efforts from all-CIS integration to the creation of a union with a smaller number of participating states, which nevertheless represent the bulk of the CIS population and economic capacity. This approach is also underpinned by the hope that the rest of the CIS states would join a successful union later on. EurAsEC was the first such agreement. This trend was strengthened in the 2000s. Since 2003, Russia has redirected its main efforts to the integration of the 'Big Four'. The main part of Russia's trade within the CIS is with Belarus, Ukraine and Kazakhstan. The 'Big Four' account for 94 per cent of the GDP and 88 per cent of the total trade flow of the Commonwealth states. Thus, the SES can be viewed as the locomotive of integration processes for the whole of the post-Soviet space.

Contemporary Russian foreign policy shows a clear understanding of Ukraine's vital role in the SES. Ukraine is the key state for Russian efforts to build up any structure of economic integration in the post-Soviet space, not only due to its economic weight but also due to its strategic location between the EU and Russia. For Ukraine, as well as for Belarus and Kazakhstan, there is a good deal of economic justification for the formation of the SES. While increasing exports and manufactured goods and agricultural products to the Russian market may be the principal justification, there are a number of other concerns of an economic nature. Both Ukraine and Belarus are interested in securing the cheap oil and gas supplies from Russia. Ukraine is concerned with Moscow's collection of value-added tax on Russian oil and gas exports according to the country-of-origin principle. The introduction of an FTA would, according to the rules of the WTO, make Russia and Ukraine switch to the country-of-destination principle, a move that could give Ukraine's budget some $800 million annually. In fact, Russia has already taken a decision to repudiate VAT for oil and gas exports to the SES member states, a move that was to cost Russia an estimated 34 billion rubles in 2005 alone.[20] As Ukraine is committed to advancing toward EU membership, an FTA is all that Kyiv wants from the CIS, whereas the mere creation of an FTA is not justifiable economically for Russia. It seems, however, that an FTA is the maximum that can be achieved in relations with Ukraine, as the country is officially striving to attain EU membership, which would be unthinkable if Ukraine were to form a customs union with Russia. Answering the question on EurAsEC during the press conference on 23 December 2004, the Russian President said that Russia was building up its relations with its nearest neighbours above all in the economic sphere. EurAsEC and SES are seen as organizations that provide a good basis for integration processes in the post-Soviet space. It has become clear from the answers that the developments in Ukraine are perceived as threatening the future of the SES.

While the SES might greatly benefit other member states, what would it mean for Russia? The economic justification seems to be substantially less strong on the Russian side. The official position is optimistic, stating that the SES will greatly benefit the Russian economy by expanding internal markets and by creating favourable conditions for investment. A closer look supports a more moderate view. If successful, the SES would lead to a common market with approximately 225 million consumers – a rise of 50 per cent compared with the internal Russian market. However, there are many limitations to this figure. First of all, in analysing the SES, one must take into consideration the fact that Russia and Belarus already have a functioning customs union. Thus, they have already reached the second stage of the envisaged CES integration. With Ukraine unwilling to move further than an FTA (and even this might depend on internal Ukrainian politics), the basis for integration will remain limited. Moreover, the common market will grow even less in terms of buying power since Russia's GDP per capita is the highest among the states participating in the CIS. To sum up, it is clear that the economic integration within the framework of the SES (or under any other umbrella organization) will not substantially enlarge the internal market for Russian producers and investors. To justify costly efforts, with the repudiation of VAT costing more than a billion dollars a year as one vivid example, the arithmetic of the Russian CIS integration must include other, non-economic variables.

These variables belong to the geopolitical and security spheres. Russia is striving to preserve and even enhance its leading role in the post-Soviet space. In the 2000s, Russia is slowly coming to accept the need for self-restriction and concentration on vital interests. Trenin argues that the major objective in the near future will come down to rearranging post-Soviet territory and establishing a centre of power under Russia's aegis.[21] Khristenko justifies integration, stating that Russia is not able to compete on its own with the principal players on the world political and economic scene. As a part of the SES, it will be able to defend its interests with more confidence based on common resources.[22] Creating a union in the post-Soviet space is meaningless for Moscow in this sense unless Russia is able to assert its leading role in it. Indeed, analysis of policies in the 2000s shows that this goal remains one of the guiding lines. The ideas upon which both the EurAsEC and the SES are based are aimed at securing Russia's leading role in these organizations. For example, according to the SES Concept, the voting power in the SES (although not in the first stage) is to be allocated according on the weighted basis. The number of votes for every participating state is to be determined, taking into account the economic potential of each state (Art. V of the SES Concept). These mechanisms ought to provide leadership for Russia in the organizations of regional integration. Among other steps intended to strengthen Russia's leading role in the post-Soviet space are the preservation of military bases and the usage of energy supplies as a means of pressure.

Old paradigms in the beginning of the second Putin presidency

The beginning of Vladimir Putin's second presidential term provides a preliminary answer to the question as to whether the trend toward the economization of Russia's foreign policy would be sustainable. It can be seen that the pragmatic spirit of raising the country's competitiveness and defending its economic interests both in the post-Soviet space and in the global arena is being restrained by the geopolitical objective of reasserting Russia's 'traditional zone of influence'; that is, to place the CIS states under Russia's indirect rule. The emphasis is on placing the 'near abroad' states under Russia's leadership and, by all means, not giving them away to the West. Thus, the current Russian foreign policy on the post-Soviet space is governed by the old, however softened, paradigm of the confrontation with the West. There was a multitude of cases in 2004 and 2005 where Russia's foreign policy was guided by the old paradigm of control over the post-Soviet space: above all, these relate to Ukraine, but also Abkhazia and Georgia.

Russia intervened in the Ukrainian presidential elections of 2004, proactively backing Victor Yanukovich. A variety of means was utilized to achieve the goal of installing a power in Ukraine that would be obliged to Moscow and responsive to its requests. First, the switch to the country-of-destination principle was realized shortly before the elections. The connection between this 'present' and the election campaign is difficult to ignore. Second, Yanukovich was backed by all imaginable means of personal support from the highest levels. Putin flew twice to Ukraine to express his support for Yanukovich's candidature. Russian politicians and officials of even higher standing repeatedly pronounced anathema against Yushchenko. Third, other financial resources were put into play, in particular for the purpose of mobilizing the Ukrainians residing in Russian territory. Moscow was covered with billboards calling upon Ukrainians to vote for Yanukovich. Fourth, Ukrainian citizens were allowed to spend 90 days in Russia without registration (up from the previous mere three-day limit). The decisions allowing double citizenship and 90 registration-free days were speedily rushed through the Russian Duma to be in time for the presidential elections in Ukraine. Having made Russians inferior to foreigners in their own country, this decision caused a wave of protest. The government felt obliged to introduce the same measure for Russian citizens as well – something completely unimaginable before, taking into consideration the officially declared war on terror and the general tightening of the screws in Russia. Fifth, Putin, together with the Turkmen and Belarusian presidents, congratulated Yanukovich on his victory after the second round of the elections, thus attempting to afford him international recognition.

The Ukrainian election campaign is not the only case showing the prevalence of the desire to regain influence in the post-Soviet space, and the perception of post-Soviet politics in terms of confrontation with the

West. Russia's backing of Abkhazia in the Georgian–Abkhazian conflict indicates the same perception of the power game in terms of indirect confrontation with the West. Since the new Georgian leadership is perceived as an agent of the West, it has been meeting a hostile attitude from Russia since the change of power in Tbilisi. The tensions are not decreasing over time. During a press conference in late 2004, Putin directly accused the Georgian leadership of 'being on Soros' payroll'.[23] During the same conference, speaking of his perception of the post-Soviet space, Putin focused on severely criticizing Western 'double standards' on the issues of human rights and elections. He mentioned Afghanistan, Kosovo, Iraq and Macedonia as examples. The President expressed his unhappiness with the so-called 'permanent revolutions' in the post-Soviet republics, which are being 'orchestrated' in some other place for this or that nation.[24]

In the 1990s, Russia was often the one to bury integration agreements in the CIS spaces. Hale elaborates on the 'logic of economic anti-imperialism' as an explanation for this phenomenon.[25] The desire to preserve fiscal discipline and to avoid the heavy expenditures needed to implement the agreements led the Russian government into sabotaging these agreements on financial grounds. Thus, Russian government officials have come to play a crucial behind-the-scenes role in stifling efforts to reunify the 'near abroad countries'. This happened, for example, with the introduction of the Ruble Zone in 1997 and with the Russia–Belarus Union in the same year.[26] It appears to be changing under Putin, however. Russia is now more decisively expressing its readiness to pay for integration, as happened in August 2004 with the decision not to levy VAT on oil and gas exported to the SES member states. The same can be observed with regard to the military bases abroad. While a number of overseas bases have been closed (Cuba, Vietnam and so on), the bases in the CIS (Armenia and Tajikistan) have been preserved and maintained. Although the role of economic factors in Russian foreign policy on CIS integration is increasing, this does not imply that Russia is guided solely by these factors. To the contrary, Russia is now ready to pay the price for reasserting its sphere of influence in the post-Soviet space. The state is ready to invest money to promote integration, and it is expecting returns in geopolitical, security and economic terms. Hence, Russia's approach to integration in the post-Soviet space in the beginning of Putin's second term is guided by a mix of motives. While the economic factor and the defence of the national economic interests will not be taken off the board completely, the geopolitical objective of reasserting the zone of influence in the 'near abroads' is coming to the foreground. The attraction of this objective is proving strong enough for Russia to be willing to accept high economic costs in order to push other CIS states towards integration under the umbrella of Moscow-written agreements.

Pushing CIS states towards integration

The only integration vehicle put forward in the beginning of the 1990s was the CIS. Russia strongly advocated this arrangement. Russian leaders pushed immediately for the organization to increase its formal powers.[27] Thus, the CIS as an institutional framework was used as a principal means for obtaining greater control and power in the post-Soviet space. Putin's era in Russian foreign policy has so far been characterized by a variety of efforts to push the CIS states towards integration. President Putin has acknowledged that the CIS has not always been effective, pragmatic and consistent. Currently, it finds itself on the threshold: either it will achieve significant advances or it will be washed away completely. The president also noted that a number of local interstate agreements of lesser scale, whether focusing on economic or security matters, worked more effectively than the CIS as a whole. Real advances were made in cases where it was possible to find mutual benefits and interests with the partners.[28] Russia is gradually becoming more sophisticated, employing both sticks and carrots in its efforts to push for integration. Instruments being used to pressure the CIS states or to give them various incentives to consent to proposals from Moscow are being drawn from three main areas, which are broadly defined as follows: first, the conclusion of integration agreements intended to create the legal and institutional framework for regional integration; second, oil, gas, and energy supplies; third, support and cooperation in military and security areas.

Integration agreements

A legal, organizational and institutional framework is expected to be created in the course of concluding plurilateral integration agreements. Moscow is pushing its neighbours to conclude agreements such as EurAsEC or SES, while not encouraging the creation of any union of which Russia is not a member. At the same time, Russia is striving by all means to assert its dominant role in the CIS. In 2004, Russia entered the Central Asian Cooperation (CAC) forum. CAC was created in 2002 and originally included the four Central Asian states of Kazakhstan, Kyrgyzstan, Uzbekistan and Tajikistan, having been the only multilateral post-Soviet body in Central Asia that excluded Russia. According to its Charter, this organization pursues regional political, economic and security cooperation. In May 2004, the heads of the member states declared their intention to build a common Central Asian market as well as international energy and transport consortia.[29] Before the Russian accession, Kazakhstan was the leading force of the CAC. This can change with the accession of Russia to the organization.

Energy supplies

The most salient areas from which Moscow draws powerful instruments to guide neighbouring states are perhaps oil and gas supplies, as well as other energy supplies. As the neighbouring states are dependant to a greater or lesser degree on Russian supplies of oil, gas and/or electricity, Russia can use a variety of sticks and carrots in this field. While still rather unusual in the 1990s, it is becoming a normal practice under Putin. One vivid example is the decision taken in August 2004 not to levy VAT on oil and gas exports to Ukraine, Belarus and Kazakhstan (that is, the SES member states). The transition from the country-of-origin principle to the country-of-destination principle for VAT payments on oil and gas exports is one of the most costly concessions that Russia is ready to make for the sake of the SES. While the exports of oil and gas to Russia's neighbours were previously subject to the levying of VAT in Russia, this VAT will no longer be levied on hydrocarbons exported specifically to the SES member states. According to the Vice Prime Minister, Alexandr Zhukov, the transition to the country-of-destination principle in relation with the SES member states would cost the Russian budget approximately 34 billion rubles ($1.17 billion) in 2005 alone. Zhukov argues that this measure will be compensated by the positive effects of the establishment of the SES.[30] As Ukraine will profit the most from this measure, it should be viewed as the payment to Ukraine for its consent to join the SES.

Gas prices are used as a powerful instrument in Russia-Belarus relations. For example, the gas price for Belarus in 2004 was settled at less than $47/TCM, which is well below world prices, although it is higher than domestic prices in Russia itself. In the second half of 2004, the two states held negotiations, which went even further. The economic expansion of Russian business in Belarus and the direct dominance of Gazprom over Beltransgaz are at stake. According to the preliminary decision already reached, some advances were made on the issue of Russian participation in the Belarusian gas industry in exchange for the promise to supply gas at Russian domestic prices. Thus, in order to acquire control over Beltransgaz, Russia is willing not only to pay by means of cash and loans but also to start selling gas to Belarus at domestic prices.[31] In addition, large-scale projects connected with massive investments can move forward not only as the goals but also as the means of foreign policy in cases when the recipient countries might be interested in their completion (as in the case of Gazprom's intention to invest in the Iran–Armenia gas pipeline).

Furthermore, the use of gas pricing as a policy tool became particularly prominent at the end of 2005. The (successful) Russian demand of $230/TCM engendered a crisis in Russia–Ukraine relations. At the same time, the price was set at $110 for Georgia and Azerbaijan. The gas price for Belarus remained unchanged ($46.68/TCM).

Also, the control over electricity supplies was used several times by Russia, most prominently in cases of switching off the Moldovan and Georgian power circuits for short periods of time in 2003 and 2004.

Military and security areas

The instruments and means of foreign policy are not restricted to economy and life support. Attempts to find an acceptable balance between geopolitical objectives and economic costs can be traced also to the security issues in Russia's CIS policies. While several military bases abroad were closed down during the Putin's first presidency (Cuba, Vietnam and so on), the beginning of the second presidency was marked by attempts to consolidate Russia's remaining military influence in the post-Soviet space. The issue of the military base in Armenia (102 division) has been settled on favourable terms, as Armenia agreed to share costs and to hand over the property rights to the land and buildings of the base in Russia. A preliminary decision was reached with Tajikistan on the transformation of the 201 division into a military base, an issue which had been debated for at least five years.[32]

Within the Collective Security Treaty Organization (CSTO), Russia has begun to supply the member states with armaments at domestic prices. A common communication system is to be established.[33] Such steps indicate the willingness to pay in order to preserve and increase Russia's influence on the post-Soviet space by means of indirect subsidization in military and security spheres.

To sum up, in the course of the 2000s Russia has started to employ a wider variety of available means to support integration agreements in which it plays a leading role. In fact, all kinds of agreements are supported, from the bilateral agreement with Belarus to the plurilateral Single Economic Space to CSTO, an organization with purely security purposes. Moreover, Russian foreign policy in the CIS can now be based on the readiness to use costly carrots in relations with its neighbours, which was not the case in the 1990s. The sophistication of contemporary

Russian foreign policy on the issue of CIS integration should not how-ever be overestimated, as it still shows an inclination to flex muscles, whether military or economic, and 'show power' as was the case with the electricity cut-offs.

The concept of multi-level and multi-speed integration and the impact of the EU experience

The Russian Federation Foreign Policy Concept,[34] approved in June 2000, refers to the concept of differing speeds and levels of integration within the CIS framework. According to this idea, integration within the CIS can pro-ceed on a flexible basis, with different states having the right to choose the 'integration packages' and to join different agreements and institutions at different times. The concept of multi-speed integration in the CIS was developed in the 1990s and defined in the crucial Presidential Decree of 14 September 1995. Art. VII of the Decree shows strong support for the model of different-speed integration. While mentioning its non-obligatory character, the Decree stipulates that the position of the CIS states in rela-tion to this model is viewed as an important factor conditioning the scope of economic, political and military assistance that Russia would be willing to render to its CIS neighbours. The concept of multi-speed and multi-level integration underlies the integration designs of the 2000s as well.

According to early agreements on the CIS (including the CIS Charter and the Agreement on the Creation of the Economic Union signed in 1993), the Economic Union was supposed to lead in stages to the CES, meaning the implementation of all four freedoms. Integration of the four freedoms had to be accompanied by concerted monetary, budget-ary, tax, customs and currency policies, as well as the harmonization of economic legislation. In other words, the CIS was supposed to be mov-ing in stages towards a full-scale EU-type common market. First, a free trade zone should have been created; second, a customs union; and, finally, economic and currency unions. This image resembled the his-tory of the creation of the EU. However, the whole process was planned to have been completed much faster – not in fifty, but rather in ten to fifteen years. Later, this vision was corroded by the real world events. It became clear that neither the scale nor the scope of the envisaged inte-gration would be reached so quickly. With regard to scope, even attempts to reach the first stage (an FTA) did not work out in practice. The second stage has been reached only by the Russia–Belarus Union. Regarding scale, the grand CIS designs comprising all twelve states were put aside in favour of agreements comprising a smaller number of participants. The reservation has always been made, however, that these smaller unions were free to be joined by other states at a later date.

In the 2000s, the EU ideal is still playing an important role in integration designs in the post-Soviet space. It is being mirrored both in the strategies and in the designs of regional integration constructed by Moscow. The Russian Middle Term Strategy towards the EU, which is intended for the period 2000–10, makes provision for the utilization of experience that was successful in the EU in the development of integration processes in the CIS area.[35] Both the EurAsEC and the SES agreements foresee a three-stage incremental development. The EurAsEC was planned to develop in three stages moving toward an economic union, although rather less comprehensive than the early CIS designs (for example, no currency union was planned from the start). The most recent integration design, the Single Economic Space (SES), is built on the same idea. It stipulates that the SES is to be formed stage by stage, taking into account the possibility of integration at differing speeds and levels (Art. II, see p. 31). Thus, at least technically both EurAsEC and SES agreements stipulate a three-stage design; that is, going from an initial free trade area through a customs union to a comprehensive economic union.

Recent integration designs are characterized by the same approach. The development is divided into three ascending stages. The sequence of stages on the way to the SES is influenced by the successful experiences of the EU. Discussing Russia's integration strategies in particular in the post-Soviet space, Khristenko draws an analogy with the 'multi-speed Europe', emphasizing the success of this concept in the EU developments of the last two decades. He assumes also that the centripetal forces of the integration agreements in the CIS will increase with time, provided positive effects become apparent.[36] However, the scope is substantially less grandiose than in the 1990s. It has become clear that the depth of EU integration is unlikely to be reached in the post-Soviet space, even in the long run. Consequently, in the first place, some advanced features of economic integration, such as the common currency, are put aside (with the exception of the Russia–Belarus Union). Second, attention is concentrated more on the mid-term goals of the first stage, such as free trade and facilitation of trade between participating states.

Now, the claim that the EU represents a technical model for the Russian designs for economic integration in the post-Soviet space does not go so far as to say that Russia wants to create a new 'EU in Eurasia'. The model role of the EU for the SES and the EurAsEC is more technical than substantial. There is a principal difference between the early European Communities and current Russian aspirations for the economic integration of the post-Soviet space. All these projects would naturally lead to the institutionalization of the leading role of Russia, thus making Russia the dominant decision maker in the organizations to be created. Such a consequence is likely, taking into account Russia's heavy weight in the politics and economics of the post-Soviet space. This situation is qualitatively different from the integration that took place in the European Communities in the 1950s and 1960s and to date. Hence, the impact of the EU is restricted to the technical modelling of the institutional designs and the planned processes of economic integration both within the EurAsEC and the SES.

Official policy on the problem of compatibility of integration processes within the CIS and with the EU

Two vectors dominate the integration agenda of Russian foreign policy: the EU vector and the CIS vector. As soon as discussion on the Common Economic Space with the European Union started in 2001–02, the problem of the compatibility of these two integration projects quickly became a serious issue to resolve. The problem is multi-faceted and by no means trivial. It includes such issues as the rules of origin and the compatibility of standards. Concerns have been raised both in the EU and in Russia. In fact, the SES has often been mentioned in CES negotiations between the EU and Russia.[37]

The official Russian position on the issue of the compatibility of Russia's EU and CIS integration vectors is that these processes are compatible and should proceed concurrently. V.A. Chizhov, Deputy Minister of Foreign Affairs, summarized the official position by saying that 'we believe that the various integration projects do not obstruct one another's progress'.[38] This view is constantly supported in speeches by the highest state officials. President Putin, giving a speech on the prospects of Russia-EU economic cooperation, stressed that 'the formation of a common economic space in Europe should not restrict the abilities of the parties to take part in different regional integration processes'.[39] Analysing Russia's official approaches to the problem, Emerson comes to the conclusion that, in the Russian view, the system should consist of two hub-and-spoke systems in which the EU should agree not to interfere with the development of CIS integration. Russia prefers a free hand to deepen CIS integration.[40] Furthermore, Putin characterized these processes in terms of 'harmonizing relations with Greater Europe':

> You know that Russia is building together with the European Union four so-called common spaces. And the first and most important of

them is an economic space. But we are planning to do the same within the CES (Common Economic Space) between Russia, Ukraine, Belarus and Kazakhstan. What does this mean? It means that we are harmonizing relations within Greater Europe. This has nothing to do with some Russian aspiration to subjugate or absorb anybody. That is rubbish.[41]

Khristenko goes into more detail, outlining the general recipe of how the SES and the CES are to be pursued concurrently. Starting with the question as to whether a successful development of the SES could impede the creation of the EU–Russian CES, the Vice Minister concludes that such a danger exists only if the union of the 'Big Four' is built without taking into account Russia's obligations regarding European partners (or vice versa). If a certain balance of interests and obligations in respect of both the EU and the CES member states is observed, then parallel development of the two spaces will be feasible. The Minister supports his argument with the examples of Mexico (being a member of NAFTA, Mexico concluded a free trade agreement with the EU) and the EU itself, which has dozens of free trade agreements with countries around the world.[42]

Conclusion

The analysis of Russian foreign policy towards the CIS in the beginning of the 2000s enables us to differentiate two periods. The years 2000–03 demonstrated a gradual movement towards a more pragmatic and balanced foreign policy. This policy recognized the importance of the defence of national economic interests by political means. Any direct confrontation was avoided, both globally and in relations with the post-Soviet states. The emphasis was put on employing the economic mechanisms of integration with the neighbouring states. The early designs of all-CIS integration agreements were removed from the table, and the designs envisaging economic integration between a restricted number of key states (Ukraine, Kazakhstan and Belarus) were high on the daily agenda. Both EurAsEC and SES agreements stipulate a three-stage design; that is, going from an initial free trade area through a customs union to a comprehensive economic union. The functionalist understanding of the process of economic integration and the experience of the European Union underlie the desire to start modestly and to move gradually toward deeper economic integration. The first two years of the second term witnessed a partial refusal to continue the same policies. Russian foreign policy began to put greater emphasis on the attainment of an indisputable position of leadership in the post-Soviet space. This space is understood as the traditional zone of influence, which is to be restored.

Russia has not yet worked out a coherent and comprehensive approach towards its regional integration and towards integration with the CIS states in particular. The latest developments show that Russia is now ready to pay the price for reasserting the sphere of influence in the post-Soviet space. The state is willing to accept high costs in order to push other CIS states towards integration under the umbrella of Moscow-written agreements. Russia is consistently pushing the CIS states toward integration. To achieve this goal, Moscow is employing a wide variety of available means. Both sticks and carrots are being used. Russia is ready to pay a high price while hoping that integration will pay off threefold – economically, in terms of security, and geopolitically – by asserting Russia's leading role in the post-Soviet space and by increasing its weight in the global arena.

Notes

1 One can encounter a multitude of names used not only in newspaper articles but also in official documents and speeches to describe this integration project of Russia, Ukraine, Belarus, and Kazakhstan. The terms Common Economic Space (CES), Single Economic Space (SES), Integral Economic Space (IES), and Unified Economic Space (UES) have all been used. These names correspond to *Obshchee* or *Edinoe Ekonomicheskoe Prostranstvo* in Russian. Gradually, the terms *Edinoe Ekonomicheskoe Prostranstvo* and Single Economic Space have become standard usage.

2 Cf. Yu. A. Borko, 'Rossiia i Evropa: kurs ili dreif?' ['Russia and Europe: Course or Drift?'], in *Kakaia integratsiia nuzhna Rossii* [*What integration does Russia need?*], (Moscow: Komitet 'Rossiia v ob'edinennoy Evrope'), 2002: 7–16. See also Yu. V. Shishkov's comment in the same volume: 32.

3 'Foreign Policy Concept of the Russian Federation', approved by the President of the Russian Federation, 28 June 2000, http://www.russiaeurope.mid.ru/RussiaEurope/concept.html

4 Russia's National Security Concept (Blueprint), approved by the Decree of the President of the Russian Federation, 10 January 2000, 24, http://www. russiaeurope.mid.ru/RussiaEurope/russiastrat2000.html

5 'Foreign Policy Concept of the Russian Federation', approved by the President of the Russian Federation, 28 June 2000. ch. 1 'General Principles', http://www.russiaeurope.mid.ru/RussiaEurope/concept.html

6 'Address of the President to the Federal Assembly of the Russian Federation', 26 May 2004, http://www.kremlin.ru/eng/text/speeches/2004/05/262021_64906. shtm

7 'Osnovnye dokumenty, reglamentiruiushie funktsionirovanie zony svobodnoy torgovli' ['Main documents regulating the functioning of the Free trade zone'], Memorandum, http://www.cis.minsk.by/russian/zon_dokm.htm

8 'Free Trade Zone of the Commonwealth's countries: main stages of establishment', Memorandum, http://www.cis.minsk.by/english/eng-zona.htm

9 V. Batyuk, 'Russia and the CIS. Does the CIS exist any more?' Conflict Studies Research Centre of the Russian Defence Academy, Working Paper Series, 1999, http://www.da.mod.uk/CSRC/documents/Russian/E103/E103, ch. 5.

10 Only 44 out of the 70 bilateral economic agreements and none of the five principal plurilateral agreements – the Commonwealth of Independent States (1991), the Economic Union of the CIS (1994), the Central Asian Economic Union (1995), GUUAM (1999), and the Eurasian Economic Community (2000) – have been implemented. Russia had by then only implemented about one-third of the economic agreements with its CIS partners. Tacis (2001), *Regional Trade Agreements among CIS Countries and WTO Accession*, available at http://www.aris.ru

11 M.B. Olcott, A. Åslund and S.W. Garnett, *Getting It Wrong. Regional Cooperation and the Commonwealth of Independent States*, (Washington, DC: Carnegie Endowment for International Peace, 1999): 230.

12 A. Schleifer and D. Treisman, 'A Normal Country', NBER Working Paper 10057, October 2003.

13 'Russia's Strategic Course in its Relations with the States-Participants of the Commonwealth of Independent States', Presidential Decree of 14 September 1995, 940.

14 B. Lo, 'Principles and Contradictions. The Foreign Policy of Vladimir Putin', in T. de Wilde d'Estmael and L. Spetschinsky (eds) *La politique étrangère de la Russie et l'Europe* (Brussels: Peter Lang, 2004): 67.

15 V.B. Khristenko, 'Making Headway to Integration', *Russia in Global Politics*, 2 (March–April 2004), http://eng.globalaffairs.ru/numbers/6/508.html

16 *Ibid.*

17 *Ibid.*

18 The Concept itself utilized the term 'Integral Economic Space'. The English translation is available under http:// www.kmu.gov.ua /control/en/publish/ printable_article?art_id=2831293

19 R.M. Cutler, 'Integration Within and Without the CIS', *Association for the Study of Nationalities Monthly, Analysis of Current Events 9*, 3 (March 1997).

20 'Za geopolitiku Rossiya otdast 34 milliarda rubley' ['Russia will give up 34 billion rubles for geopolitics'], *Rosbalt*, 28 July 2004.

21 D. Trenin, *New Priorities in Russian Foreign Policy: 'Project CIS'*, 2004, available at www.carnegie.ru

22 V.B. Khristenko, 'Making Headway to Integration', *Russia in Global Politics*, 2 (March–April 2004), http://eng.globalaffairs.ru/numbers/6/508.html

23 Press conference of the President of the Russian Federation, V.V. Putin, Moscow, Kremlin, 23 December 2004, http:// www.kremlin.ru/eng/speeches/ 2004/12/23/1806_81700.shtml

24 *Ibid.*

25 H. Hale, *Russian Fiscal Veto on CIS Integration*, PONARS Policy Memo 15, 1997, http://www.csis.org/ruseura/ponars/policymemos/pm_0015.pdf

26 *Ibid.*

27 M. B. Olcott, A. Åslund and S.W. Garnett, *Getting It Wrong. Regional Cooperation and the Commonwealth of Independent States* (Washington, DC: Carnegie Endowment for International Peace, 1999): 11.

28 'Putin konstatiroval skoruiu smert SNG' ['Putin the near death of the CIS'], *Kommersant*, 130(2969), 20 July 04.

29 S. Salimov, 'Moskva usilit svoe vliianie v Centralnoy Azii', *Nezavisimaia Gazeta*, 30 August 2004.

30 'Za geopolitiku Rossiia otdast 34 milliarda rubley' ['Russia will give 34 billion rubles for geopolitics'], *Rosbalt*, 28 July 2004.

31   *Kommersant*, 155(2994), 24 August 2004.
32   S. Martirosyan, 'Moskva perekhodit v kontrnastuplenie' ['Moscow launches a counter-offensive'], *Rosbalt*, 10 August 2004.
33   *Ibid.*
34   'Foreign Policy Concept of the Russian Federation', approved by the President of the Russian Federation, 28 June 2000, http://www.russiaeurope.mid.ru/RussiaEurope/concept.html
35   'The Russian Federation Middle Term Strategy Towards the European Union (2000–2010)', http://www.eur.ru/en/p_245.htm
36   V.B. Khristenko, 'Making Headway to Integration', *Russia in Global Politics*, 2 (March–April 2004), http://eng.globalaffairs.ru/numbers/6/508.html
37   Interview with Alexey Slizkov, Mission of the Russian Federation to the European Communities, 19 March 2004, conducted by the author.
38   V.A. Chizhov, Deputy Minister of Foreign Affairs of the Russian Federation, Statement at the International Conference, 'Wider Europe: Enlarging Tansborder Cooperation in Central and Eastern Europe', 11 November 2003, Press Release, 32/03, www.russiaeu.org
39   V.V. Putin, Speech at a meeting with representatives of the European Round Table of Industrialists and the Round Table of Industrialists of Russia and the EU Mission of the Russian Federation to the European communities, Press Release, 38/03, 2 December 2003, www.russiaeu.org
40   M. Emerson, *The Wider Europe Matrix* (CEPS Paperback, 2004): 29.
41   Press conference of the President of the Russian Federation, V.V. Putin. Moscow, Kremlin, 23 December 2004, http://www.kremlin.ru/eng/speeches/2004/12/23/1806_81700.shtml
42   V.B. Khristenko, 'Making Headway to Integration', *Russia in Global Politics*, 2 (March–April 2004), http://eng.globalaffairs.ru/numbers/6/508.html

3
Russia's Pursuit of its Eurasian Security Interests: Weighing the CIS and Alternative Bilateral–Multilateral Arrangements

John P. Willerton and Mikhail A. Beznosov

During a joint press conference with the Armenian President in Yerevan, March 2005, Russian President Vladimir Putin publicly acknowledged what had long been assumed about the original logic and role of the Commonwealth of Independent States (CIS) in the transformation of the post-Soviet states, commenting:

> The stated aims were one thing, but in reality the CIS was formed in order to make the Soviet Union's collapse as civilized and smooth as possible and to minimize the economic and humanitarian losses it entailed, above all for people.

Western observers had long been sceptical about the viability and utility of the CIS as related to the security, economic and other policy needs of the former Soviet Union (FSU) states, and Putin's remark appeared to fully legitimate this scepticism.[1] Yet, the Russian President went on to discuss the valuable role the CIS played in 'exchanging information and discussing general problems, general political, humanitarian and administrative issues'. Indeed, he went further in emphasizing the CIS's potential to address common regional problems and he expressed his desire that FSU states continue to utilize it:

> There are a great many problems to deal with and the CIS provides a forum for the leaders of our countries to meet regularly, discuss these

problems, take rapid measures to resolve them and then seek solutions either at the bilateral level or through the integration organizations ... we definitely should keep the CIS going and I think we all have an interest in this, regardless of the political views of this or that force either coming to power or losing power in this or that country at the given moment.[2]

The years since 1992 have witnessed the emergence of a wide array of multilateral and bilateral arrangements addressing the diversity of domestic and security concerns of the FSU states. Although the CIS was, in the early years, the most important forum bringing together all of the non-Baltic FSU states, other multilateral forums and a wide array of bilateral agreements have arisen to augment it.[3] While the CIS has, at one point or another, addressed the full range of policy concerns confronting the FSU states, more area-specific multilateral forums (for example, the Eurasian Economic Community and the Shanghai Cooperation Organization) and focused bilateral agreements (for example, the Russian–Armenian Mutual Military Infrastructure Agreement, 2002, and the Russian–Kazakh Agreement on Interactions in the Process of Exporting Military Related Merchandise to Third Countries, 2004) have become important settings for the more detailed addressing of specific sets of issues. This is certainly true of one critical policy area – regional security – and we focus on this issue area as we examine the position of the CIS, as nested among other bilateral–multilateral arrangements, in Russia's Eurasian security calculations.

Since the Soviet collapse, unilateral and regional security questions have been central to the foreign policy decision-making process in all FSU states, and most certainly in Russia.[4] Security issues encompass a complex range of issues, from broader strategic issues, to common infra-structural needs, and more concrete technical needs. The first CIS pro-nouncements and treaties addressed security issues, with various security-relevant institutions and many dozens of treaties, protocols and decisions issued in the aftermath. Taken together, the sizeable array of agreements and arrangements that emerged in the CIS's first dozen years reflects both the commonalities and important differences that charac-terized the twelve CIS member states as they manoeuvred and crafted their post-Cold War security positions. We analyse this set of CIS secu-rity agreements, in the process illuminating both the accomplishments and the limitations of CIS regional security cooperation. Our study, part of a larger project that entails creating and analysing a database of all

CIS treaties for the period 1992–2004, is intended to examine the dynamics of regional security and economic negotiations among the FSU states. A varied set of divergent domestic and geo-strategic interests animated the negotiating positions and actions of the twelve non-Baltic FSU countries but, under the rubric of the CIS, a set of common institutions and agreed-upon policies were crafted that represented an important component in all of these states' security structures.

Many observers have correctly questioned the long-term substance and significance of CIS arrangements,[5] especially as regards security, but we believe they merit attention as they have been an important focus of the foreign and security policy rhetoric and actions of Russia and other FSU states. While illuminating the content and significance of the security treaties negotiated in the CIS's first dozen years, we also argue that these security arrangements must be nested in the broader context of the FSU states' other bilateral and multilateral arrangements. Often more concrete and intrusive in the arrangements made and obligations incurred, these focused bilateral and multilateral agreements – when combined with the broader structures and policy preferences set out in CIS treaties – add up to form a more comprehensive and coherent security whole. We rely on the bilateral dealings involving the FSU's regional power, Russia, with five other FSU countries – Armenia, Belarus, Kazakhstan, Kyrgyzstan and Tajikistan – to further explore our expectations. Each of these states has important security issues involving Russia, each has been willing to engage Moscow in protracted negotiations and, accordingly, each has been able to craft a series of bilateral security arrangements with the FSU hegemon. At the same time, each of these states has been an active member of the CIS, each has engaged most if not all security structures and agreements, and each has continued to be committed to the CIS's core defence agreement, the Collective Security Treaty. Combined with Russia, these states offer a useful focus for considering the summed value of both CIS and bilateral treaty arrangements for the realization of more comprehensive FSU regional security. Meanwhile, we can concomitantly consider the evolving interests and perspectives of Russia, which has consistently struggled to reconstruct its regional power base while reasserting its regional leadership position.[6] Thus, an examination of both (1) CIS security treaties and (2) bilateral agreements involving a focused set of FSU states permits us to set out a more complete picture of Russia's and other states' post-Soviet security calculations and arrangements.

The universe of CIS security treaties: a glass half-full or half-empty?

During its almost fifteen-year existence, the CIS has been involved in a countless number of meetings and negotiations. Spanning a wide range of government officials and diplomatic representatives with its central organizational structure and its numerous treaties, agreements and protocols, the CIS formally appears as among the most developed inter-governmental organizations. In reality, much less of real substance has been implemented, with the Western scholarly literature – and Russian and FSU observers themselves – effectively documenting multilateral constraints and the meager organizational-policy accomplishments.[7] Nevertheless, the 12 CIS member-states have been involved in many high-profile, regularized consultations, their meetings yielding hundreds of treaties and accords, with the commitment of member states' resources, however limited, matched by the creation of selective multi-lateral institutions and combined forces (among the most important, the CIS 'peace-keeping' forces).[8]

While not contesting the 'common wisdom' about the powerful constraints operating on the 12 CIS member states as they have sought common understandings, policies and institutions, we desire to identify what this multilateral forum has accomplished in the all-important area of national and regional security. As part of a larger project on regional trade agreements and regional intergovernmental organizations, we culled all available published and web sources (including the official CIS website in Minsk) for CIS treaties negotiated during the period 1992–2004.[9] A thorough search yielded more than 1400 CIS documents of varied kinds, many of which involved relatively formal bureaucratic paperwork. More than 500 documents had been adopted by the CIS Council of Heads of State, the organization's top policy-setting body, while more than 900 were products of the CIS Council of Heads of Government. Of all these documents, more than 200 required either member states' ratification or implementation for inter-state procedures to go into effect.[10] We view these roughly 200 documents as legally binding treaties.[11] Among these 200 documents, 53 were found to involve security issues. These 53 treaties represent, to the best of our knowledge and effort, the total population of formally negotiated CIS security treaties, albeit with dozens of other related protocols, accords and support documents that touch upon more narrowly defined issues.[12] Having coded these treaties utilizing a detailed instrument involving over sixty questions, we were able to assess the formal products of over a dozen years of posturing and hard bargaining among Russia and other CIS member-states.[13]

What emerge from an analysis of this database of CIS security treaties are the contours of a regional security institutional-policy shell, composed of a number of interconnected components which, taken together, constitute a foundation for interested member states, most notably the regional hegemon, Russia, to advance their unilateral security interests. These interconnected components include, first, broad understandings and strategic definitions reflective of collective judgements and shared perspectives. Second, they include selective institutional arrangements designed to cope with often narrowly defined policy dilemmas. And, third, they include focused collective policy statements and ad hoc multilateral measures oriented toward concrete tasks or problems. Recalling that a fundamental operating norm of the CIS is the ability of all member states either to engage in or exit from any multilateral negotiations, with no obligation to sign or ratify resultant treaties, the 'exit option' permits member states complete flexibility and freedom of manoeuvre.[14] From a collective CIS perspective, this signifies that no arrangement or decision is binding on all members, so each CIS institution or treaty constitutes the agreed-upon interests of a separate and distinguishable subset of the entire CIS membership. Thus, all of the 53 negotiated security treaties represent individual understandings and arrangements relevant to a self-selected subset of the entire CIS membership, and binding on the signatory states to the extent that these states subsequently ratify and implement the final document. Taken together, the 53 treaties do, however, reveal a comprehensive regional security foundation that can be further developed through (1) additional CIS agreements and/or (2) other bilateral-multilateral arrangements. We contend that the 1992–2004 record of CIS development and treaty outcomes suggests that Russia and other FSU states are keen on using bilateral means to effectuate concrete regional security goals that transcend this multilateral foundation. As a result, both CIS and FSU bilateral developments must be considered to illuminate more fully the FSU regional security architecture.

In analysing signed CIS treaties, an important caveat is in order. Unlike with the case of negotiated bilateral agreements, we understand that the products of often prolonged CIS negotiations do not automatically yield fully worked out policies or immediately viable institutions.[15] These CIS treaties reflect the signatory states' individual and collective goals, expectations and hopes. Since the collective security arrangements resulting from CIS deliberations and actions cannot and will not exceed what is set out in the final documents, these signed treaties represent an important formal manifestation of individual and negotiated collective preferences, and thus are more reflective of FSU regional security potential than of accomplished policy.

Security issues addressed

From the beginning, FSU leaders and officials have emphasized the critical role of the CIS as a forum for exchanging information and perspectives, for illuminating problems, and for finding common policy responses. As Table 3.1 reveals, over twelve years of negotiation produced a sizeable number of treaties dealing with nearly all facets of post-Soviet Eurasian regional security. Core security issues involving weaponry and conflict were addressed in the earliest negotiated documents, as were more concrete problems such as natural disasters and immigration. It may be ironic that 21, or roughly 40 per cent, of all security treaties have no specific substantive focus, but this reflects the reality that these were complex multilateral negotiations and the fact that much of what was accomplished involved posturing and the general illumination of security questions, without more specific decisions or directed policies. Many of these 'non-specific' security treaties were signed in the CIS's early years, most of them set out general goals and consensus thinking around the theme of 'collective security', and they generally reflected the sort of high-profile public posturing that we have associated with meetings between CIS heads of state and heads of government.

Table 3.1   Security issues addressed by CIS security treaties, 1992–2004

Issue	No. of treaties addressing issue*	Earliest	Latest
Terrorism	13	1992	2004
Conventional weapons and small arms	12	1992	1998
Interstate war	10	1992	2003
Ethnic conflict	8	1992	1996
Territorial disputes	7	1993	2001
Biological and chemical weapons	6	1992	1998
Intrastate war	6	1992	2003
Nuclear weapons	5	1992	1995
Drug trafficking	3	1995	1998
Immigration	2	1995	1998
Natural disasters	2	1992	1998
Disease	1	1998	
Treaties with no specific substantive focus	21		
Total no. of treaties	53		

* The treaty numbers do not total 53 because many treaties addressed multiple security issues.

It is not surprising that nearly 25 per cent of all security treaties involve conventional weapons and/or small arms, while another 25 per cent touch upon issues of terrorism. These are two fundamental security areas important to all FSU states, but the 'logic' of how those security areas were addressed through the CIS meetings and deliberations varied greatly. The control of conventional and small weapons was an immediate post-Soviet concern, and it was more amenable to multilateral action. Early treaties in this area set out broad goals, the development of common CIS forces, and the organization of command structures, with one treaty providing specifics on the coordination of conventional forces in Europe (15 May 1992). Through the following six years, additional agreements built on this base, factoring in border issues (especially with non-CIS states), the creation of a common air defence system, and information exchange programmes. All of these conventional and small arms treaties were signed in the 1990s, the last being signed in 1998. In similar fashion, the 6 treaties touching upon weapons of mass destruction (biological, chemical, or nuclear) were also negotiated in the 1990s, but these dealt with narrowly constructed technical issues such as border and transit issues, safety procedures and information exchange. Only 2 treaties signed in 1995, one addressing the concept of collective security and the other discussing ways of deepening military cooperation among CIS member states, dealt with broader issues involving weapons of mass destruction.[16] Thus, whereas conventional and small arms treaties dealt both with broad strategic issues and with narrow technical considerations, those that even just touched upon weapons of mass destruction did so only in so far as various infrastructural and technical arrangements were relevant to these types of weapons.

The CIS has also addressed issues of terrorism since its earliest days, with the increasing importance of this issue area necessitating ongoing negotiations that continued into the 2000s (with 4 of these 13 treaties being signed during President Putin's tenure). What CIS negotiations accomplished – and failed to accomplish – in this all-important area is reflective of both the potential and the limitations inherent in this multilateral forum. In 1992, several treaties addressed broader security questions relevant to terrorism, including the first steps toward creating unified armed forces and the identification of measures entailing the use and non-use of threat and force among and within member states. Yet looking beyond these initial documents in the CIS's first year, most treaties with a component on terrorism had narrow foci of interest, involving information exchange and/or infrastructural concerns (for example, transit control, especially concerning borders with non-CIS

states). The two 'omnibus-like' treaties of 1995 that we referred to earlier –
dealing more broadly with collective security and expanded military
cooperation – only include passing references to control of terrorism.
But the 4 treaties of the early 2000s addressed more narrowly defined
and timely matters (for example, the situation in Afghanistan in the
wake of the 2001 US invasion) and the further standardization of
relevant CIS procedures vis-à-vis those of the OECD and the UN.
Over time, treaties with broader intergovernmental understandings
gave way to more narrow concrete agreements, and where the former
generally entailed nonactionable statements, the latter involved
implementable decisions.

A final area of policy interest involves a set of treaties addressing
interstate war (10 treaties) and territorial disputes (7 treaties). Again,
beginning with the 15 May 1992 Treaty on Collective Security that laid
out broad thinking on a wide range of security issues, these documents
concerned force arrangements, collective security procedures, measures to
deal with potential crisis situations (including the concept of a unified air
defence), and steps to bolster and maintain external borders. Those specifically addressing territorial disputes were more specific in their content,
including detailed understandings on observing the sovereignty, territorial integrity, and inviolability of member states' borders, and specific
arrangements regarding the support of collective peace-keeping forces
(for example, 2000 and 2001 treaties involving such forces in Abkhazia).

Organization-integrated services funding

Two thirds of the 53 CIS security treaties were signed in the organization's first five years (see Table 3.4, column 1). We have noted that a
good number of these early documents involved posturing and general
principles and goals, with these treaties generally signed by most or all
member states. Other documents had a narrower, more technical focus,
but while all member states participated in negotiations (including
hesitant participants such as Turkmenistan and Ukraine, who were
engaged as observers), those states formally signing the resultant documents varied on a treaty-by-treaty basis. As a result, the significance of
individual treaties and sets of treaties varied considerably, a point to
which we will return in the next section as we consider the individual
member states' engagement in the CIS. A review of the chronology of
CIS security treaty construction reveals a flurry of activity in the early
years (1992–93), culminating in a number of important treaties signed
in 1995–96. Broad common understandings having been reached, and
selected infrastructural and technical issues having been addressed,

there was a significant drop in treaty production in subsequent years, with security treaties in the late 1990s and early 2000s generally constituting either (1) an updating or expanding of treaties and arrangement already in place (and most especially involving the early documents that set out broad principles, as with collective security), or (2) narrowly constructed documents directed toward specific issue concerns (for example, a June 2001 document fine-tuning military–industrial cooperation). As we will see, the drop in CIS treaty production and the narrowing of the foci of these fewer treaties came as the number of bilateral treaties among FSU states (and most particularly with Russia) grew.

The potential value of CIS negotiations and treaties in enabling member states to better link and coordinate selected capabilities and infrastructures is revealed by the fact that 29 of the 53 security relevant treaties entail some level of integration of common services. By such technical integration we have in mind more unified standards and joined capabilities. We contend that after the CIS's first years, this was a major role for these multilateral deliberations and, as Table 3.2 reveals, such integration involved a diversity of concerns, such as achieving standardization of measurements, equipment and capabilities; the provision of linked technical services; and the development of scientific

Table 3.2 Types of integration in common services, CIS security treaties, 1992–2004

Type of service	No. of treaties wrt type of integration*
Standards or standardization	16
Technical services	16
Scientific services	14
Transportation	13
Education and training	12
Industrial project services	8
Telecommunications	7
Tax services	4
Health services	3
Immigration service	2
Crime control service	1
Environment	1
Public administration	1
None specified	24
Total no. of treaties = 53	

* The treaty numbers do not total 53 because many treaties addressed multiple types of integration.

Table 3.3   Types of organizational structures specified in CIS security treaties, 1992–2004

Organizational structure	No. of treaties wrt given organizational structure*
Executive assembly/general council/ general participatory body	13
Executive body	11
Secretary-general/executive president	4
Official language(s) specified	4
Regular meetings	2
None	23
No. of treaties = 53	

* The treaty numbers do not total 53 because some treaties contained multiple organizational structures.

services, and comparable and interconnected educational and training programs. While some treaties entailed linking infrastructural capabilities such as telecommunications, others involved coordinating such national services as immigration and crime control services. On balance, these more concrete documents were agreements that were more likely to be subsequently implemented.

Yet another indicator of potentially more binding linkages is the emergence of governing bodies and organizational structures, which we also find in slightly over half of the CIS security related treaties (see Table 3.3). Fifty-seven per cent of the security treaties contain provisions for creating such structures, with general participatory or executive bodies specified in most such cases. Such executive and/or deliberative bodies could facilitate information exchange and discussion, with the longer-term potential for heightened policy coordination and joint decision making among member states. The operative word, however, is 'potential', because the reality that many security treaties were not implemented means that far fewer organizational structures were actually created than intended. In fact, the most important governing bodies created (for example, the Council of Collective Security, the Council of Defence Ministers and the Council of Foreign Ministers) have essentially served as forums for the exchange of information or discussion of policy preferences.

When we add up all these and related dimensions of CIS construction we do not find a trend over time toward more binding institutional arrangements or the evolution of the CIS as an increasingly integrative regional entity (see Table 3.4). First, as already noted, most CIS treaty 'output' was produced during the organization's first five years, whether in terms of total number of security treaties (68 per cent), security treaties with an issue focus (72 per cent), treaties dealing with organizational structures (77 per cent), treaties advancing integration in an issue area (65 per cent), or treaties with set funding (75 per cent). Multilateral activity waned as the focus shifted to bilateral negotiation. Moreover, as we move from least to most intrusive and resource demanding arrangements, from the simple generation of treaties to the generation of treaties with fixed funding, the number of signed treaties diminishes: from a total of 53 security treaties, the totals drop to 32 with a specific issue focus, to 30 with organizational structures, to 20 with intended integration in any issue area, to only 12 with fixed funding. And as regards funding, in those cases where funding is discussed in a treaty, it is left to member states to make their own choices; there is no regulating or enforcing entity.

Finally, beyond the question of implementation of signed documents – and we have already noted this is an important question – the cumulated integrative value of CIS security treaties and related institutions is affected by individual member states' preferences in signing finalized agreements. Given the ever-present 'exit option', most of these 53 treaties did not garner the unanimous support and signatures of all 12 member states. As levels of CIS engagement varied across member states, we must at least briefly consider these member states' levels of commitment to signed documents as we evaluate the cumulative value of the resultant CIS security arrangements.

Varying levels of engagement

The CIS 'exit option' enabling each member state to determine for itself its level of engagement, both in the organization as a whole and in specific treaty arrangements, permitted even the most sceptical FSU states to remain engaged. Contrasting domestic and security needs yielded a variety of policy preferences among member states. The states' assessments of Russian interests and actions were important, along with the attention they gave to the role the CIS and other bilateral arrangements assumed in enhancing regional security while preserving the states' political and economic independence. As Table 3.5 indicates, half of the CIS members, Armenia, Belarus, Kazakhstan, Kyrgyzstan, Russia and Tajikistan, signed all, or nearly all, of the 53 security treaties. Moreover, in separating out those 11 'omnibus-like' treaties with multiple security issues, these states signed all, or nearly all, of them. In contrast, the

Table 3.4 CIS security treaties, 1992–2004

Year	Total no. of treaties	No. of treaties in which specific issue is addressed	No. of treaties wrt organizational structure	No. of treaties wrt integration in any issue area	No. of treaties wrt fixed funding
1992	14	10	10	0	6
1993	4	2	2	1	1
1994	2	1	1	0	0
1995	9	5	7	8	0
1996	7	5	3	4	2
1997	0	0	0	0	0
1998	4	3	4	2	2
1999	1	0	1	1	0
2000	3	1	1	1	0
2001	4	3	1	1	0
2002	1	0	0	0	0
2003	1	1	0	0	0
2004	3	1	0	1	1
Total	53	32	30	20	12

Table 3.5 CIS member states' security treaty signings, 1992–2004

	No. of treaties signed	No. of the 11 treaties wrt 3 or more separate security issues signed
Kazakhstan	53	11
Russia	53	11
Kyrgyzstan	52	11
Tajikistan	51	11
Armenia	50	10
Belarus	48	10
Uzbekistan	40	8
Georgia	35	5
Ukraine	30	4
Azerbaijan	29	2
Moldova	23	5
Turkmenistan	22	3

Total no. of treaties = 53.

remaining six members, Azerbaijan, Georgia, Moldova, Turkmenistan, Ukraine and Uzbekistan, were more cautious in initialling final security documents, with Moldova and Turkmenistan signing fewer than half of all treaties and the 11 identified omnibus-like documents.[17] It is no coincidence that five of these more 'reluctant' member states formed the informal political-economic-security group GUUAM that, for more than a half-decade, represented the major multilateral challenger in the FSU to the CIS and its leading member, Russia. Nor is it a coincidence that all of those member states noted earlier as especially engaged with the CIS and its security products simultaneously pursued extensive and more intrusive bilateral security arrangements with Russia.

Fully appreciating the achievements and limitations of CIS multilateral negotiations requires sensitivity to the varying levels of commitment made by individual member states to this multilateral forum. Examining the 53 multilateral security treaties, we find that, by and large, most members were willing to initial agreements setting out broad goals or understandings, while there is considerable variance in members' signings for treaties with more concrete security ends. For instance, when we look at the subset of security treaties touching upon terrorism, the member states' engagement varies in accordance with their divergent security perceptions and needs. All member states initialled agreements dealing with civil aviation (1995), measures regarding the situation in Afghanistan (2001), and the standardization of CIS measures with the OECD and UN (2004). However, a number of member states (for example, Azerbaijan, Moldova, Turkmenistan and Ukraine) consistently abstained from signing agreements on border transit and control issues and on the creation of unified forces, while others (for example, Georgia and Uzbekistan) selectively abstained from signing some of these agreements. These are states that are worried about Russian hegemonic interests and the potentially intrusive role of CIS multilateral arrangements guided by a Russia-led bloc of members. Overall, we find numerous, often major, gaps in CIS regional security structures that reflect member states' selective engagement. At the most fundamental level, there is the inability of this intergovernmental forum to expand fully and make concrete the Collective Security Treaty set out in the CIS's early days. In the absence of a full and effective collective treaty, more focused bilateral security arrangements – especially with the regional hegemon, Russia – will prove critical in filling the gaps left from CIS multilateral activities, and it is to these bilateral arrangements that we now turn as we consider the fuller regional security architecture for the FSU–CIS states.

Bilateralism thrives

In contrast to the challenging circumstances that have complicated CIS multilateralism, FSU bilateral relationships have proven to be more resilient in the management of many of the FSU–CIS states' contemporary security politics. Russia's bilateral security arrangements with selected CIS member states are the key elements in today's CIS security architecture, and these arrangements have in many ways come to take precedence over FSU multilateral collective defence arrangements as states have endeavoured to craft more efficiently agreements and structures fine-tuned to their specific security needs. We argue that many countries take the view that well-defined dyadic relationships are more effective in the current international security environment: rapid structural changes in this environment make reconciling the interests of multiple actors within multilateral frameworks too complex and uncertain.

Within the FSU–CIS space, bilateral security arrangements between Russia and Armenia, Belarus, Kazakhstan, Kyrgyzstan and Tajikistan, while emergent in the Yeltsin period, enjoyed revitalization in the Putin period. This occurred despite the fact that bilateralism came to be challenged by ideas and efforts to develop sub-regional and multilateral security structures. Indeed, these bilateral alliances proved to be remarkably adaptive to new security challenges. In addition to our database of CIS treaties, we are also developing a comparable database of FSU bilateral treaties, and we focus here on those bilateral security treaties that involve the six states that have been most engaged in CIS treaty and institution construction and that signed the CIS Collective Security Treaty (CST): Armenia, Belarus, Kazakhstan, Kyrgyzstan, Russia and Tajikistan. We are interested in the bilateral arrangements linking Russia with these other five CST states.

Table 3.6 summarizes these bilateral security treaties, distinguishing totals for the Yeltsin and the Putin (beginning with his prime minister-ship in August 1999) periods. Each of the five countries initialled more than ten bilateral security treaties with Russia, the number signed per year averaging slightly over five for both the Yeltsin and the Putin peri-ods. The relatively lower total number of Russian–Belarusian treaties might be somewhat unexpected in light of the intense negotiations that have characterized this bilateral relationship since the Soviet collapse, but it is explained by the fact that since 1999 there have been a number of security arrangements developed by the governing bodies of the Union State of Russia and Belarus that are not included here (13 related to security issues).

Juxtaposing the chronologies of these bilateral treaty totals with multilateral treaty totals for the CIS (Table 3.7) suggests the intercon-nection between the two bilateral and multilateral processes. The years 1994 and 1995 entailed more than two dozen bilateral agreements being initialled between Russia and other CST signatories, while the CIS – after the first years of negotiations and organization construction – was experiencing its first institutional crisis. Some FSU states, such as Ukraine, were already expressing concerns about entwining multilateral obligations at a time when Russia was making its first serious effort to revive its regional and international leadership role.[18] There was a

Table 3.6 Bilateral security treaties signed by Russia with other collective security treaty members, 1992–2004

	No. of treaties signed 1992–99*	No. of treaties signed 1999–2004*	Total n
Armenia	11	8	19
Belarus	8	3	11**
Kazakhstan	10	7	17
Kyrgyzstan	7	7	14
Tajikistan	9	7	16
Total	45	32	77

* First column is January 1992 to August 1999; second column is August 1999 to 2004.
** Does not include security arrangements of the Union States.

Table 3.7   Bilateral security treaties signed by Russia with other collective security treaty members and multilateral security treaties signed by CIS member states, 1992–2004

	No. of bilateral security treaties signed by CST member states	No. of multilateral security treaties signed by CIS member states
1992	3	14
1993	4	4
1994	15	2
1995	11	9
1996	4	7
1997	7	–
1998	1	4
1999	4	1
2000	7	3
2001	–	4
2002	3	1
2003	–	–
2004	12	3
Total	77	53

discernable drop in CIS security treaty production, while some signed documents were left unimplemented. Likewise, in 2000 and then again in 2002–04, there was a burst in bilateral treaties. First, the Kosovo crisis of the late 1990s prompted a renewed focus on regional security concerns by the Russian political establishment, while growing scepticism over the effectiveness of CIS security structures in the post-9/11 geopolitical environment was conducive to increased bilateral activity. An overall comparison of the bilateral and multilateral treaty production trends for the 1992–04 period suggests that greater promise is associated with bilateral arrangements when multilateral structures seem not to be working.

What do we find in these bilateral agreements and how do they augment what was realized in CIS multilateral treaties? First, a vast majority of the 77 bilateral agreements dealt with very specific issues ranging from legal and economic concerns to the protection of deployed Russian military personnel. In this regard, they supplemented or built upon CIS structures and agreements. Many early bilateral treaties mostly regulated legal issues; for example, the status of Russian forces serving in particular countries or procedures for employing local military personnel to serve or work at Russian bases (for example, in Armenia, Kyrgyzstan and

Tajikistan). Most such treaties were signed in the early to mid-1990s, with some being amended in the late 1990s and early 2000s. Several important bilateral treaties regulated the use of anti-aircraft and anti-missile defence systems as well as various space related facilities. One of the most strategically important bilateral treaties was a 1995 Russian–Belarusian agreement on the procedures for the construction, utilization and maintenance of the Centre for Early Missile Warning in Baranovichi. Another strategically important agreement was a 1994 Russian–Tajik treaty regulating the use of the 'Nurek' Fibro-Optical Centre for the control of space. One of the urgent tasks confronting Russia in the early 1990s was to create a legal basis for maintaining and using the city of Baykonur and its rocket launching infrastructure. A 1995 Russian–Kazakh agreement accomplished this end, with a series of additional bilateral treaties (over a dozen) addressing a variety of related concerns as well as border protection. In addition, a variety of bilateral treaties regulated the export of military production (for example, Russian treaties with Belarus (2000), Kyrgyzstan (2003) and Kazakhstan (2004)), as well as other economic aspects of military production (for example, creation of joint enterprises for the production of military hardware).

Individually, each FSU–CIS partner of Russia had particular areas of interest that were reflected in the bilateral treaties signed. For Armenia, most agreements dealt with aspects of Russian military bases on its territory, while for Tajikistan, most agreements concerned the regulation of Russian troop deployments and border guard units on its territory. Similar military concerns characterized Russian–Kyrgyz treaties, while the vast majority of Russian–Kazakh agreements were related to the rent or mutual use of military testing grounds. Overall, these states significantly linked their security with Russia. Armenia and Belarus signed full-scale treaties on friendship, cooperation, and mutual assistance in 1997, Kyrgyzstan signed a comprehensive military cooperation agreement in 2002, and Kazakhstan concluded a similar agreement in 2004.

Why have bilateral security arrangements seemingly outperformed CIS multilateralism? One important factor is the effective withdrawal of several member states from a core CIS agreement, the 1992 Collective Security Treaty. From 1998 onward, a number of these states (Azerbaijan, Georgia, Moldova, Ukraine and Uzbekistan) began seeking a different security dimension that would be absent of Russian dominance, and the loose common military structure GUUAM was an important result of this quest. Some pointed to the potential for turning GUUAM into a structure with a common military-industrial complex, with Ukraine playing a major role thanks to its large military industry. There was also the potential for creating a different multilateral peace-keeping force devoid of a Russian presence to fight what was termed 'an aggressive separatism' in such regions as Nagorny-Karabakh, Abkhazia, South Ossetia and Transnistria. The GUUAM states assumed that CIS peace-keeping forces would be unable to address these problems adequately, in view of the potential for Russian meddling.

Other factors also help explain the thriving of bilateral arrangements tying selected CIS states with Russia. One reality is that bilateralism has simply been more flexible; it permitted Russia and other CIS states to address security threats on a case-by-case basis, taking into account sub-regional variations in the FSU–CIS security environment. Domestic level factors were also pertinent. Ideas about multilateralism, which may compete with bilateralism, were relatively new when compared to established and time-tested bilateralism. The impact of multilateral ideas on domestic bureaucratic structures of the CIS member states could be best described as slow and evolutionary, rather than transformative. Since alliances had been the dominant form of Soviet security relationships with allies since 1919, national security establishments in the FSU–CIS had grown familiar and comfortable with managing alliances and dealing with new security challenges through them.

Ultimately, bilateral security agreements helped fill the void left from the continuing absence of full-scale multilateral security arrangements realized through the CIS. Despite years of negotiations and a number of signed documents committing CIS member states to craft a collective security regime, no working regional collective security organization was in place. The signed documents did not stop the civil war in Tajikistan, nor did they prevent violence in Nagorny-Karabakh and Abkhazia. The CIS agreements did play a role in legitimizing Russian military presence in some of these conflicts, eventually leading to localization of military activity and finally to ceasefires. Indeed, in the twelve years of its application the Collective Security Treaty arguably did help to avoid significant wars on CIS territory. But this consequence did not lead to the creation of a reliable defence environment for all 12 CIS members.

Finally, a primary reason why CIS security treaty construction did not result in a full-scale collective defence system involved Russia's own power and security preferences. Member states' concerns about state sovereignty and fear of Russian hegemony kept the CIS firmly committed to a soft institutionalism that precluded real security interdependencies. The GUUAM countries' rejection of CIS collective security arrangement effectively destroyed the possibility for a 12-state security environment and created the potential preconditions for interstate conflict.[19] In the face of these continuing challenges, Russia felt forced to create its own border defence and regional security, and it has done so primarily via bilateral means. Other FSU states have been similarly motivated (for example, Armenia and its concerns that the military consolidation of GUUAM would cut its access to Russia). Overall, the new collective security arrangements individually linking Russia, Armenia, Belarus, Kazakhstan, Kyrgyzstan and Tajikistan appear to have better prospects, taking into account that this grouping is almost congruent with the Eurasian Economic Community (only Armenia is not a member) and Customs Union.

Putin, the CIS and expansive bilateralism

Multilateral security arrangements developed under the auspices of the CIS entailed broad understandings of regional security and more narrowly focused agreements addressing a wide variety of more technical needs. The all-important 1992 Collective Security Treaty set out a general perspective on FSU regional security to which nearly all parties were agreed, but it was followed by numerous more narrowly crafted agreements seldom signed and implemented by all members. From the CIS's earliest days, there was strong opposition among many member states toward the possible creation of a unified military command. Indeed, even the attempts to further develop a CIS collective security concept made after the 2001 US attack on Afghanistan and destruction of the Taliban regime failed to take shape, leaving the CIS devoid of a fully-fledged collective defence system.

Throughout this period a number of CIS member states were actively developing bilateralism based on the notion that their security interests were better advanced via separate relationships with relevant states, especially Russia. Yet there is a difference between what might be termed 'narrow bilateralism' and 'extended bilateralism'.[20] Those adopting narrow bilateralism regard their bilateral relationships as sufficient and appropriately self-contained; indeed, relationships to be isolated from one another and not to be compromised in multilateral contexts. In the first years of CIS evolution there were relatively few signed bilateral security arrangements among these states, as FSU states attempted to employ multilateralism as a security paradigm. The FSU bilateralism of these early post-Soviet years was 'narrow', with an overwhelming preference to try to use collective action: the Collective Security Treaty was the major example of this strategy's implementation.

However, in the late 1990s there was a shift in the paradigm of FSU regional security toward expansive bilateralism. By 'expansive bilateralism' we mean constructing bilateral arrangements as nested within multilateral contexts; that is, developing bilateral linkages that are conducive to – or prone to – broader linkages that become multilateral in their policy significance.[21] The end result is a multi-tiered regional security system that brings together different types of policy coordination among states, including bilateral, multilateral, sub-regional and regional arrangements. The emergence of GUUAM and the concomitant reactive policies of Russia and other CIS member states played key roles in this paradigm shift. The value of this multi-tiered system explains why Russia has not abandoned its enthusiasm for promoting multilateral arrangements, even given ongoing concerns about their effectiveness. The multi-tiered approach also helps explain Russia's efforts to maintain and strengthen its bilateral security arrangements with individual FSU–CIS states during the past decade.

Momentum for Russian policy makers to settle on a multi-tiered approach to regional security came with the formation of the new Putin regime, and it is evinced in a number of important foreign and security policy documents that came early in the Putin administration: a National Security Blueprint (January 2000), a revised version of the Military Doctrine of the Russian Federation (April 2000), and a Foreign Policy Blueprint (June 2000). Taken together with statements by the new president and other government officials, these documents indicated both long-standing and changing emphases in Russian FSU–CIS policy. Regarding foreign and security goals, the CIS, at least nominally, remained at the top of Russian priorities. The Foreign Policy Blueprint clearly stressed the importance of the CIS: 'One priority area in Russia's foreign policy is to ensure the conformity of multilateral and bilateral cooperation with the member states of the Commonwealth of Independent States (CIS) to national security tasks of the country'. The document continued: 'The emphasis will be put on the development of good-neighbourly relations and strategic partnerships with all CIS member states. Practical relations with each of them should be structured with due regard for reciprocal openness to cooperation and readiness to take into account in a due manner the interests of the Russian Federation, including providing guarantees of the rights of Russian compatriots.' Meanwhile, the April 2000 Military Doctrine assumed what was termed 'the collective security system within the CIS framework' and 'the need to consolidate the efforts to create a single defence area and collective military security'. The June 2000 Foreign Policy Blueprint described the key features of current Russian policy on CIS integration in a more comprehensive manner, articulating a more pragmatic and flexible approach in advancing the concept of 'different-speed and different-level integration within the CIS framework'. Overall, the expectation was that Russia would significantly determine the parameters and character of interaction among FSU states, both in the CIS as a whole and in narrower arrangements – for instance, the Eurasian Economic Community, the Common Economic Space, the Customs Union and the Collective Security Treaty.[22] A related priority task would involve the continued strengthening of the Union State of Belarus and Russia as the 'highest form' of integration of two sovereign states.

It could be argued that this 'multi-level and multi-speed integration' of the Putin period is a new recognition of the desired reality of CIS integration that has drawn many Moscow decision makers since the early 1990s. Former Russian Foreign Minister Igor Ivanov described the rationale for adopting this combined approach:

> The entire history of the creation of various integration structures shows that without a solid bilateral base of relations, it is difficult to come to multilateral forms of cooperation. For any form of multilateral cooperation presupposes delegation of a part, insignificant perhaps, but still a part of sovereignty to multilateral agencies ... We will actively develop bilateral ties, and as these grow stronger, the possibilities will broaden for multilateral cooperation within the CIS as well.[23]

Overall, the move toward more efficient bilateralism is accompanied by the intent to make CIS integration more beneficial for Russia. Defence Minister Sergei Ivanov emphasized this point when he stated:

> I believe it is already clear to all that integration should not be an end in itself. Integration should be in pursuit of specific steps, benefits or shortcomings, but to try to draw everyone in, as it was, perhaps, in the past when some tried or hoped to get everyone in a single group, is quite simply unrealistic.[24]

FSU–CIS regional security interests have been advanced through both multilateral and bilateral means. Nearly a decade and a half of extensive negotiation has yielded a complex set of arrangements that represent varying levels of collective security for different groups of FSU–CIS states. With no state surrendering its sovereignty, and a resurgent Russia continuing to assert its 'natural' regional leadership role, any region-wide collective security arrangement will have to be sufficiently flexible to maintain all states' active engagement. The multi-tiered approach that Russia and other FSU states have taken has a logic that permits engagement with unilateral discretion. In this regard, the CIS's past achievements and future promise should not be discounted. Our analysis of the multilateral CIS security architecture of the period 1992–2004 reveals that a workable foundation of understandings and arrangements was laid. Only time will tell whether an expansive bilateralism, grounded in a decade of past treaties and buoyed by the energy of the Putin regime, will further advance that multilateral foundation.

Notes

1   We thank Gary Goertz of the University of Arizona, and Kathy Powers, Tatiana Vashchilko and Logan Kincheloe of Pennsylvania State University for their assistance in the construction of the CIS treaty dataset and in the completion of this chapter.
2   'Press Conference Following Russian-Armenian Talks', *Yerevan*, 25 March 2005, President of Russia Official Web Portal, www.kremlin.ru/eng/text/speeches/2005/03/25
3   A. Åslund, *Building Capitalism: The Transformation of the Former Soviet Bloc*, (Cambridge: Cambridge University Press, 2001).
4   I.S. Ivanov, *The New Russian Diplomacy* (Washington, DC: Brookings Institution Press, 2002).
5   Z. Brzezinski and P. Sullivan (eds), *Russia and the Commonwealth of Independent States: Documents, Data, and Analysis* (Washington, DC: Carnegie Endowment for International Peace, 1997); M.B. Olcott, A. Åslund and S.W. Garnett, *Getting It Wrong: Regional Cooperation and the Commonwealth of Independent States* (Washington, DC: Carnegie Endowment for International Peace, 1999).
6   D. Lynch, *Russian Peacekeeping Strategies in the CIS* (New York: Palgrave Macmillan: 2000); J.P. Willerton, 'Regional Leadership Amidst Power Contraction: Russia and the FSU', *Soviet and Post-Soviet Review*, 25, 1, 1998 (published spring 2000), 83–100.
7   For example, L.K. Metcalf, 'Regional Economic Integration in the Former Soviet Union', *Political Research Quarterly*, 50, 3 (1997) 529–49; D. Trenin, *The End of Eurasia: Russia on the Border Between Geopolitics and Globalization* (Washington, DC: Carnegie Endowment for International Peace, 2002); J.P. Willerton and G. Cockerham, 'Russia, the CIS, and Eurasian Interconnections', in J. Sperling, S. Kay and S.V. Papacosma (eds), *Limiting Institutions? The Challenge of Eurasian Security Governance* (Manchester: Manchester Press, 2003) 185–207.
8   A.C. Lynch, 'The Realism of Russia's Foreign Policy', *Europe-Asia Studies*, 53, 1 (2001) 7–31.
9   The Gary Goertz–Kathy Powers Regional Trade Agreements as Security Institutions project, which includes data collection and analysis for all major regional trade agreements for the period of the 1960s through the early

2000s. For an overview, see K. Powers and G. Goertz, 'Regional Trade Agreements as Security Institutions Project: Challenges in Coding Multi-Issue Treaties', Paper presented at the Annual Meeting of the American Political Science Association, Washington, DC, September 1–4, 2005.

10 See Spravka o ratifikatsii dokumentov, http://www.nau.kiev.ua/ 1014/345/ 1014_3450_1.html

11 Our understanding of a treaty as a document (1) that is designated by certain labelling (that is, convention, treaty, agreement or accord, along with related protocols and amendments), (2) that entails the establishment of intergovernmental bodies, (3) that is identified as binding by reliable sources (for example, by a secretariat or published legal analysis), and (4) that includes a text which is in conformity with accepted terminologies of legally binding agreements and is informed by the definitive discussion provided by Ronald B. Mitchell, 'International Environment Agreements: A Survey of Their Features, Formation, and Effects', *Annual Review of Environmental Resources*, 28 (2003), 429–61, especially 432.

12 Such support documents, whether entitled decisions, protocols, or amendments, are generally declarative, provide technical details on institutions or policies, and lack the complex legal structure expected of binding treaties. While often providing useful information about the composition of administrative structures, the rotation of leadership within the CIS, and other bureaucratic matters, these documents are not included in our population of treaties.

13 Goertz-Powers RTA/Protocol Treaty Coding Sheet, version 5.1: 9 January 2005.

14 H.A. Welsh and J.P. Willerton, 'Regional cooperation and the CIS: West European lessons and post-Soviet experience', *International Politics*, 34, 1 (March 1997), 33–61.

15 Former Russian Foreign Minister Igor Ivanov has written that of the 164 documents adopted by the Council of Heads of State and Council of Heads of Government for the period 1991–98, only seven had gone into full effect (as of 1 February 2000); see I.S. Ivanov, *The New Russian Diplomacy* (Washington, DC: Brookings Institution Press, 2002), p. 83.

16 'Agreement on the Concept of Collective Security Among Member-States' and 'Agreement on the Basic Directions of Deepening Military Cooperation Among Member-States', both signed 10 February 1995 by all CIS members except Azerbaijan.

17 Turkmenistan's decision at the 26 August 2005 CIS summit in Kazan to downgrade its formal affiliation to associate member was yet another sign of its hesitancy in engaging this multilateral forum.

18 The fact that Moscow decided to declare an independent Russian army in spring 1992 was an early reflection of its unilateral interests separate from multilateral CIS arrangements. This decision significantly undercut the prospects for a unified CIS military command.

19 It might be further argued that the GUUAM arrangements could even provoke such conflicts, with the potential for this group of states to ask for NATO assistance. The 2005 departure of Uzbekistan raised serious questions about GUUAM's long-term viability.

20 See Ashizawa 2003, Hoare 2003, and Tow 2003; K. Ashizawa, 'Japan's Approach toward Asian Regional Security. From "Hub-and-spoke" Bilateralism to "Multi-tiered", *Pacific Review*, 16, 3 (2003) Special Issue,

361–82; M. Hoare, 'The Prospects for Australian and Japanese Security Cooperation in a More Uncertain Asia-Pacific', Land Warfare Studies Centre, Working Paper 123 (September 2003): 22, http://www.defence.gov.au/army/lwsc/Publications/WP%20123.pdf; W. Tow, 'U.S. Bilateral Security Alliances in the Asia-Pacific: Moving Beyond "Hub and Spokes" ', Paper presented to the Australasian Political Studies Association Conference, University of Tasmania, Hobart, 29 September–1 October 2003; mhttp://www.utas.edu.au/government/APSA/WTowfinal.pdf

21   It could be argued that the USA made an important transition from narrow to expansive bilateralism in the post-Cold War era.

22   The Shanghai Cooperation Organization, founded in June 2001 and including five FSU–CIS states (Kazakhstan, Kyrgyzstan, Russia, Tajikistan and Uzbekistan) and China, is another more recent Eurasian intergovernmental forum addressing comparable security, economic and other issues.

23   Report by Igor Ivanov, Ministry of Foreign Affairs of the Russian Federation website.

24   Sergei Ivanov, quoted on Russian television, Moscow, 12 February 2001, BBC Monitoring.

Part II
The EU and the Post-Soviet Space

4
The Clash of Integration Processes? The Shadow Effect of the Enlarged EU on its Eastern Neighbours

Tom Casier

Introduction

The Eastern enlargement of the European Union has fundamentally redrawn the map of Europe. Together with the extension of its borders, the EU is facing an extension of both its impact and its responsibilities in the wider Europe. The enlarged EU now borders several former Soviet Republics and members of the Commonwealth of Independent States (CIS). Some of these new neighbours have made membership of the European Union a strategic priority. Even if the EU cannot offer them a prospect of membership, it has an increased responsibility towards them: a responsibility to create stability, a responsibility to mitigate the negative impact of enlargement on these outsiders and a responsibility to take up its role as a regional political force. At the same time, the EU plays a more active political role, mainly pursuing stability around the enlarged EU, in the framework of its new European Neighbourhood Policy (ENP).

This chapter reflects on how this increased responsibility and growing role of the EU on the territory of the Western CIS is overlapping, and possibly clashing, with other integration initiatives as well as with Russian interests. It first investigates the impact of the EU on its direct neighbourhood and the paradoxes that EU enlargement has created. It then critically analyses the ENP as an escape route from these paradoxes. The focus then shifts to EU–Russia relations, which will be a highly determining factor for the outcome of the ENP towards the CIS republics. Finally, the chapter analyses how two separate and incompatible integration processes, within the EU and within the Commonwealth of Independent States (CIS), risk collision.

The impact of enlargement on the new neighbours

The shadow effect of the European Union

The EU's 'presence'[1] in the world is determined by much more than its foreign policy activities alone. The EU is, on one hand, an international actor with a proactive foreign policy pursuing implicit or explicit objectives. On the other hand, the EU has a certain impact, especially on its neighbourhood, because of its mere existence. Therefore an analytical distinction needs to be made between the EU's intended and unintentional impact.

The unintentional impact may manifest itself in two different ways. First, internal policies produce certain externalization effects. The rules of the internal market, for example, have effects on companies who wish to export to the EU or invest in the EU. They have to live up to the environmental, safety and technical standards of the Union if they want to safeguard their export. In the same way, competition policy may affect business operations across the borders of the EU. The acquisition of Honeywell by General Electric, both American companies, was rejected by the European Commission in 2001 because it would distort free competition within the Single European Market. The subsidies and income support granted under the Common Agricultural Policy in turn produces the effect that certain agricultural goods enter the word market at low prices, thus disrupting local markets in some developing countries. These externalization effects have been present since the very start of the European integration process.

Second, the EU exerts 'a gravitational pull'[2] in international relations. It is regarded as a model of integration, of pooling and balancing interests between states. It is an example of how to overcome conflicts by transferring a part of national sovereignty. Or, alternatively, the EU attracts because of the wealth the internal market generates or because of the economic opportunities it provides. In this sense, the European Union is more important for what it is than for what it does.[3]

This effect is particularly present in the immediate geographic proximity of the EU, where its sheer presence is confining the options of third states. At the same time, though, the EU also actively exports norms and practices, thus further increasing its presence in the area. I label this double impact of the EU on its immediate neighbouring states the 'shadow effect', as if the Union is casting a shadow over its new neighbours. The shadow effect means that the EU has a direct impact on the countries in its geographic proximity. This effect is partly unintentional, partly steered. Moreover, it is a differentiated effect. Not all countries are equally vulnerable to the impact of the EU. The degree of asymmetrical dependency on the EU determines to what extent a country can escape the impact.[4] Countries with a geographic location in the proximity of the EU and highly asymmetrically dependent on the EU are most likely to undergo the shadow effect. This is of tremendous importance for the new neighbours of the EU: it is an extreme determinant of whether they have alternative political, economic and (soft) security options but turn towards the EU. Exactly at this point, the Eastern enlargement of the EU has redrawn Europe's map drastically, as the two giants of the continent, the European Union and the Russian Federation, are now potential direct competitors. They both have a huge impact on the 'countries in between',[5] they both have interests in the area and they both are sources of carrots and sticks affecting domestic politics and policies in these states.

The paradoxes of enlargement

The distinction between intended and unintentional impact is crucial to the analysis of the effect of enlargement on the EU's new Eastern neighbours. First of all, enlargement unintentionally alters the power relations between states and the way in which interests of different countries converge or diverge. This can largely be assumed to be a side-effect. As a consequence, the autonomy of third countries to make their own choices is confined. This unintentional externalization effect is clearly visible in the securitization of external borders and the new visa regimes which were introduced as a result of the integration of the Schengen *acquis* by the new member states.

Second, the EU consciously shapes norms, practices and institutions in the new neighbouring countries. This can be done in a very direct and explicit way; for example, by including human rights clauses in bilateral treaties. It can also be done in a more indirect way; for example, by imposing certain standards for goods exported to the single market.

The 2004 enlargement has extended the EU's shadow effect to the East, but has also increased the effect. Though this may not be the intended outcome, enlargement inevitably has created new dividing lines. The enlargement of May 2004 was the biggest enlargement in the history of European integration. It augments the EU population with some 80 million inhabitants and extends its territory to almost 4 million square kilometers. The EU, with 25 members, counts 450 million inhabitants. The 'other Europe' (roughly following the Council of Europe as a criterion) comprises approximately 360 million people, but they represent a national income that is only a fraction of that of the EU.

The unintentional outcome of enlargement is, thus, a two-speed wider Europe.

If we consider that the initial goal of European integration is to create stability and structural peace in Europe, enlargement is characterized by a fundamental ambiguity, which can be summarized in two paradoxes. I speak of paradoxes because enlargement has created a situation in which the EU is forced to act if it wants to remain true to its founding principles.

The first paradox is intrinsic to the deepening of integration: more integration inside the EU complicates a close involvement of third countries. This is most visible in the case of free movement of persons: while internal borders disappear, external borders are reinforced, better secured and harder to cross. This paradox may therefore be labelled the 'Schengen paradox'. According to the Copenhagen criteria, the accession states had to integrate the Schengen *acquis* into their legislation. Countries such as Poland, for example, had to impose visa obligations for Ukrainians travelling to its territory, whereas in the past the latter could cross the border without many formalities. With an estimated 30 million border crossings yearly, the consequences of the extension of the visa regime to the new member states are enormous.[6]

A second paradox, the 'insider/outsider paradox', is specifically a consequence of Eastern enlargement. With the accession of ten new member states, it becomes more and more problematic not to be part of the Union. The outsider states inevitably undergo profound effects of European integration. As the EU grows bigger, their alternatives diminish and it becomes harder (or more costly) to escape the impact of the EU. There are fewer non-EU countries in the immediate neighbourhood to trade with or to travel to without visa. With an EU of 25, 27 or more members, third countries will have little choice but to orient their export towards the EU. New tariffs apply for trade with countries that have recently joined the EU. In some sectors this may have serious consequences.

The politicization of the EU's regional role

The unintentional impact is often complemented by an intentional, goal-oriented foreign policy. European Foreign Policy often functions as a tool to either mitigate the 'side-effects' of the EU or to reinforce them. Recently, we have seen the EU taking up a more explicitly political role in its neighbourhood.

This politicization of the EU's international role is not new. We have seen an incremental politicization of international agreements of the EU over recent decades, clearly visible in the differences between the Lomé Convention with the ACP countries and the Cotonou Convention.[7] But as a result of different tendencies this evolution has recently gained momentum, especially in regional foreign policy. First of all, it is inextricably linked to the development of CFSP during the 1990s and the creation of ESDP, which gave the EU a more explicit foreign policy role to play and made decision-making procedures more flexible. Second, it is the result of increasing responsibility of the EU in the new geostrategic situation in Europe created by enlargement. Third, it flows from the increased visibility of the enlarged European Union. Finally, the new Central and East European member states have oriented the EU's foreign policy more to the East. As it is their major concern to stabilize their Eastern neighbours, they have pushed the EU towards a more active political engagement in the area. This was most clearly visible in the case of the Orange Revolution in Ukraine in 2004, where Poland was diplomatically very active and pushing the EU to play an active role.[8]

Mitigating the effects of enlargement: the European Neighbourhood Policy

Driven by fears of instability around the enlarged EU and by the danger of new dividing lines in Europe, the Union has developed its own specific, differentiated policy oriented towards its new neighbours around the Mediterranean and in Eastern Europe. The first step was taken with the launch of the Wider Europe/New Neighbour initiative in May 2002. This initiative was the first step towards the development of a more coherent policy baptized 'European Neighbourhood Policy' (ENP) in the Commission's Strategy Paper of May 2004. It is an attempt to develop a privileged relationship with neighbouring states without offering them the prospect of membership:

> The objective of the ENP is to share the benefits of the EU's 2004 enlargement with neighbouring countries in strengthening stability, security and well-being for all concerned. It is designed to prevent the emergence of new dividing lines between the enlarged EU and its neighbours and to offer them the chance to participate in various EU activities, through greater political, security, economic and cultural cooperation.[9]

The ENP builds on 'mutual commitment to common values' and departs from a 'common set of principles', but differentiates among the partner countries.[10] Action plans per country outline the priorities and serve as a point of reference for the next three to five years. Progress will be monitored by country reports. They are expected to lead to the negotiation of European Neighbourhood Agreements. Additional support is provided by a new European Neighbourhood Instrument.[11]

The ENP is aimed at countries around the Mediterranean (Algeria, Egypt, Israel, Jordan, Lebanon, Libya, Morocco, Syria and Tunisia as well as the Palestinian authority), in Eastern Europe (Ukraine, Belarus and Moldova) and since 2004 in the Caucasus (Armenia, Azerbaijan and Georgia).[12] The Balkan states are not included, because they are expected to become members of the EU at some point in the future, an evolution underlined by the official candidate status of both Croatia and the Former Yugoslav Republic of Macedonia (17 December 2005).

In contrast to earlier blueprints on the wider Europe, Russia is not part of the ENP. The Russian Federation was granted a special status as 'key partner of the EU'.[13] The Strategy Paper recognizes that 'Russia and the enlarged European Union form part of each other's neighbourhood',[14] thus acknowledging the equivalence of both.

ENP: main characteristics

The main strategic objective of the ENP is, in the words of Romano Prodi, to replace 'an arc of instability' with a 'ring of friends'. Its aim is simultaneously to avoid the enlarged EU being confronted with instability on its borders and that enlargement leading to new forms of polarization. No doubt there are also hidden strategic and economic objectives.

ENP is a subfield of European Foreign Policy, but is quite unique as it is overarching different policy fields in all three pillars, from CFSP and Common Commercial Policy to 'Freedom, Security and Justice'. What are the main characteristics of ENP that set them apart from other forms of foreign policy and from the process of integration as such?

First of all, ENP is a prototypical example of 'structural foreign policy'. In contrast to traditional foreign policy, structural foreign policy proactively shapes the external environment.[15] The aim is to create a favourable or stable external environment by – in the words of Ikenberry – socializing third countries by stimulating common values and cooperation. In contrast to a traditional possession-goals oriented foreign policy, the time frame is long-term. The ENP is an explicit attempt to structure the immediate neighbourhood along the dominant principles and norms of the EU. The goal is to involve the new neighbours in a selected number of policy areas, thus socializing them in the longer term into an extended form of European cooperation.

The EU, in other words, invests a lot in shaping its immediate external environment in its own image.

The core of this structural foreign policy is 'political conditionality'.[16] Though the concept of conditionality originally stems from international financial institutions such as the IMF, it refers in the EU context to a foreign policy instrument to give incentives to a third country to comply with certain rules or norms.[17] Certain conditions are imposed and the targeted country is rewarded or sanctioned in the case of (non-)fulfilment. In other words, it is an instrument for rule or norm transfer attempting to change the institutional practices, policies and behavior in the target country by offering or withholding rewards in the case of (non-)compliance. The rewards may take different forms: preferential trade, association, membership, financial aid, free movement and so on. Conditionality is at the heart of many international agreements the EU has concluded, often in the form of clauses on democratization or respect of human rights, but also on economic reforms. It is a central element in the Cotonou Convention with the ACP countries, but also forms the backbone of the accession process, with the Copenhagen criteria stipulating the essential conditions for qualification for EU membership. Although the rewards in the case of the ENP differ drastically – as membership is excluded – this policy is based on a similar form of conditionality.

Second, the ENP is a differentiated policy which allows countries to be approached in very different ways. The extension of certain forms of EU cooperation across the border in a differentiated way is nothing new, as such. The European Economic Area, for example, extends most of the Single European Market to third countries without the other benefits and duties of membership. In the same way, the Schengen zone includes non-EU members Norway and Iceland. A customs union involving Turkey was already provided for in the Association agreement of 1963 but was only established in 1996. There has thus been a long tradition of associating countries closely with the European integration process. Often these countries are linked to EU cooperation through agreements; financial aid and the awarding of all sorts of benefits, such as preferential trade tariffs or the granting of market economy status. A multi-speed Europe, exceeding the borders of the EU, has thus been a reality for long.

What is a major innovation, though, is that the 'one size fits all' approach, in which a similar policy was developed for a whole area (for example, the Central and East European candidate member states), has been replaced by a tailor-made approach. This is not surprising if one takes into account the great diversity of the countries involved both in size and in economic strength, political system or culture. Understandably one approaches Ukraine in a different way than Syria, Israel or Morocco.

Third, the ENP is characterized by a low level of institutionalization. In the words of Prodi, the new neighbours would 'share everything but the institutions'. The proximity policy and the priorities laid down in the different Action Plans are developed by the EU in dialogue with the neighbour state, but generally try to avoid the establishment of new institutions.

Fourth, the ENP is a dynamic policy. It is in essence a framework that allows for uneven progress by different countries and in different fields. As target countries fulfil more and more conditions, this framework will further develop.

Finally, the European Neighbourhood Policy (ENP) is in essence an EU-centric policy. It reflects the norms and values of the European Union and aims at exporting them to third countries. This is clearly apparent from the European Neighbourhood mechanisms, which mainly involve financial assistance and country reports, through which the EU monitors the progress in bilateral relations and the political, economic and social situation of the country involved.

ENP: an assessment

The ENP represents a fundamental strategic shift from extending stability to exporting stability. The European integration process is, in origin, a project about the creation of structural peace and stability in Europe. Starting off with six founding members, this project has gradually been extended to other European countries. The model of stability that was generated through European integration and cooperation was thus extended through enlargement. When communism collapsed in 1989, the EU was confronted with the huge challenge of creating stability in Central and Eastern Europe. The European Council of Copenhagen in 1993 very explicitly chose to do so by offering the former communist satellite states the prospect of membership. This prospect was made dependent on clear conditions – the Copenhagen criteria. The ENP, however, explicitly rules out this possibility. As Verheugen, then Enlargement Commissioner, put it: 'Membership perspectives are not on the table. Full stop.'[18] This is a break with the past. The ENP is an attempt to export stability and security in a new way. By developing privileged relationships with neighbouring countries, but simultaneously excluding membership, the EU fundamentally changed the Copenhagen strategy. The model of stability will no longer be extended by admitting new members, but stability will be exported by partially integrating or socializing third countries into European values and forms of cooperation, without offering them an entrance ticket to the club. The success of this strategy remains to prove its effectiveness. It will be argued later in this chapter that the ENP either risks leading to a compelling logic of enlargement or failing because incentives are too weak to trigger real reforms.

Churchill said 'democracy is the worst form of government, except for all the others that have been tried': one might be tempted to regard the ENP as the worst possible form of proximity policy, except for all other options. Its chances of success are doubtful, it confronts neighbouring countries in Eastern Europe with difficult choices by not offering the prospect of membership and it deprives the EU of its most important instrument for creating stability; namely, enlargement. On the other hand, in the current political climate, where public opinion and many political leaders tend to take a negative stance towards further enlargement, it might be the only possible option. Certainly within the European Commission, the ENP may be regarded as a temporary policy until the time is ripe for further enlargement. In this sense, it also performs the function of a test lab for future membership.

One of the major challenges is that the ENP interferes with Russia's strategic interests. Therefore its success will depend on the development of EU–Russia relations.[19] In the next section of this chapter, the relations between the two giants and their impact on the countries in between will be analysed.

Russia–EU relations

Russia: global disengagement but regional assertiveness

Contrary to the dominant perception of Russia as an increasingly assertive international player, its foreign policy in the post-communist era has been characterized by global disengagement in military terms and a re-engagement in economic terms. On one hand, Russia has closed military bases in Cuba and Vietnam and has accepted far-reaching arms reductions. Its current military budget is only a fraction of that of its former rival, the United States. On the other hand, especially under Putin the economization of foreign policy has become a top priority. Russia uses its economic strengths (oil and gas resources in the first place) as a political weapon, but also aspires to integration into the global economy. Putin regards integration into an increasingly global economy as a necessity, a vital long-term interest. The words he spoke at the APEC summit in Shanghai in 2001 exemplify his conviction: 'I think we must not be afraid of globalization. This is an objective process. I say so as a citizen of a country, which suffered more than anybody else from isolation. There is nothing worse than isolation.'[20]

Russia's foreign policy since the late 1990s is based on a paradox. Russia has the ambition to restore its status as a great power, but is driven by its fear of isolation. Or, as Anatol Lieven puts it: 'Putin's external policies are founded on a frank recognition of Russia's weakness.'[21] Russia wants its post-communist identity as a 'normal' country to be recognized and to be acknowledged as a member of the community of Western states.[22] The EU and its member states play a crucial role in this. Russia's first fear is to be isolated in Europe. The European Union exerts a very strong magnetic force upon the states surrounding it. Moreover, trade and geographic proximity make it an evident partner.

As a result, Russia's foreign policy is following a two-track approach.[23] Its policy towards the EU and the West in general is largely pragmatic and cooperative. It aims at close cooperation with the EU. Ever since the Medium-term strategy, the Russian Federation has declared itself to be a European country and the EU a vital partner.[24] The policy towards the other CIS states, on the other hand, is more coercive and more differentiated. Russia makes full use of its dominant position, but will do so in different ways and degrees depending on the target country.

Russia–EU relations: a win–win partnership?

Considered over the longer term, relations between the EU and Russia have steadily become closer. Of course, there have been many ups and down. In 2004 and 2005, the EU and Russia clashed over a number of issues, from Russian concerns over the impact of EU enlargement, over the hostage crisis in Beslan, to the tensions over Georgia and, most of all, the presidential elections in Ukraine. Notwithstanding these obvious ups and downs, the overall relationship continued to be based on a 'strategic partnership'. There is a continuous 'commonality of interest among the member states of the EU'[25] towards Russia, as well as a mutual interest for the EU and Russia to have a structural partnership. Notwithstanding critical voices in both Brussels and Moscow, leaders on both sides were always eager to reconfirm their commitment to a strategic partnership.

The framework of the structural partnership is put down in a number of key documents. The bilateral Partnership and Cooperation Agreement (PCA) was signed in 1994 and entered into force in 1997. It creates a framework for cooperation and a structure for consultation. In 1999, the EU presented its Common Strategy on Russia.[26] The 'common strategy' was a new instrument created by the Amsterdam treaty to increase the consistency of the EU's external policy. The fact that the Common Strategy on Russia was the first to be adopted is significant. The document is aimed at strengthening 'the strategic partnership between the Union and Russia', an objective fully in line with the rhetoric of involving Russia in European affairs. That same year, Russia presented its 'Medium-term Strategy for Development of Relations between the Russian Federation and the European Union (2000–2010)'. In this document, Russia presents itself as a European country and a partner of the EU. The document pleads for pan-European cooperation based on collective security and free trade.

At their summit in St Petersburg in May 2003, the Russian Federation and the EU agreed to create four 'common spaces': a common economic space; a common space of freedom, security and justice; a space of research, education and culture; and one of external security. The existing bilateral institutional framework has been reinforced in view of this, with the conversion of the Cooperation Council into a Permanent Partnership Council.[27] The road maps to create these common spaces were adopted at the Russia–EU summit in Moscow 2005.

The structural partnership between the EU and Russia is underpinned by a number of mutual economic and political strategic interests. On the EU's side, the strategic interests are reflected in the European Security Strategy, which puts forward two core objectives.[28] One is to create stability around the enlarged Union. The other one is effective mutilateralism. To create stability across its new Eastern borders, cooperation with the Russian Federation is totally unavoidable. When it comes to multilateralism, the EU and Russia are pretty much on the same line. While Putin has largely followed the pragmatic policy line of Primakov, he changed the emphasis from multipolarity to multilateralism.

The main political-strategic interest for Russia has to do with its fear of isolation. To avoid potential isolation on the European continent, the inevitable partner for cooperation is the EU. It is the most crucial factor of integration in Western and Central Europe. It is not only the dominant economic power, but also an important political factor. The EU shapes, more than any other organization, the architecture of the new post-Cold War Europe. A close partnership with the EU – hand in hand with the close bilateral relations Moscow maintains with many European capitals – thus might yield strategic benefits. It forms an attractive alternative for cooperation with NATO, as it is less of a direct threat to long-term strategic interests and might eventually provide a security architecture with a less prevalent role for the USA.

In the economic field, one may discern a growing interdependence between the Russian Federation and the EU.[29] The latter is highly dependent on Russia's energy resources. Moreover, the Russian market opens plenty of opportunities for trade and investment. The other way around, the importance of the EU for Russia is even more obvious. The EU is Russia's number one trading partner.[30] Russian exports to the EU have climbed to 54 per cent following the 2004 enlargement. If Russia succeeds in establishing a free-trade area with the EU, it would be given access to a huge market of 450 million consumers, where it can sell products whilst enjoying a considerable advantage in labour costs.

Tensions over enlargement

The overall balance of EU–Russia relations appears to be rather positive. Russia and the EU have not only incrementally developed a structured form of cooperation in different areas, they have also taken a pragmatic stance and have shown their willingness to compromise. Nevertheless, there have been signs of growing tension. Several of them can be traced back to the Eastern enlargement of the EU and the extension of its role as regional force to the East. Moscow has voiced concerns over the big bang enlargement on several occasions. In early 2004, Foreign Deputy Minister Chizhov handed over to the EU ambassadors a list of 14 concerns. They ranged from delaying EU import tariffs and lifting restrictions on sensitive Russian goods, visa requirements for Russian citizens travelling to the EU, to the status of the Russian-speaking communities in the Baltic states. Also the position of Kaliningrad, a Russian enclave in the enlarged European Union, was a contentious issue.

Many Russian concerns were related to the economic impact of the Eastern enlargement. Because of the existing trade flows between Russia and the Central and East European Countries, the expansion would increase Russia's dependence on the EU. The automatic extension of the Partnership and Cooperation Agreement with the EU to the ten new member states would confront Russia's exports to these countries with higher import tariffs, higher technical and hygiene standards for its products, and make the export of steel more difficult. Russian estimates expected the cost of EU enlargement for the country to amount to 150 million euros.[31]

Most of the frictions related to the Eastern enlargement of 2004, however, were solved as accession grew closer. Already, at the Brussels EU–Russia summit of 11 November 2002 an agreement was reached unexpectedly smoothly on Kaliningrad. The agreement mainly consisted of a facilitation of the transit procedure and documents.[32] In 2004, just a few days before the enlargement, an agreement was reached that provided for compensatory tariff adjustments, the adaptation of EU–Russia steel agreements, special antidumping measures and a facilitated visa issuance.[33] A protocol was signed on 27 April 2004, extending the PCA to the ten new member states.

Harder to grasp, at this stage, is what the strategic and political impact of enlargement will be. No doubt, the 2004 enlargement has increased the EU's interests in Eastern Europe and made it a more visible and active player. While many of the new member states have a strong interest in maintaining stability on the EU's Eastern borders, most of the newcomers belong to the more critical member states who favour a tougher stance towards Russia. As a result, countries such as Poland tend to promote closer cooperation with new Eastern neighbours, such as Ukraine, while favouring a more critical position vis-à-vis Russia.

The Eastern enlargement of the Union has no doubt increased mutual distrust. Russia was very concerned over growing European influence in CIS countries. The position of Russian minorities in the Baltic states has been an issue of concern for a long time. Notwithstanding their accession to the EU, Russia still has not signed border agreements with Latvia and Estonia.

The EU felt more and more uneasy about 'the emergence of a more assertive and generally well articulated Russian foreign policy vis-à-vis the new independent states'.[34] The European Parliament produced a very critical report in 2004 on relations with Russia.[35] This report was followed by a Communication of the European Commission, in which it *inter alia* recommends the Council to defend EU interests more vigorously and take a more frank critical stance towards 'universal and open values, such as democracy, human rights in Chechnya, media freedom and some environmental issues'.[36]

Especially for Moscow, unwelcome regime changes in Georgia and Ukraine in 2004 fed the looming distrust and reinforced mutual perceptions of unwanted interference. In Ukraine, the EU played an exceptionally prominent role. Pushed by the Polish government, Javier Solana played a crucial role in brokering a final deal, breaking the deadlock in which the Orange Revolution found itself.

From the EU perspective the events in Ukraine were feeding fears of 'Russia's drift to a bloc mentality' and 'a zero-sum attitude to cooperation with the European Union in [its] New Neighbourhood Countries'.[37] From the Russian point of view, the EU attitude towards the presidential election was perceived as part of a long term strategy to increase its influence in Western CIS states.

EU enlargement has thus clearly led to a growth of conflicting strategic interests between the two giants. Whether this will affect the structural relationship between Russia and the EU in the longer term remains to be seen. As argued above, their partnership holds a lot of potential for a win–win situation. Both continue to need each other: Russia to avoid isolation and to export its goods, the European Union to secure its energy supplies and stability on its Eastern borders. Taking into account the longer-term evolution of their partnership (pragmatic and based on the willingness to cooperate) and the recurring political insistence on both sides that they continue their 'very constructive dialogue',[38] there is not too much reason for pessimism.

Analyzing the wider Europe after enlargement

Since the collapse of communism, the wider Europe has been characterized by two different integration processes: the expansion of the (West-) European integration process to Central and Eastern Europe and the attempt to set up a new form of cooperation in the former Soviet space in the form of the CIS. While the former is based on the pooling of sovereignties and hard law, the latter is based on Russian leadership and soft law.[39] These two processes have largely existed in isolation. There has been little osmosis between the two, and even less so an attempt to fuse them. Now the two processes, different in nature, risk clashing – posing new strategic challenges.

Two separate integration processes

Notwithstanding the strategic partnership between Russia and the EU and their intense trade relations, post-communist Russia has found itself in relative isolation in terms of European integration.

This partly results from missed opportunities. One may wonder – embarking on normative ground – whether Europe has not missed unique historic opportunities to anchor post-communist Russia solidly in a process of wider European integration. In the same way as it was a far from evident choice and huge challenge to integrate West Germany into firm, supranational structures only a short while after the Second World War, it would have required enormous creativity to involve Russia, the 'former enemy', in a process of deep European cooperation. The recent plea of the former British ambassador to Moscow in 'Europe's World' to consider making Russia a member of the EU may be rather daring, but it indicates that the mental exercise has not been done seriously before.[40]

But also, choices made by Russia have been determining factors. The country occupies a position within the processes of integration and cooperation in wider Europe which is particular in two respects. First of all, as it appears from the Medium-Term strategy, Russia's view of Europe is based on two pillars: the European Union on the one hand, and the Russian Federation on the other. The latter is the leading force within the Commonwealth of Independent States. This is a sort of imbalance. Making abstraction of political realities, it would have been more logical if the EU and the CIS had been counterparts. In the mindset of Russian foreign policy makers, however, the EU and Russia are considered to be Europe's two giants. They should seek to establish forms of pan-European cooperation – as they do, for example, in the framework of the Four Common Spaces. The CIS only comes in second, under the leadership of Russia. It confirms the leading role Russia seeks for itself within the CIS area.

Second, Moscow refused to be part of the European Neighbourhood Policy of the European Union. Though originally part of the Wider Europe Initiative and earlier blueprints of the ENP, the Russian Federation has silently boycotted participation in the ENP. Moscow considers the ENP to follow too much of a one-way approach, reflecting the interests of the EU. Russia was instead awarded the special status of key strategic partner outside the ENP framework. By recognizing explicitly that the EU and Russia belong to each other's neighbourhood, Russia is recognized as a fully equal partner of the EU.

The clash of two integration processes

The two processes set in after the collapse of communism in Central and Eastern Europe are at a point where they meet and potentially risk clashing. One process is the expansion of West European models of political, economic and security cooperation towards the East. This process has, to a large extent, been the result of the attractiveness of the European Union as a model of integration and welfare, and of NATO as hard security guarantee. It has drawn the former satellite states of the Soviet Union and the Baltic Republics into the magnetic field of EU and NATO. The other process is the attempt of the Russian Federation to maintain its influence over the CIS states. Russia first conceded and gave up its sphere of influence in Central Europe. Later, it grudgingly gave up the Baltic states. Simultaneously, however, Moscow reinforced its assertive role as a regional actor, keeping control of the other former Soviet Republics. It did not hesitate to use the dependency of these states on Russian energy supplies as a political weapon. The yearly recurring conflicts of oil and gas supplies are a case in point. Moscow applies differential oil and gas tariffs for the CIS states, which are clearly inspired by political reasons.

Since enlargement, the 'neighbourhoods' of Russia and the EU overlap, but the role played by both is highly different.

First, the strategies of both actors differ strongly. Russia relies on coercive means of power, exploiting the dependency of the states in the Near Abroad. The EU, on the other hand, – as argued above – impacts on its neighbouring countries for what it is, more than for what it does. Its latent economic power is only partly transferred into actual power. Pushed by enlargement, the EU now more actively seeks to promote democracy and convergence towards its rules and norms through the ENP and the mechanisms of conditionality. As Kubicek argues, the political role of the EU in Ukraine was minimal before the Orange Revolution.[41] Only with the advent of the ENP and the hopes of new reforms, did the EU start to play a more active political role in Ukraine. The instruments underlying the ENP, however, are persuasive rather than coercive, as they refrain from hard threats to force countries', obedience merely offering benefits in return for compliance. Some authors argue that this policy is not necessarily a milder or less targeted form of foreign policy. It can be regarded as a form of 'soft imperialism' or 'soft interventionism'.[42]

Second, the two regional forces have different interests in the area. While the EU has a clear interest in stability in the countries 'in between' by involving them more closely in the European integration process and its trade regime, Russia has a clear interest in keeping the regimes in this area relatively weak and isolated, in order to maintain its dominance. An increase of trade flows between the EU and Ukraine, for example, would decrease the latter's dependence on trade with Russia.

Third, the – now overlapping – integration processes in the CIS and the EU and its neighbourhood are different in nature. The EU model is based on the pooling of sovereignties, on seeking compromises. Moreover, in a constructivist approach, the EU can be regarded as a community of values, committed to stability, structural peace and liberal values.[43] In the case of the CIS, cooperation is based much more on bilateral relations between Moscow and the other capitals. It is hard to discern a community of values. The CIS countries embody a wide variety of political regimes. Moreover, there are clearly overlapping and contradictory tendencies in the cooperation between CIS states. Several of them have made EU membership a strategic objective. Though not very influential as an organization, the establishment of GUAM[44] was a clear reflection of the will of the Western CIS countries to escape the dominance of Moscow and seek closer cooperation with the West.

An important consequence of this growing overlap of neighbour-hoods, integration processes and interests is that the double track approach in Russian foreign policy (pragmatic versus the West; coercive in the Near Abroad) comes under strain. If interests clash over the 'common' neighbourhood, it becomes much harder to maintain the cooperative and pragmatic attitude towards the West. Or put differently, two vital interests of the Russian Federation risk clashing: safeguarding its dominance in the CIS and maintaining a constructive, pragmatic partnership with the EU.

Which of the two prevails will depend on many factors. First, it will depend on internal political developments. How will Russian politics further develop, especially in the post-Putin era? What will be the impact of the current crisis on the EU's credibility as an international actor? Will the EU be capable of maintaining its consistency? Will some new member states, such as Poland, increase the EU's role in Eastern Europe or will they act as a brake on CFSP? Second, political develop-ments in the countries in between are of crucial importance. With the Orange Revolution in Ukraine, we have witnessed that the interests of the EU and Russia tend to clash most if the situation on the ground is changing. Last but not least, the evolution of EU–Russia relations is a determining factor. The balance between the two giants will, inter alia, depend on the development of the Russian economy and the EU's energy dependence.

But, equally important, the further evolution of the ENP will be a highly significant factor. If the ENP is effective, it risks becoming the victim of its own success. If a neighbouring country successfully fulfils the conditions imposed by the EU, it will be difficult to keep member-ship from the table. The conditionality that underpins the ENP might generate a compelling logic, eventually leading to pressing demands for membership.[45] The EU might easily entrap itself by making a growing number of commitments. This entrapment is particularly likely, as few moral arguments will be left to refuse membership to, for example, a successfully reforming Ukraine, in a scenario where Turkey has entered the Union.

Conversely, the ENP might fail because it is not capable of delivering incentives that are sufficiently strong to cause drastic reforms and effec-tive rule transfer. As Schimmelfennig and Sedelmeier have argued in their study of enlargement, a number of factors determine the potential success of external incentives for rule transfer.[46] These factors include credibility (is the EU credible in its promise to deliver the rewards?), size (is the vague prospect of 'privileged relations' a sufficient incentive?), time frame (can the rewards be offered fast enough to maintain the momentum of reforms?) and domestic adoption costs (what effect does the ENP have on domestic opportunity costs and veto players?). The fact that the prospect of membership is withheld may cast doubt on the EU's chances of successfully transforming its neighbouring countries through a policy of conditionality. Heather Grabbe, for example, argues that conditionality has mainly been successful in gate-keeping; that is, the conditions imposed by the EU have mainly been effective when used as an instrument to guard accession.[47]

Moreover, the ENP gives the EU an explicit role and responsibility, and a high visibility outside its own territory. Especially in the Western CIS, it risks clashing with the interests of the Russian Federation. The effectiveness of conditionality might be undermined by 'cross-conditionality'.[48] If similar benefits can be obtained from an alternative source at lower costs (for example, no drastic changes in the power structure) the target country may be tempted to comply with the latter. Russia is such an alternative source of incentives and rewards in the countries in between, and thus a competitor for the ENP.

The situation of the countries in between is not very different from a Ukrainian cartoon I saw in the late 1990s. Ukraine was in front of three doors. The first two doors, of the EU and of NATO, remained firmly closed. The third door, that of the Russian Federation, was wide open and a beautiful woman tried to seduce Ukraine to come inside. Because of the ENP, the door of the EU is now ajar. The question is whether the EU will offer Ukraine enough of a glimpse of what's behind the door to keep it waiting without giving in to Russian temptations.

Conclusion

As a result of the biggest enlargement in the history of European integration, the 'shadow effect' of the EU on its new Eastern neighbours has increased dramatically. The options of the latter have been constrained because of the geographic proximity of and dependence on the EU. Enlargement has unintentionally created two paradoxes. First, the inclusion of new member states implies that external borders shift to the East and that strongly secured borders are established roughly between the EU and the CIS countries. This change in geopolitics makes it harder to involve the EU's new neighbours in the process of European cooperation and integration. With Eastern enlargement, this paradox has become more problematic than before, because it becomes harder for 'outsiders' to escape the 'shadow effect' of the EU. In order to create stability on its borders and to mitigate the effects of enlargement on its neighbours, the EU has developed its European Neighbourhood Policy. This policy represents a breakaway from the Copenhagen strategy, which provided for the extension of stability by allowing new members into the Union, towards a strategy of exporting stability without enlarging.

The ENP has increased the political role and visibility of the EU in the Western CIS. As a result of enlargement, Russia and the European Union have overlapping neighbourhoods, in which their interests may well collide. Whereas the EU has a strategic interest in stability in this area, Russia has an interest in keeping the regimes in the Western CIS relatively weak and dependent on Moscow. As developments in the CIS depend strongly on bilateral relations with Moscow, the key to the strategic future of the area lays in the development of the triangular relation between the EU, Russia and the countries in between. Three developments will be of crucial importance. First, how will the overlap of neighbourhoods affect Russian foreign policy? Conflicting interests in the countries in between put Russia's two track foreign policy – pragmatic towards the West and coercive towards the CIS states – under strain. Secondly, what will be the outcome of the ENP in Eastern Europe? It may be feared that the ENP will either generate a compelling logic leading to enlargement or will fail altogether because it is not capable of delivering incentives strong enough to trigger off drastic reforms. Finally, will the strategic partnership between the EU and Russia be undermined because of clashing interests in the Western CIS? The latter may suggest that there is not too much ground for pessimism, as their relation remains to based on a strategic and economic win–win partnership. The Orange Revolution in Ukraine has demonstrated that clashing interests may provoke tensions, but do not necessarily undermine the structural partnership.

Notes

1 In studies of European Foreign Policy, the concept of presence refers to 'the ability to exert influence, to shape the perceptions and expectations of others' (D. Allen and M. Smith, 'Western Europe's Presence in the Contemporary International Arena', *Review of International Studies*, 16, 1 (1990): 19–37). See also R. Ginsberg, *The European Union in International Politics. Baptism by Fire* (Oxford: Rowman & Littlefield, 2001): 46 ff.

2 H. Maull, 'Europe and the New Balance of Global Order', *International Affairs*, 81, 4 (2005): 775–99 (779).

3 *Ibid.*: 778.

4   S. Lavenex, 'EU External Governance in Wider Europe', *Journal of European Public Policy*, 11, 4 (2004): 680–700.

5   M. Light, S. White and J. Löwenhardt, 'A Wider Europe: The View from Moscow and Kyiv', *International Affairs*, 76, 1 (2000): 77–88.

6   J. Batt, 'The EU's New Borderlands', Working Paper (London: Centre for European Reform, 2003): 12.

7   F. Petiteville, 'Exporting "values"? EU external co-operation as a "soft diplomacy" ' in M. Knodt and S. Princen (eds), *Understanding the European Union's External Relations* (London: Routledge, 2003): 127–41 (132).

8   P. Kubicek, 'The European Union and Democratization in Ukraine', *Communist and Post-Communist Studies*, 38 (2005): 269–92.

9   Commission of the European Communities, 'Communication from the Commission. European Neighbourhood Policy', Strategy Paper, Brussels, 12 May 2004, COM(2004) 373final: 3.

10 *Ibid.*: 3.

11 Commission of the European Communities, 'Communication from the Commission. Paving the Way for a New Neighbourhood Instrument', Brussels, 1 July 2003, COM(2003) 393final.

12 Belarus will only fully benefit from the ENP once it has established a democratic form of government. Normal relations with Libya will only be established after the country has accepted the Barcelona *acquis*.

13 Commission of the European Communities, 'Communication from the Commission. European Neighbourhood Policy', Strategy Paper, Brussels, 12 May 2004, COM(2004) 373final: 4.

14 *Ibid.*: 6.

15 S. Keukeleire, *Het buitenlands beleid van de Europese Unie* (Deventer: Kluwer, 1998): 169 ff.

16 K. Smith, *European Union Foreign Policy in a Changing World* (Cambridge: Polity, 2003).

17 J. Checkel, 'Compliance and Conditionality', ARENA Working Papers, WP 00/18, 2000.

18 Verheugen quoted in M. Emerson, 'EU neighborhood policy "too low gear", *European Voice*, 27 May–2 June 2004: 15.

19 R. Aliboni, 'The Geopolitical Implications of the European Neighborhood Policy'. *European Foreign Affairs Review* (2005) 10: 1–16 (14).

20 Vladimir Putin, APEC Summit, Shanghai, 19 October 2001, quoted in Igor Zevelev, 'Russian and American National Identity, Foreign Policy, and Bilateral Relations', *International Politics*, 39, (December 2002): 447–65 (453).

21 A. Lieven, 'The Secret Policemen's Ball: the United States, Russia and the International Order after 11 September', in *International Affairs*, 78, 2 (2002): 254.

22 F. Splidsboel-Hansen, 'Russia's Relation with the European Union: A Constructivist Cut', *International Politics*, 39 (2002): 399–421.

23 See also: A. Pravda, 'Foreign Policy', in S. White, A. Pravda, Z. Gitelman (eds), *Developments in Russian Politics 5* (Basingstoke: Palgrave, 2001).

24 [Russian government], *Medium-term Strategy for Development of Relations between the Russian Federation and the European Union (2000–2010)*, October 1999, (Unofficial translation), http://presidency.finland.fi/frame.asp

25 Emerson, M., 'Russia and the EU – From an Awkward Partnership to a Greater Europe?', *CEPS/IISS European Security Forum*, 2004: 1–14 (2).

26 European Council, 'Common Strategy of the European Union of 4 June 1999 on Russia', *Official Journal*, L 157, 24/06/1999: 1–10.

27 The institutional framework now consists of: Summit meetings twice a year, a Permanent Partnership Council at Ministerial level, Cooperation Committees at senior officials level, Sub-committees on technical issues, and a Joint Parliamentary Committee (EU–Russia Summit, 2003).

28 European Council, *A Secure Europe in a Better World. European Security Strategy* Approved by the European Council held in Brussels on 12 December 2003 and drafted under the responsibilities of the EU High Representative Javier Solana, electronic version.

29 F. Splidsboel-Hansen, 'Trade and Peace: A Classic Retold in Russian', *European Foreign Affairs Review*, 9 (2004): 303–22.

30 The other way around the Russian Federation is the fifth trading partner for the European Union. Energy resources account for 55 per cent of EU imports from Russia.

31 Kosachev, quoted in *Moscow Times*, 3 February 2004.

32 EU–Russia Summit, 'Joint Statement on Transit between the Kaliningrad Region and the Rest of the Russian Federation', Brussels, 11 November 2002, electronic version.

33 Joint Statement on EU Enlargement and EU–Russia Relations, Brussels, 27 April 2004, electronic version.

34 External Relations Commissioner Ferrero-Waldner, speaking to the Foreign Affairs Committee of the European Parliament, 25 January 2005.

35 European Parliament, 'Recommendation to the Council on EU–Russia relations' (2003/2230(INI)), 26 February 2004, electronic version.

36 Commission of the European Communities, Communication from the Commission to the Council and to the European Parliament on Relations with Russia, Brussels, 10 February 2004, COM(2004) 106 final.

37 External Relations Commissioner Ferrero-Waldner, speaking to the Foreign Affairs Committee of the European Parliament, 25 January 2005.

38 Foreign Minister Lavrov at the meeting with the EU Troika in Luxemburg, (Minister Lavrov, Press Conference, 28 February 2005).

39 R. Dragneva, 'Is "Soft" Beautiful? Another Perspective on Law, Institutions, and Integration in the CIS', *Review of Central and East European Law*, 29, 3 (2004): 279–324.

40 R. Lyne, 'Russia in the EU? We should never say never', *Europe's World*, (Spring 2006): 38–41.

41 P. Kubicek, 'The European Union and Democratization in Ukraine', *Communist and Post-Communist Studies*, 38 (2005): 269–92.

42 B. Badie, 'Sovereignty and Intervention', in W. Carslsnaes *et al.* (eds), *Contemporary European Foreign Policy* (London: Sage, 2004): 155–69.

43 F. Mayer and J. Palmowksi, 'European Identities and the EU – The Ties that Bind the Peoples of Europe', *Journal of Common Market Studies*, 42, 3 (2004): 573–98.

44 GUAM was originally established in 1997 as GUUAM and consisted of Georgia, Ukraine, Uzbekistan, Azerbaijan and Moldova. It was aimed to

counterbalance Russian influence. In 2002, Uzbekistan withdrew from the organization.

45   F. Schimmelfennig, 'The Community Trap: Liberal Norms, Rhetorical Action and the Eastern Enlargement of the European Union', *International Organization*, 55, 1 (2001): 47–80.

46   F. Schimmelfennig and U. Sedelmeier, 'Governance by conditionality: EU rule transfer to the candidate countries of Central and Eastern Europe', *Journal of European Public Policy*, 11, 4 (2004): 661–79.

47   H. Grabbe, 'How does Europeanization affect CEE governance? Conditionality, diffusion and diversity', *Journal of European Public Policy*, 8, 6 (2001): 1013–31 (1020).

48   F. Schimmelfennig and U. Sedelmeier, 'Governance by conditionality: EU rule transfer to the candidate countries of Central and Eastern Europe', *Journal of European Public Policy*, 11, 4 (2004): 661–79.

5
Russia, the CIS and the EU: Secondary Integration by Association?

Holger Moroff

Introduction

Cooperation among states and regional organizations can take on various forms. Governance modes vary from supranational to intergovernmental; material policies may include trade, common markets, the environment, and fundamental rights, from soft security issues to military, strategic politics and geopolitics. How does cooperation take place and why are regional organizations such as the European Union (EU) interested in associating with other regions or states? The following contribution tries to develop an answer by focusing on the EU's *Ostpolitik*.

First, after a brief comparison of the EU and the CIS, we will consider the case of Russia, which is important from an EU perspective and in light of cooperation between the EU and CIS. Second, we develop a research agenda for analysing what informs the EU's thinking about its Eastern neighbourhood in general and Russia in particular, applying the concept of soft security. Third, we will discuss the first empirical findings and the division of competencies for various soft security issues and numerous internal constraints of EU external policy towards Russia, before we delineate concrete cooperation structures with Russia. Finally, the main forms of cooperation will be compared and assessed concerning their transferability to the interregional level between the CIS and the EU.

Different species of regional associations

Comparing the present state of the EU and the CIS, one might be tempted to conclude that these two political entities belong to different species of regional integration, rendering cooperation or even mutual association difficult. By institutional design, decision-making modes and identities vary considerably. While the EU has a strong suprana-tional streak, this dimension is virtually absent in the CIS. The most prominent forms of the transfer of sovereignty in the EU are powerful supranational institutions such as the EU Commission's first pillar right to be the sole initiator of legislation, the member states' qualified majority vote on the majority of these initiatives in the EU Council, as well as the Parliament's veto power over the same fields. In these internal market-related matters, no single member state has veto power. Cooperation builds upon a shared understanding of a positive-sum game played in an essentially non-hierarchical, bottom-up policy-making environment with a focus on regulatory policies of low political salience.[1]

The CIS, in contrast, is dominated by Russia, its most powerful member state. A strong veto power, an intergovernmental set up and a hierarchical, top-down policy-making mechanism set it apart from the entity it was originally aiming to imitate – the EU. In theory, the CIS has potentially strong supranational institutions such as the Economic Court or the Executive Committee, able to issue directly applicable instructions (analogous to EU regulations). Beyond this, it has a political-strategic dimension through its Council on Collective Security. However, these high aims contrast sharply with the few substantive results thus far. Neither the 1994 Free Trade Agreement nor the common agricultural market, envisioned in 1997, has been implemented.[2] Inside the CIS a trend of more restricted regional agreements such as GUUAM, EEU and CAEU has emerged during the late 1990s and led to greater internal variation rather than unity.[3]

How can these different species cooperate? Why should they do so, and what is the limit of such a relationship? Given that EU bilateral approaches toward the post-Soviet space have dominated interregional ones, in addition to the fact that one hegemonic actor on the CIS side determines its fate, it seems most revealing to focus on the forms of asso-ciation between this central state within the CIS and the EU. Thus, Russia–EU relations will be taken here as a partial indicator for possible CIS–EU relations, despite more recent EU attempts to differentiate between the Western and Eastern parts of the CIS.

In the process of the EU structuring and harmonizing relations with its neighbours, Russia was singled out as a special case from the begin-ning. In what could be called a double *Ostpolitik*, Russia has always offered something to CIS countries – if only as a token of good relations – whenever the EU granted new privileges to those countries between itself and Russia. Some examples are the European agreements for candidate countries, their final EU membership, the two rounds of NATO enlargement and most recently the EU Neighbourhood policy. They all were accompanied by new or special contracts with Russia. Moreover, Russia was the first country with which a Partnership and Cooperation Agreement was negotiated, the only non-WTO state receiving compensation for losses due to trade diversion after Finland and Sweden entered the European Union, the first for which a Common Strategy was designed, the first CIS country in which the European Investment Bank became active and with which negotiations on visa facilitations were opened. The EU took all these initiatives, thus underlining its attitude of being actively involved in shaping the situation.

Originally, the EU preferred interregionalism over bilateralism, but since the CIS lacked a legal personality it could not serve as the contracting counterpart to replace the CMEA (Commonwealth for Mutual Economic Assistance) in the 1989 trade agreement. Instead, bilateral PCAs, comprising trade issues and multilevel political dialogue modelled on European agreements with candidate countries, were concluded with all post Soviet successor states save the three Baltic countries.[4] Despite the single EU financial instrument (Technical Assistance to the Commonwealth of Independent States, referred to as TACIS) for all, a process of differentiation emerged from the beginning. Most of the money has gone to the Western parts of the CIS, with Russia receiving almost one third of the funds.[5] Second, a further degree of differentiation in treatment of CIS countries can be seen in the fact that the PCAs for Ukraine, Russia, Moldova and Belarus contain an evolutionary clause for an eventual free trade area, which is lacking in the other PCAs as well as the new concept of a common economic space with Russia (see Chapter 6 by Vahl). Now we find that the Western CIS (Ukraine, Moldova and Belarus) is dealt with within the European Neighbourhood Policy – a unified bilateral framework – and relations with the Central Asian states are regulated by the 2002 Strategy Paper[6] promoting regional cooperation. Meanwhile Russia is singled out for special bilateral treatment within the framework of four common spaces.

What can this latter cooperation beget? What do the two sides want from each other, where do interests run parallel and where do they diverge or contradict each other? Against the backdrop of a double asymmetry – the EU as an economic giant but political dwarf and Russia as an economic dwarf but a politically unified actor and strategic giant – three dimensions need to be assessed. Economic interests can best be captured by a realist cost-benefit analysis. Political interests are both based on identities and institutions, the former calling for a constructivist, the latter for a liberal regime theoretical approach.

Economic interests

Opening the circle of integration to the ring of countries around the EU involves, first and foremost, granting access to the internal market. Direct financial assistance is of secondary importance because the EU has not been designed as a strong redistributive system.[7] Since the vast majority of Russian exports to the EU consist of oil and gas and do not face any tariff or non-tariff restrictions, further market access would not affect these exports. It thus provides a fairly weak bargaining chip.[8] The EU, on the other hand, exports mainly finished goods to Russia, for which further market openings would be advantageous especially since Russian tariffs are, on average, much higher than the EU's.

Political identities

Russia's self perception as a great power – at least regionally, in strategic and economic terms – means that it tends to restrict the sovereignty of its neighbours but does not accept restrictions on its own sovereignty. Whereas EU member states are accustomed and willing to cede or share sovereignty in a post-national policy setting, Russia is keen on preserving it by whatever means. Two contrasting sets of behaviour flow from such different outlooks on international cooperation. The first is a problem-solving oriented, positive-sum game, realizing common gains. The latter is a zero-sum game, where Russia's gain is the West's loss and vice versa. Interestingly, the Russian government insinuates that the EU operates according to the same logic towards its neighbourhood as Russia does, though with different means, when it suggests that Western money sponsored these NGOs that have apparently undermined or are subverting pro-Russian forces in Ukraine, Belarus, Moldova, Georgia and so on.

Political institutions

On the institutional side, it might be argued that a common forum for discourse changes and eventually harmonizes the outlook of the participating actors through continuous communication. The PCA has provided such a platform since 1997 (see p. 102 on how policy objectives are pursued). If access is one indicator of influence, we must state that Russia enjoys a privileged position indeed. No other third country – not even the USA – has as many meetings on ministerial, administrative and parliamentary levels as Russia. Input and opportunities for voicing opinions are certainly provided. Yet, although the institutional infrastructure is in place, it is lacking substantive traffic. Participants often give the impression that both sides are talking past each other or are at cross purposes rather than charting common ground.[9] Thus, patterns of institutional interaction and lines of communication do not always cover fault lines of association.

What forms and limits of association are conceivable? This calls for an answer to the question: What constitutes an optimal political and economic integration area or sector of integration? However, no easy and objective answer is at hand. Neoclassical economists would argue that integration on a global scale would be optimal with a view to realizing economies of scale and comparative advantages, as well as an efficient international division of labor. Less ambitiously, one could state that optimal forms of international cooperation between non-state entities (that is, the EU and the CIS) should at least be functional in the sense that gains from parallel or complementary interests can be realized and conflicting interests resolved non-conflictually.[10]

Russia seems to be particularly prone to cooperating in the fields where it can be an active player (the security field and on issues of high politics), which leads to an intrinsic politicization of its external relations. The EU, however, is mainly interested in expanding its regulatory regimes into the neighbourhood as a precondition for internal market access and societal security.[11] It is thus rather interested in depoliticization. There are also numerous institutional reasons for this discrepancy. The EU can act best in the technical terrain without high political or media salience. This is because the EU proffers a system of diffuse power sharing with a consensual diplomatic, rather than a confrontational, politically charged discourse, which it cannot handle or sustain since it has no such strong political mandates. For the EU, it is thus extremely difficult to obtain a clear political mandate from its member states for pro-active international behaviour on high politics issues. In contrast, Russia is characterized by a highly (re-)centralized and hierarchical political leadership, which makes for the opposite of diffusely pooled sovereignty and power sharing.

After next drawing out a research agenda able to answer three central questions connected to the EU's Ostpolitik, we will look at the general internal EU conditions for policies towards its surroundings before the EU's particular interests and problems with Russia are discussed in a framework of depoliticization and desecuritization. Since the EU is better equipped through its bottom-up decision-making system to deal with non-political issues, it tends to export its low politics approach, focusing on soft and human security, as is borne out through a comparison of various EU policies towards Russia.

The EU's *Ostpolitik*: a research agenda

The EU is developing a new policy towards its Eastern neighbourhood. This section aims at providing an analytical frame for studying the Europeanization of security concepts and its expression in the EU's policies towards Russia. There is a special focus on the internal conditions and external effects of the Union's Eastern neighbourhood policy. In a first step, the EU's own approach to security will be delineated by identifying and interpreting core documents. The question of how these ideas inform relevant actors within the EU institutions will be addressed subsequently as part of an analysis that looks at the interaction patterns between the EU and Russia in an overall effort of projecting stability through cooperation and association. Finally, we will assess whether and when the experiences gained within the framework of the Northern Dimension can fruitfully be applied to the evolving policies towards the EU's new Eastern neighbourhood and Russia.

First, we wish to sketch out an applied research agenda, which aims at bridging the gap between the highly specialized and continuously updated policy reports and the more broad sweeping academic volumes with greater theoretical reach but lesser operational relevance. This should be divided into three parts addressing the following questions: What is considered a soft security threat? Why has the Union developed as a major actor in these new external policy fields? How are these policy objectives pursued and jointly implemented with Russia through a process of external multi-level network governance?

What is considered a soft security threat in the EU's neighbourhood?

This question hinges on the perception of interdependence[12] and should be analysed through the critical lens of security studies, drawing on the Copenhagen School's concept of 'securitization'[13] and using social constructivist methods of discourse analysis when identifying and interpreting relevant EU documents. From this perspective, securitization is not necessarily linked to objective external threats but is the outcome of framing processes in political discourse and practices by which an issue becomes defined as a security problem requiring political action according to public and elite opinions.[14]

Extending the zone of security around Europe forms one major objective of the EU as manifested in its security strategy.[15] Russia will be both an indispensable partner in securing the EU's immediate neighbourhood as well as a source of potential soft security threats within this neighbourhood itself. Engaging Russia will thus be of utmost importance for the EU. The former European Commission president, Romano Prodi, has set out a vision of the EU offering its neighbours 'everything but institutions'. The aim is to promote the emergence of a 'ring of friends' across Eastern Europe and the Mediterranean. Europeanization is here understood not only as standardization from Brussels, but as the diffusion and consolidation of ideas and practices in the European governance network[16] as it straddles the borders between members, candidates and associated neighbours.

Why has the EU developed as the major actor?

This question is concerned with how the EU is expanding its sphere of governance in those areas that have become 'securitized' inside the Union and where it sees itself as vulnerable to developments in third countries of its Eastern neighbourhood. The understanding that the Union is better equipped to tackle underlying transborder problems in its vicinity both mirrors internal competences and projects them externally. This neofunctionalist expression of path dependency[17] should be taken further by looking at the role conceptions of and for the Union as manifested in the principles and commitments for achieving and retaining an 'area of freedom, security and justice' (Title IV TEC), which might be taken as the basis for going beyond the borders of the Union proper in an extended effort to fulfil this primarily domestic task. This is especially true for the whole gamut of soft security risks – for instance, in areas of justice and home affairs, the environment, pollution, nuclear safety, health, migration, crime and corruption. Here, a structured analysis could fruitfully draw on neofunctionalist theories, showing how domestic competencies spill over into external policies by analysing the institutionalization of the Union's new soft security agenda.

Why and how is the EU interacting with third countries on soft security issues in its Eastern neighbourhood in general and Russia in particular? This is the guiding question for a demanding research agenda, leading to answers that should be useful for the further development of the Eastern Dimension within the European Neighbourhood policy. The examples set by the Northern Dimension Initiative can serve as a model for future policy options and provide a case in point where the EU Commission can gain foreign policy competences through programmes such as Interreg III, Phare CBC and Tacis CBC as well as by participating in regional and sub-regional organizations without strict and clear mandates from the EU Council.[18] The main hypothesis to be tested is whether the EU's low politics approach through cooperation in fields such as the environment, pollution, nuclear safety, health, migration, crime and corruption reinforces EU soft security concepts inside the Union and can provide a path for altering Russian approaches towards security internally as well as in the overlapping common neighbourhood of the EU and Russia.

How are policy objectives pursued?

To answer this question, one should look at how this agenda is implemented through concrete policies in the neighbourhood. A special focus might be Northern Dimension policies both to demonstrate the functioning of multilevel network governance in 'nearby' external relations[19] and to test whether the particular mechanisms developed here are suitable for engaging Russia in that process. Two theoretical approaches lend themselves to such a study; namely, multi-level governance[20] and foreign policy analysis.[21] The main difficulties in this area are associated with problems of cross-pillar coordination on the EU side and the concrete negotiation and governance management bringing the Commission, member and candidate states and neighbourhood countries together at one table on national, sub-national, state and NGO levels, thus leading to 'fuzzy policies around fuzzy borders'.[22] The concrete coordination and implementation methods have been described as bottom-up processes in low policy fields that have the potential of both alleviating problems at hand and changing the thinking on security and the openness of policy processes in the 'target' countries, and especially in Russia.[23]

Analytical approaches that conceptualize the Union as a relatively coherent actor[24] – focusing on the whole rather than the individual parts – can be juxtaposed with theoretical approaches that work from the bottom-up by looking at all individual units, actors and pillars.[25] Similarly, while some assume that member states' interests are driving the process of Europeanization, others maintain that preference formation is influenced by ideas, role conceptions and institutions beyond the national state level.[26] As far as the analysis of concepts and the development of the external competence to act are concerned, the first two parts of the research agenda should be focused on holistic approaches. When it comes to the process of concrete policy developments and implementations, the research focus must centre on the interplay of individual units, actors and pillars. Thus, the earlier bird's eye perspective should be complemented by a more detailed mole's perspective on the bottom-up processes.

Empirical analysis and first findings

A more detailed overview of the three questions developed above will put flesh on the bones of this research by (1) pointing to the development of the soft security concept; (2) looking at some of the challenges facing the Eastern Dimension in the context of EU policy towards Russia; and (3) analysing concrete dialogue and cooperation structures as provided by the PCA. Finally (4) EU policies will be compared while giving some indications of how the Northern Dimension policy frame functions as a model.

Risk prevention, neighbourhood and the concept of soft security

In its 1998 study of possible scenarios of how Europe might look in the year 2010, the Forward Studies Unit of the European Commission developed one particularly bleak outlook in its chapter entitled 'Turbulent Neighbourhoods'.[27] It spoke from a siege mentality as an expression of the fear Europeans might then feel towards the world beyond their borders, conceived of as beset with ethnic tensions, a gradually disintegrating Russia, environmental degradation, epidemics and proliferating international crime, all inextricably interlinked and leading occasionally to terrorist incidents inside the Union. With its methodology of anticipatory hindsight, looking back at the present European Union from an imaginary vantage point in 2010 they note: 'In its state of general languor, the European public did not notice all the new military and soft security threats on the Union's doorstep.'[28] Future historians would then describe the EU policy reactions as a failed attempt to implement an effective *cordon sanitaire* strategy also against the neighbouring regions uncontrollable deluge of migrants and refugees.

The current EU policy on the external frontier is dominated by justice and home affairs considerations, giving apparent credibility to the image of a fortress Europe. However, a general uncertainty about the definitive external limits of the EU and the attraction exercised by the EU on its neighbouring states has the effect of giving the external frontier aspects that are more analogous to old imperial frontiers rather than those of a nation state:

In very general terms Member States have certain basic principles in common (rule of law, parliamentary democracy, respect for human rights, private property as the basis of market economies). The significance of the external frontier is different according to the degree to which the neighbouring state adheres to these principles. For example, the external frontier with Switzerland and Norway is viewed differently from that with Morocco and Russia.[29]

Consequently, the EU's policy towards its direct neighbourhood is one of projecting those basic principles shared by the EU's member states. It is, consciously or not, an attempt at making its proximate vicinity more similar to itself, creating and reproducing a socio-political landscape of centre/periphery. This, in relation to Russia, does not only have to do with the great economic asymmetries in the EU's favour,[30] but also a strong path dependency as a result of the painstakingly negotiated *acquis communautaire* in various policy fields, which, for reasons of internal rigidity and inertia, cannot be changed easily, even if the negotiating partner is of equal or even larger economic size.[31]

Some of the Commission officials[32] who had produced the dreadful scenario of turbulent neighbourhoods also contributed to the Commission's communication on conflict prevention of mid-2001, as well as its dossier on 'Wider Europe', March 2003, which proposes a neighbourhood policy for the coming decade. This might have contributed to providing the negative backdrop before which a whole array of soft security measures were summoned up to confront and avert such appalling prospects. Soft security issues loom large in the Commission's conflict prevention concept and its new neighbourhood policy, as well as in its Security Strategy of December 2003 and in the Commission's communication on 'Security Research – the next step' of September 2004. Among other things, the Commission calls for action against environmental degradation, the spread of communicable diseases, population flows and human trafficking as well as support for democracy, the rule of law and civil society.[33] The explicit aim is to project stability into the Union's direct neighbourhood. It is noteworthy that the first and foremost means of pursuing this goal, according to the Commission paper, is through the 'strengthening of regional cooperation in a wider context', thus indirectly according a pilot function to the Northern Dimension policy frame.

Internal constraints and external effects of EU policies

We also find three cardinal geographic directions towards which the EU has developed distinct policies; namely, a 'Mediterranean Policy' towards the south, a 'Northern Dimension' towards the north-west and most recently an 'Eastern Dimension' towards eastern Europe and the western CIS has been proposed. All of them are now part of the EU Neighbourhood policy.

From the perspective of the single member states, questions arise as to whose particular neighbourhood is more important and who lobbies for whom: this in turn gives rise to internal conflicts over funds and attention. Examples are the proposed setting up of a Mediterranean Bank as a branch of the European Investment Bank (EIB), which was blocked mostly by Northern member states, while EIB lending to Russia, Ukraine and Moldavia is usually met with reservations from southern member countries.[34] Through EU membership, countries acquire a virtual neighbourhood at the other end of Europe's geographical reach. Thus, we find that Finland has established a Mediterranean desk in its foreign office and staged a conference on the topic since it became an EU member. This also means that the number of opinions, voices, and actors in the Union's Common Foreign and Security Policy (CFSP) has increased manifold through successive enlargements. Who would have asked Portugal about European policies towards Russia, for example, if it were not for its EU membership and the fact that theoretically every country has the same voice?

One needs to turn at this point from the internal difficulties, jealousies and rivalries that a multidimensional neighbourhood policy entails towards the substantial underlying aims which are equally valid for all corners of the EU's proximity policy. First and foremost, the EU wants to avoid creating new dividing lines, arising from an eastward shift of the EU borders with enlargement. Fulfilling this goal means, effectively, squaring the circle. The economic and social divide will inevitably increase and not be bridged, for the amounts of structural and other funds made available for the accession countries will not be matched at all by TACIS or cross border funds from pre- and post-accession aid. The economic reorientation will always be towards the centre and not the periphery, even within the EU, not to mention the outer peripheries of the EU. The centre, in this case the EU, has a tendency and history of incorporating its outer periphery. This is a natural process; no member state wants to be cut off from its neighbours by an EU – meaning Schengen – border. The latest example is set by Poland's proposal of an Eastern Dimension, providing for the eventual membership of Ukraine, Belarus and Moldova. But where does it or where should it end? Is it a process of natural organic growth or geographic over-extension?

Intermediate space

The EU's new Eastern neighbourhood might be viewed by some as contested[35] in the sense that it is an 'in between' space of two large powers, the one being in relative decline – Russia, the other on the rise – the EU. Thus, the concept of a 'double periphery' or an overlapping 'near abroad' brings Russia into play and the Polish proposition for an Eastern Dimension policy of the EU highlights Russia as the main 'other'.[36] The Polish initiative speaks of eventual EU membership for Ukraine, Belarus and Moldavia as being dependent on the direction of their political and economic developments. Russia, however, is painted differently and labelled a definite outsider also for its apparently non-Western mode of political and economic transformation. Old EU member states such as France and Germany are perceived (rightly or wrongly) to have conducted a 'Russia first' policy, but that this will change after Eastern Enlargement.[37] Though understandable, this position is slightly unreasonable, especially as regards the role of Russia in the Balkans. Neither a solution to the Kosovo question nor the peacekeeping in Bosnia-Herzegovina would have been possible without some degree of Russian support. It might be true that Russia, as many other states, uses the EU for its purposes; for example, by keeping the problem of Russian minorities in the Baltic states on the agenda and the Kaliningrad question open – also in order to have a foot in the door of EU policies such as 'Schengen' – with the ultimate aim of securing visa-free travel for all Russians. As the Kaliningrad question exemplifies, many offers of turning a region into a more prosperous zone through special trade privileges or assistance by the EU were stalled in Moscow apparently for fear of fuelling separatist tendencies.[38] However, one might also view this as a functional *realpolitik* approach to problem steering, aiming not at solving problems but rather at keeping them alive as useful bargaining chips for later. Differences between Brussels and Moscow in conceptualizing strategic foreign policy concepts should also be noted: whereas the former believes in positive-sum games and views its own integration process as a prime example, the latter takes a more zero-sum game approach where the gain of one side is inevitably the loss of another. In other EU attempts to engage Russia through the PCA and the Northern Dimension, an incompatibility of administrative structures has revealed the difficulties of practical interaction.[39] Whereas on the EU side many questions are tackled and decided on at the expert level, the Russian experts' mandate seems rather limited and contingent upon constant approval of superior administrative layers, which makes even technical collaboration difficult.[40] Thus, such a low politics approach might profit from engaging non-state and non-hierarchical actors as well as adopting the Northern Dimension efforts.[41] These 'Northern' experiences might thus be usefully applied to problems involving Russia in one way or another further south.

The evolving concept of an Eastern Dimension policy as championed by Poland might open up other routes to move closer to the EU.[42] This is especially true as new forms of association below the membership level are currently discussed in Brussels. Ultimately that will also mean swallowing decisions made in Brussels without sitting at the table where they are made.[43] Given that the Eastern neighbourhood is perceived to be a central hub of cross-border illegal activities such as smuggling, trafficking in human beings or arms and drugs, cooperation with the EU in the field of Justice and Home affairs might very well be the greatest bargaining chip as funds are being made available for the new neighbourhood (see proposed financial instrument from 2007 onwards) and the prospect of common spaces leading up to an extension of the single market are discussed as carrots in the evolving conditionality regime of the Union.

The EU's interests and goals as regards Russia

All initiatives shaping the relationship between the EU and the Russian Federation in the 1990s were introduced by or reflected in the EU's concepts. In the words of the former Russian ambassador to the EU, Vladimir Shemiatenkov, the 1990s were the 'golden age' for the European bureaucrats working on Russia.[44] Everything the EU proposed, usually following initiatives of the Commission, was sooner or later accepted by the Russian side: the Trade and Cooperation Agreement of 1989, the PCA of 1997 as well as the idea of a Common Economic Space under the condition of Russia's membership in the WTO, which was included into the PCA in 1999.

From the Russian perspective these initiatives fell on fertile ground for three reasons: (1) Gorbachev promoted maximum cooperation with the EU; (2) the extremely cooperative Russian attitude during the Yeltsin presidency, driven by the 'Westerners' within the administration and by fears of Russia's isolation from the West, supported the EU's efforts; and (3) the weakness of the Russian state and the lack of a post-Cold War grand strategy facilitated EU policy making toward Russia considerably.

The EU's policy toward Russia has to be considered an integral part of its *Ostpolitik*, which rests on two pillars: the Eastern Enlargement and the partnership with Russia.[45] Both policies have been developed during the 1990s as a reaction to the geo-strategic changes after the Cold War and the transformation of the Eastern European states.

A concrete change in the EU's set of policy concepts for Eastern Europe and Russia alike was the break with the Washington consensus,[46] which was based upon the idea that privatization and market liberalization as well as democratization were the core elements of the transformation process. Aspects institutionally and legally aimed at backing up this transformation played a less important role. The dominance of the Washington consensus is due to the fact that, at the beginning of the 1990s, the G7 granted responsibility for coordinating foreign assistance concerning Russia to the International Monetary Fund, the World Bank and the European Bank for Reconstruction and Development.[47] This consensus was reflected by the distribution of money within the EU's TACIS programme. Until 1995, most of the money was spent on measures supporting privatization and market liberalization. However, after the PCA came into force in 1997, measures supporting the rule of law and its control instruments gained more prominence. The first changes in the EU's strategy, such as adding new aspects complementing the former concepts, could already be observed in 1993. Whereas in 1991 the creation of a market economy constituted the EU's main goal, Brussels added the development of liberal democracy in 1993, and the EU placed additional focus on the rule of law in 2000.[48] Once formulated, the elements of EU policies have not been abandoned; rather, they have been sustained and complemented by new ones. Thus, the development of both a foreign economic as well as strategic-political policy toward Russia is characterized by a strong degree of path dependency.

As it is the EU's main goal to prevent creating new dividing lines across Europe through its Eastern Enlargement, its policy toward Russia aims at bringing Russia closer to west European standards of democracy, a market economy and the rule of law.[49] However, given the lack of a membership perspective, the EU's political influence on Russia remains rather limited. Moreover, Russia is a strategic partner for the EU on global security issues, whose support potentially improves the EU's power as an actor in international relations. These facts explain why the EU is so interested in engaging Russia in a continuous high-level political dialogue, in spite of depoliticizing virtually all bilateral issues by rather technical problem-solving approaches.

Structures of cooperation and dialogue between the EU and Russia

In October 1992, the Council of Ministers officially authorized the European Commission to start negotiations with the Russian Federation on a Partnership and Cooperation Agreement.[50] During the eighteen-month negotiations, the EU proved its flexibility, as it widened its mandate twice: first, in order to meet Russian demands for including the option of a free-trade area and, second, it provided for the opportunity of granting Russia the status of a transitional economy.[51] As the accession negotiations with other Central and Eastern European countries started at that time, the European Parliament, the Council of Ministers as well as the Commission intended to afford Russia further cooperation in order to prevent new dividing lines.[52]

References to common values in the preamble of the PCA is based upon the Charter of Paris of 1990 and contains a commitment to political and economic liberties, the promotion of international security and peace, the appreciation of democratic and constitutional principles as well as the protection of human rights.[53] With the inclusion of Paragraph 107, the EU was successful in introducing the principle of political conditionality (see also Chapter 6), allowing both parties to suspend the agreement if one violates common values since the latter are considered integral parts of the treaty.[54]

The PCA provided for the institutionalization of the political dialogue between the EU and Russia. However, large parts of the agreement are concerned with trade issues such as the granting of most favoured nation status for the majority of Russian products and the question of establishing a free-trade area.

Presently, the depth and frequency of the EU's meetings with Russia is the highest among all third countries with which the EU conducts formal relations, surpassing even the frequency of contact with the United States. The head of the EU department within the Russian foreign ministry, Vladimir I. Seregin, speaks of approximately 42 meetings a year taking place on different levels and in varying formations.[55]

Forms and forums of dialogue between the EU and Russia can be divided into four categories: (1) those concerned with economic relations between the two partners; (2) consultations regarding foreign and security policy; (3) consultations dealing with justice and home affairs. These three categories replicate the internal three-pillar structure of the EU and project it onto relations with third countries. Concrete modes of dialogue can be found in Articles 6–9 and 90–7 of the PCA. The dialogue between members of the European Parliament and the Russian State Duma constitutes the fourth category.

Biannual EU–Russia summits, annual EU–Russia Cooperation Councils at the ministerial level, biannual cooperation committees involving senior officials as well as subcommittees at the expert level and officials which convene upon request, belong to the first category of these dialogue structures. Although summits and meetings of the Cooperation Council often focus on foreign policy issues, these conversations usually lack substance and concrete results on foreign policy questions, generating mostly declarations of merely symbolic value.

The second category deals with issues related to the EU's second pillar, CFSP and ESDP. Conducting regular contacts with the Russian foreign minister the High Representative for CFSP, Javier Solana, is at the top of the actors' pyramid on the EU side in this area. In addition, political directors of the foreign ministries of EU member states and Russia meet either in the 25 + 1 or in the troika + 1 format. The latter has prevailed until now for reasons of efficiency and it forms the basis for the Permanent Cooperation Council established in 2004. The troika + 1 format can reflect the capital formation of the Political and Security Committee (PSC), which was established 2000 by the EU summit in Nice. Both this capital PSC troika and the regular PSC ambassadors meet with Russian representatives. Furthermore, working groups within the Council of Ministers can meet with their Russian counterparts in the troika format if demanded.

A third category of dialogue concerns questions of justice and home affairs, which belong to the intergovernmental third pillar of the EU. The EU delegation is chaired at the levels of the EU–Russia Cooperation Council and in the subcommittees by the country holding the six-monthly EU presidency. Although always present, the Commission only plays an observing role. By contrast, in the fields of asylum, visa and immigration as well as the Schengen *acquis* (which was transferred to the *acquis communautaire* by the Treaty of Amsterdam and thus became part of the first pillar), the Commission bears chief responsibility. Due to the international efforts to combat terrorism in the wake the September 11 attacks, questions of internal security in cooperation with Russia have gained increasing importance. Since 2003, ministers of justice and the interior have held regular meetings with their Russian counterparts on the basis of the 30 + 2 format. However, this format was not sustained after the EU's Eastern Enlargement, which would then have included 52 representatives.[56] Furthermore, we find a special troika format in the field of justice and home affairs, which involves the ministers of justice and of the interior of the present and the future presidency as well as a representative of the Commission, rather efficient. It met for the first time in April 2001 in Stockholm.

The parliamentary cooperation committee, which consists of members of the European Parliament, the Duma and the Russian Federation Council, constitutes the fourth dialogue structure between the EU and

Russia. According to the PCA, the parliamentary delegations meet twice a year. Moreover, the heads of the committee delegations and their deputies meet additionally two times a year. As a result, a small circle of Russian and European parliamentarians convene four times a year in order to hold consultations.

Special cases of Russia–EU cooperation are two groups of high-level experts. One group meets as part of the 'energy partnership', established by the Paris EU–Russia summit in 1999. The other group meets within the project of a 'Common European Economic Space' (CEES), which was set up at the Moscow summit in 2001. Although the Commission's responsibilities pertaining to energy questions are rather limited, it chairs both expert groups. As both projects have been added to the PCA, they provide evidence for the open and evolutionary character of the PCA, whose framework allows for new concepts and consultation formats.

The forums and mechanisms of dialogue mentioned above suggest that the patterns of EU–Russia relations are very complex. They reflect the internal structure of the EU and transfer it into the EU's external relations. As a result, this organizational setting forces partners of the EU to adjust to these structures. However, the problems in dealing with the EU arise not only from its complex and static legal order, which causes a lack of flexibility in European foreign relations. Furthermore, the rotating presidency provides for a dynamic that tempts each new presidency to introduce new initiatives. Thus, almost every EU–Russia summit stages new projects and initiatives at different levels of interaction, thereby leading to a confusing variety and partially overlapping activities. This 'stop and go' dynamic is not only due to the desire of the rotating presidency to develop its own profile, but is also a due to the logic of the media, which conveys the results of institutionalized summit meetings to the public. According to this, new initiatives are the best way to make a summit meeting appear successful. Consequently, officials from both sides sometimes lose track of the multitude of rhetorical actions[57] and question the substance of new initiatives primarily designed to catch media attention.

Hence, the St Petersburg EU–Russia summit on 31 May 2003 called for a simplification of these patterns of interaction. The governments decided to replace the annual Cooperation Council by a Permanent Partnership Council (PPC). As the PPC is to meet more frequently and in different formats, this step provided for greater flexibility and strengthened the forum at the ministerial level. The PPC 'should act as a clearing house for all issues of our cooperation.'[58] Undoubtedly, the discussion of all questions related to the PCA in one forum is an enormous step forward. However, the division remains between foreign economic policy and the political dialogue.[59] The different ways of handling EC and EU issues on the European side thus prevents a coherent foreign policy dialogue.

Due to different views on its format, the first meeting of the PPC took place only one year after it was envisioned. While Russia preferred a 25 + 1 format, the EU considered the troika + 1 format to be the best solution. Eventually the latter was accepted and the PPC convened in the troika + 1 format in May 2004. The importance of this formal question derives from the fact that a 25 + 1 format would have provided Russia with direct access to all EU member states simultaneously, thus allowing Russia to play off certain member states against others. By contrast, the current format requires that member states coordinate their views and find a common position in advance, which is then represented by the troika. In addition to increased practicality, this process provides for a greater coherence in the EU's policy toward Russia. This discussion can be viewed as analogous to the creation of the NATO–Russia Council, which was established on 28 May 2003 and is conducted in the 19 + 1 format. Nevertheless, NATO member states still discuss central issues without Russia, as this format is reduced to less relevant political questions. Given the new quality in NATO–Russia relations, it seems to be only a matter of time before Russia's ties to the ESDP will be strengthened by institutional measures. France has already proposed an EU–Russia Security Council.[60]

The Council of Ministers takes the lead in political dialogue between the EU and Russia, with the presidency responsible for preparing and conducting numerous meetings. Support for the presidency comes from the High Representative for CFSP, the Secretary General and the European Commission. The High Representative seems to play an executing role and not primarily a leading one. Since numerous member states have strong interests regarding Russia, the High Representative is granted less room for manoeuvre than in other cases; for example, on the Balkans. Questions pertaining to Russia's participation in CFSP actions dominate the agenda of the political dialogue. Here, common interests exist particularly in those fields not concerning direct bilateral questions between the EU and Russia. Advanced cooperation can be witnessed in the field of disarmament strategies, policies toward the Near East and Afghanistan, questions of a nuclear North Korea and in the global fight against terrorism. In particular in the Israeli–Palestinian conflict, the EU has proven to be an equal partner for Russia, the United States and the United Nations within the Middle East quartet. Moreover, the EU's policy in the Balkans was in considerable measure backed by Russia, even though support was more symbolic than material. By contrast, questions pertaining to Chechnya, Eastern Enlargement of the EU and its new neighbourhood policy give rise to controversies.

Oscillating between inclusion and exclusion, the EU appears in its policy towards Russia as an actor granting partial participation rights. This kind of inclusion and 'circumclusion' might contribute to defusing potential conflicts. The density of consultations between the EU and Russia is a first indicator for a process of inclusion through intensified dialogue. Moreover, the concept of the 'four common spaces' provides additional forms of inclusion. However, the EU's insistence on the strict Schengen-regime constitutes a clear tendency of exclusion. The trade-off between the EU's efforts to prevent new dividing lines across Europe as a result of its Eastern Enlargement and the EU's own security needs not only remains relevant, but is likely to shape the future of EU–Russia relations.

Associating with Russia: policies in comparison

With the first round of Eastern Enlargement, the EU Common Strategy on Russia (CS) came to a close. It was perfunctorily prolonged in hope of new CFSP policy instruments promised by the EU constitutional treaty, which was put on ice after the failed referenda in France and the Netherlands. Now it is likely to be replaced by a new policy instrument resembling those Action Plans, drawn up during 2004 for the EU's other neighbourhood countries, except Russia, who refuses to be treated like any other neighbour but nevertheless participates in the financial instruments of the ENP. What should be next for Russia? How has the CS instrument fared in comparison with the PCA – up for renewal, renegotiation or replacement in 2007 – and the Northern Dimension? Which structures of engagement with Russia should be further developed, which abandoned?

Policy methods and instruments – a mixed bag and a mixed blessing

Three main EU policy initiatives have structured the EU's relationship with Russia. In their broad policy aims they overlap for the most part, but in their set-up and means they differ considerably. One rough categorization according to the number of actors involved reflects already the whole gamut of possibilities in international relations: a unilateral CS, a bilateral PCA and a multilateral Northern Dimension. Thus far, the CS had mainly fulfilled an internal coordinating function aiming to bridge the EU's dual external policy structure: it thus performs an inward looking exercise which has little relevance for actual policies. The contractual nature of the PCA constitutes the formal venue for direct engagement between the two sides and has seen a significant expansion of its agenda in recent years, including soft security issues and the new security dialogue (see above). It remains the centrepiece of the Union's policy towards Russia and provides a clear road map for greater economic and political association. Closely related to this is the Union's assistance programme for Russia (TACIS), which since the mid-1990s concentrates on providing the legal and technical infrastructure to make Russia a trading partner across the board and not just for energy. A more informal multilateralism involving some member states, the Commission and all countries of the Baltic Sea area has developed within the Northern Dimension, which has slowly turned into a platform for various soft security policies and a frame of reference for some international financial institutions' activities in the region. This originally empty shell has incrementally built up content and serves as a basis for 'low politics' and concrete public/private/civil society part-nerships in cross-border cooperation within the region.[61] Adding Belarus to the list of Northern Dimension countries, as has recently been suggested by Sweden (very much like Kaliningrad), was taken up as a central issue at a later stage. This could provide grounds for contacts about 'technical' issues on the level below the political leadership, who would thus not receive any further legitimacy. This kind of flexibility is the greatest asset of the whole Northern Dimension approach and might be successfully applied to draw the north-western regions of Russia closer to the Union and its soft security standards.

Though Russia is arguably the most important partner for the EU in Europe, it is not equally important to all member states. Among the larger ones, Germany has the strongest economic and political interests. Advocating these special interests in a strong fashion would certainly raise fears about an 'unholy' alliance. Whereas other member states can and do articulate their views on delicate issues such as Kaliningrad, Germany prefers to keep a low profile so as not to wake sleeping dogs. Also, one has to ask how the results of these interest vectors, which each member state represents, have changed in force and direction with Eastern Enlargement and who will advocate or distract Russian causes thereafter. Attitudes in foreign affairs are not always based on a sobre cal-culus of costs and benefits, not even for some self-professed policy elites. Historical experiences feed the emotional dispositions of the former Soviet satellite states that now have a say in the Union's policy towards

Russia. One case in point could be a deterioration of the situation for the Russian-speaking minority in Latvia and Estonia. The positions of the new member states towards Russia will have to be reassessed as a track record becomes discernable.

The question of potential Russian EU membership should also be addressed, if only in order to be prepared for a surprise move in Russian policy, even though there seems no remote intention of joining. However, the issue calls for at least some internal theoretical thinking if strategic thinking is to be taken seriously. The three most common arguments rejecting such a possibility are that most of the Russian territory lies in Asia, its size would totally unbalance the EU, and its population would give it a dominant position in the European institutions (Parliament and Council).[62] Interestingly, all these arguments apply to another country which is already a candidate; namely, Turkey. After accession negotiations with Turkey were opened in October 2006, who could prevent Russia from applying, and with which arguments once economic and democratic transformation has reached a satisfactory level and the security and defence issues are settled?[63] The only true *realpolitik* reason seems that it would upset the delicate power balance among current EU member states. But then, those states have always claimed that the EU is not about the old balance of power conceptions. If taken seriously, some present member states might fall victim to their own rhetoric.[64] In any event, if the EU should decide to keep Russia out, then Russia must be handled within an overall framework of a comprehensive neighbourhood policy, so as to avoid haggling in the Council about whose particular neighbourhood is more important and who should receive greater attention and benefits.[65] However, as the Russian government itself keeps emphasizing, Russia is too important and distinct a partner for it to be lumped together with countries such as Belarus, Ukraine or Moldova. Thus, a special relationship must be institutionalized to cover this special part of the EU's ever closer Eastern neighbourhood.

A Northern Dimension for the East?

Russia is both an object of and an actor in the EU's evolving neighbourhood policies. The only way to bridge this object/subject divide is through cooperation on both high and low political levels. Whereas the Northern Dimension serves as a prime example of low politics engagement alongside TACIS, the regular summits and troika visits represent a high politics top-down approach of agreeing on what should be on the common agenda and what constitutes common threats. At the same time, the EU and Russia are somewhat competitive actors in their over-lapping neighbourhood. It is through strategies laid down by the Northern Dimension that the two powers could become cooperative actors rather than competitive ones. This multilateral and multi-level approach deviates significantly from the ENP, which is essentially bilat-eral. The merged collective actor on the EU side with its considerable dif-fuseness could contribute to softening the unitary Russian actor by making it mirror certain EU organizational structures and policy aims. Thus, it is already a case for fruitful analysis of Europeanization on mul-tiple levels such as its internal conditions and its external effects. How the 25-member EU actors, as with the Commission, can be merged into one, and how the opposite side – in this case Russia – responds by taking over organizational patterns as well as the *acquis* in its four common spaces, is the prime question in their future relationship.

Conclusion

The choice between interregional and bilateral relations with East European countries was an important one in the early 1990s. Offering EU membership to a large number of these countries, the bilateral approach eventually dominated the accession process and structured the EU's relations with these states. Should the post-socialist space – or what is left of it outside the EU – form its own regional grouping with which the EU could then interact meaningfully? It is certainly appealing to think that the CIS could provide enough cohesion and develop suffi-cient governmental clout to stabilize and foster peaceful cooperation in the post-soviet space. However, the EU has not been ready – by chance or choice – to actively support such a development, which would have inevitably also cemented Russian hegemony in that region. Instead, the EU preferred dealing with these countries on a one by one basis. This pref-erence is also visibly carried over into its new neighbourhood policy. The EU will be unilaterally granting partial and passive participation rights in its common market and financial programmes to ENP coun-tries. Avoiding this 'passivity trap', with voice- and choice-less neigh-bours will be the major challenge for the EU, at least when dealing with its largest neighbour – Russia. The Northern Dimension has provided sufficiently positive experiences in giving non-EU countries a say in some EU policies without prejudice to the *acquis communautaire* through a process of open multilateral policy coordination. It thus falls in between interregional and bilateral cooperation approaches. Expanding its mode of governance might be a third choice worth making.

Notes

1 M. Jachtenfuchs (ed.), *Europäische Integration* (Opladen: Leske & Budrich 2003).
2 C. Dupont and H. Engelen, 'Elusive Interregionalism: The EU and Eastern Europe', in V. Aggarwal and E. Fogarty (eds), *EU Trade Strategies* (New York: Palgrave Macmillan 2004): 169.
3 *Ibid.*: 170.
4 For political reasons, the PCAs with Belarus and Turkmenistan are not in force.
5 C. Dupont and H. Engelen, *op. cit.*: 171.
6 EU Council, 'Strategy Paper 2002–2006 and Indicative Programme 2002–2004 for Central Asia', October 2002 (accessed at http://europa. eu.int/comm/external_relations/ceeca/rsp2/02_06_en.pdf on 10 February 2006).
7 Such a strong redistributive component can be found in the German system of transfer payments from poor to rich states of the federation, aiming at equal standards of living in all parts.
8 For detailed Russian export statistics, see H. Smith 'Russia and the European Union', in H. Smith (ed.), *Russia and its Foreign Policy* (Saarijärvi: Aleksanteri Institute 2005): 152. Russia would, of course, export more (semi-) finished goods if the EU had lower tariffs or non-tariff restrictions. Thus, Russia fought hard to have the quota for steel imports raised as part of a compensation package for the trade diverting impact of the EU's Eastern enlargement on Russia. However, even if most favoured nation status (according to the WTO) were granted to Russia for all its products, it would not change the predominance of energy in its export structure. To quote Russia's long serving ambassador to the EU, Vladimir Shemiatenkov:

> The data demonstrate that the backbone of the new Russian business class is the exporters of energy and raw materials who, by definition, are indifferent to the [WTO] accession issue. The exporters of steel, non-ferrous metals and chemicals are in favour of the accession because they count on easing the pressure of anti-dumping procedures. As for the exporters of machinery and equipment, who are supposed to be the 'bridegroom' at the WTO 'wedding', these are manifestly inconspicuous. In other words, Mr. Putin is negotiating the WTO membership on behalf of a non-existent section of the Russian business class, which is expected to emerge in the future. (V. Shemiatenkov, 'EU–Russia: The Sociology of Approximation', (Brussels: Aleksanteri Institute 2003) accessed at http://www.ecsanet.org/ecsaworld6/ contributions/session2/Shemiatenkov.doc on 10 February 2006).

9 Interviews with Coest delegates (EU Council working group on Eastern Europe and Central Asia) and Russian officials in June/August 2005.
10 Whether this is possible not only depends on the material substance, strength and direction of these interests, it is also contingent upon the internal forms of interest generation and aggregation – whether autocratic/ etatist, neocorporatist/consociational or pluralistic/competitive – within the EU and Russia and how they are expressed in their respective systems of foreign policy governance. Analogous to the democratic peace hypothesis, it could be argued that only states – or political entities with their own foreign policy capacity such as the EU – that have similar patterns of vertically

interlocking society-state/government relationships can fully cooperate in compatible ways.

11 For the concepts of societal, soft and human security, see H. Moroff, 'Introduction and Theoretical Considerations', in H. Moroff (ed.), *European Soft Security Policies – The Northern Dimension*, (Helsinki/Berlin: Ulkopolitiinen Institute, 2002): 24.

12 R.O. Keohane and J.S. Nye, *Power and Interdependence* (Boston: Little, Brown, 1977).

13 B. Buzan *et al.*, *Security: A Framework for Analysis* (Boulder/London: Lynne Rienner, 1998).

14 H. Moroff, *op. cit.*: 12–36.

15 Council of the EU, 'A Secure Europe in a Better World – European Security Strategy', Brussels, 12 December 2003 accessed at http://ue.eu.int/uedocs/cmsUpload/78367.pdf on 10 February 2006.

16 J.P. Olsen, 'The many faces of Europeanization', in *Journal of Common Market Studies* 40/5 (2002): 921–51.

17 P. Pierson, 'The Path to European Integration. A Historical Institutionalist Analysis', in: *Comparative Political Studies*, 29/2 (1996): 123–63.

18 H. Moroff, *op. cit.*: 201–27.

19 M. Filtenborg *et al.*, 'An Alternative Theoretical Approach to EU Foreign Policy. "Network Governance" and the Case of the Northern Dimension Initiative', in: *Cooperation and Conflict*, 37/4 (2002): 387–407.

20 B. White, 'The European Challenge to Foreign Policy Analysis', in *European Journal of International Relations*, 5/1 (1999): 37–66.

21 I. Manners *et al.* (eds), *The Foreign Policies of European Union Member States* (Manchester: Manchester University Press, 2000).

22 T. Christiansen *et al.*, 'Fuzzy Politics Around Fuzzy Borders: The European Union's "Near Abroad"', in: *Cooperation and Conflict*, 35/4 (2000) 389–415.

23 H. Moroff, *op. cit.* 150–227.

24 H. Smith, *European Foreign Policy: What It Is and What It Does* (London: Pluto Press, 2002).

25 C. Bretherton *et al. The European Union as a Global Actor* (London: Routledge, 1999).

26 T. Risse *et al.*, ' "Something Rotten and the Social Construction of Social Constructivism: Comment on Comments"', in *Journal of European Public Policy*, 6/5 (2001): 775–82.

27 European Commission, Forward Studies Unit, 'Scenarios Europe 2010 – Five Possible Futures for Europe, Working Paper (Brussels 1998): 45–52. Also published as *European Futures: Five Possible Scenarios for 2010*, Gilles Bertrand *et al.* (Cheltenham: Elgar, 2000).

28 *Ibid.*: 46.

29 A. Malcom, 'Frontiers of the European Union', in *Advancing the Union: Report by the Independent Commission for the Reform of the Institutions and Procedures of the Union* (London: ICRI, 2000): xiii.

30 M. Vahl, 'Just Good Friends? The EU–Russian "Strategic Partnership" and the Northern Dimension', CEPS Working Paper 166, (Brussels, 2001): 7–8, accessed at http://shop.ceps.be/downfree.php?item_id=76 on 28 November 2006.

31 A case in point is provided by the Uruguay Round negotiations between the EU and the USA, where it was virtually impossible to ask the EU to open up

again a number of positions that had been agreed on by all member states for the Commission's negotiating mandate.

32 Interviews with Commission officials and Policy Unit officials in Brussels, March 2003.

33 European Commission, 'Communication from the Commission on Conflict Prevention', COM(2001) 211 (Brussels, 2001): 4–6, accessed at http://ec.europa.eu/comm/external_releations/cfsp/news/com2001_2001_211_en.pdf on 28 November 2006.

34 H. Moroff, 'The EU's Northern Soft Security Policy: Emergence and Effectiveness', in H. Moroff (ed.), *European Soft Security Policies – The Northern Dimension*, Helsinki/Berlin: Ulkopolitiinen Institute 2002): 150–227.

35 See M. Emerson, *The Elephant and the Bear* (Brussels: CEPS 2001).

36 For the concept of 'otherness' in EU-Russia relations, see I.B. Neumann, *Russia and the Idea of Europe: A Study in Identity and International Relations*, (London: Routledge, 1996).

37 See Institut für Europäische Poltiik (ed.), *Enlargement/Agenda 2000-Watch*, 6 (2003) accessed at: http://www.iep-berlin.de/publik/enlargement-watch/ on 10 Feb. 2006.

38 L. Fairlie et al., *Are Borders Barriers? EU Enlargement and the Russian Region of Kaliningrad* (Berlin/Helsinki: Finnish Institute of International Affairs and Institut für Europäische Politik, 2001).

39 H. Moroff, 'Die Politik der EU gegenüber Russland: Kohärenz in der Vielfalt', in M. Jopp *et al.* (ed.), *Europäische Außen- und Sicherheitspolitik – intergouverne-mentaler Club oder kollektiver Akteur?* (forthcoming).

40 Interview with Head of European Department in Russian MFA, V. Sergenin, Potsdam, March 2004.

41 See H. Moroff, *op. cit.*

42 Interview with Mrs. Koleschka, European Correspondent in the Polish MFA, Warsaw, December 2003.

43 A prime example of such association is the European Economic Area – though it is not the EU keeping countries like Norway out, rather the EEA countries choose not to fully join the EU.

44 V. Shemiatenkov, *EU–Russia: The Sociology of Approximation* (Brussels 2003) accessed at http://www.ecsanet.org/ecsaworld6/contributions/session2/Shemiatenkov.doc on 10 February 2006.

45 H. Timmermann, 'Die Europäische Union und Russland – Dimensionen und Perspektiven der Partnerschaft', in *Integration* 19/4 (1996): 195–207.

46 W. Franzen, Haarland, H.P. and Niessen, H.J. *Transformationsbarometer Osteuropa 2001* (Frankfurt a.M: Campus-Verlag, 2001): 23–5.

47 I. Kempe, 'Die EU als Modernisierungspartner für Russland', in O. Hillenbrand, *Der schwerfällige Riese: Wie Russland den Wandel gestalten soll* (Gütersloh: Verlug Bertalsman SK-J King 2003): 279.

48 For an evaluation of the TACIS programme, see *ibid.* 291.

49 H. Haukkala, 'Two Reluctant Regionalizers? The European Union and Russia in Europe's North', UPI Working Paper 32 (Helsinki: Ulkopolitiinen Institute, 2001): 7.

50 H. Höhmann *et al. Auf dem Weg zu neuen gesamteuropäischen Strukturen? Die Europäische Gemeinschaft, Russland und die GUS* (Cologne: Bundesinstitut für Ostwissenschaften und Internationalen studien, 1992): 42.

51   Y. Borko, *Rußland und die Europäische Union: Perspektiven der Partnerschaft* (Cologne: Bundesinstitut für Ostwissenschaftliche und Internationale studien, 1996): 8–11.

52   Interestingly, this step set the precedence for a distinct policy towards Russia as it foreclosed on membership in the medium-term.

53   J. Gower, 'Russia and the European Union', in: M. Webber (ed.), *Russia and Europe: Conflict or Cooperation?* (Basingstoke: Macmillan 2000): 66–98.

54   H. Timmermann, *op. cit.*: 203.

55   Interview on 8 April 2004 in Potsdam.

56   Press Release 7933/03 of the EU Council on the 6th Cooperation Council of 15 April 2003 in Luxemburg, accessed at: http://ue.eu.int/Newsroom on 10 February 2006. See also H. Timmermann, 'Russlands Außen- und Sicherheitspolitik: Die europäische Richtung', in *Aus Politik und Zeitgeschichte*, 16–17 (2003): 22–30.

57   For the concept of rhetorical action, see F. Schimmelfennig, 'The Community Trap: Liberal Norms, Rhetorical Action, and the Eastern Enlargement of the European Union', in *International Organization*, 55/1 (2001): 47–80.

58   Joint Declaration 2003 of the EU–Russia summit in St. Petersburg 31 May 2003, accessed at http://europa.eu.int/comm/external_relations/russia/sum05_03/js.htm on 10 February 2006.

59   'The political dialogue structures should be streamlined. We agreed to launch a focused discussion in this respect.' *Ibid.*

60   According to H. Timmermann, *op. cit.*: 29, a bilateral French–Russian Security Council and a bilateral German–Russian task force for security issues has existed since 2002. Both bodies were concerned with issues like North Korea, the Near East and disarmament initiatives (interview with Gernot Erler, Foreign Office Coordinator for German–Russian civil society cooperation on 8 April 2004 in Potsdam). Whether these institutional projects thwart a strategic security partnership between the EU and Russia, or whether they support it indirectly, is difficult to assess. If discussions within these two bodies provide preparation and support for CFSP, they can be seen as bilateral supporting measures complementing a common EU policy.

61   See H. Moroff, 'The EU's Northern Soft Security Policy – Emergence and Effectiveness', in H. Moroff, *op. cit.*

62   See F. Riccardi, 'A Look Behind the News', *Bulletin Quotidien Europe* 8224, 3, 4 June (2002): 3.

63   On this front, much has been achieved already. See M. Webber, 'Third-Party Inclusion in European Security and Defence Policy: A Case Study on Russia', in *European Foreign Affairs Review*, 6 (2001): 407–26.

64   Very much like Schimmelfennig (*op. cit.*) demonstrated for the Eastern Enlargement project.

65   See European Commission, 'White Paper on Governance – Policies for an Enlarged Union, Group Report 6, (Brussels 2001): 22–6 accessed at: http://europa.eu.int/comm/governance/areas/group12/report_en.pdf on 10 February 2006.

6
EU–Russia Relations in EU Neighbourhood Policies

Marius Vahl

Introduction: patterns in the development of EU–Russia relations

The European Union (EU) and Russia are today closer than ever before, and the relationship plays an increasingly prominent role in both EU and Russian foreign policy. A 'deepening' and a 'widening' of EU–Russia relations has taken place over the last decade. An intensification of the political dialogue at all levels has resulted in negotiations on enhanced cooperation across an increasingly wide range of policy areas. This has resulted in a number of contractual agreements, which has institutionalized and enhanced the bilateral relationship.

But progress has been slower than had been anticipated in the early- to mid-1990s.[1] The process from political dialogue and the launch of new cooperative initiatives to the conclusion and implementation of bilateral agreements has been very drawn out. A recurring complaint from the EU is that Russia fails to implement agreements reached with the EU, most notably and persistently the Partnership and Cooperation Agreement (PCA) itself, but also concerning secondary bilateral agreements, multilateral treaties and other international commitments. Combined with the broadening scope of the relationship, this has resulted in an increasingly overcrowded agenda with a growing number of outstanding and/or unresolved issues.

Furthermore, significant progress has been achieved mainly on secondary issues. Grand initiatives to 'strengthen the strategic partnership' have failed to materialize and the stated long-term objectives, such as a free trade area, seem almost as distant today as they did a decade ago. Overall, there have only been modest changes to the basic regimes underpinning the relationship, such as the lowering of trade barriers in the mid-1990s. In other areas, however, the fundamentals have moved away from the stated long-term objectives. This has, notwithstanding the recent agreements on visa facilitation and readmission, been most notable concerning the movement of people.

Greater interdependence between the EU and Russia has been accompanied by growing friction and disagreement between the two sides, with the intrusion of high politics on issues that could have been resolved at the technical and senior officials level; for instance, the matter of transit between Kaliningrad and mainland Russia. Discord has frequently occurred in the 'new' policy areas of EU competence such as in Justice and Home Affairs (JHA) and foreign, security and defence policy (CFSP and ESDP), and most notably over EU enlargement to Central and Eastern Europe, as well as on the economic agenda which dominated the relationship for much of the 1990s. While enlargement was treated with benign neglect by Russia for much of the 1990s, Moscow became increasingly sceptical of its consequences for Russia as the accession of the new member states drew closer. Growing EU activism in Russia's 'Near Abroad' through the development of the European Neighbourhood Policy (ENP) targeting Russia's neighbours and partners in the Commonwealth of Independent States (CIS) has also been regarded with scepticism.

Divergences between the EU and Russia in terms of their fundamental political and economic systems are increasing as a result of the growing authoritarianism in Russia. As tensions between the EU and Russia have grown, Russia has become an increasingly contentious issue within the EU, both among the member states and between the EU institutions. Recent years have seen the emergence and ascendancy of actors within the EU that are more critical of developments in Russia, calling for a unified EU line with a greater emphasis on adherence to common values as a precondition for further cooperation.

This is often interpreted by Russian leaders and experts as a result of the accession of Central and Eastern European countries to the EU, which 'have integrated into Europe with all their inferiority complexes, Russophobic complexes first of all'.[2] While the new member states are certainly playing a role in shaping policy towards Russia, it should be noted, however, that the Commission and the Council secretariat were calling for a tougher line in early 2004. This has further considerable support among many 'old' member states such as the Nordic countries, Austria and to some extent Britain. Furthermore, the European Parliament has over the years been consistently in favour of a harder line vis-à-vis Russia, calling on the EU to give greater emphasis on 'values' as opposed to its material and commercial 'interests'. Even if its formal powers remain limited in foreign policy, its growing clout and assertiveness within the EU system could push the Council and the Commission towards a greater emphasis on 'common values' as a pre-condition for a strategic partnership with Russia. In spite of disagreements on specific issues, there is a broad consensus in the EU on the need to respect common European and universal values in order to develop a real strategic partnership.

This narrative of the development of bilateral relations is presumably familiar to most students of EU–Russia relations. The principal assump-tion in this chapter is the rather self-evident assertion that EU–Russia rela-tions do not take place in a vacuum, and that comparative perspectives are required to assess the past, present and future of EU–Russia relations. Indeed, this seems particularly important to understand this bilateral relationship in so far as the 'strategic partnership' between the EU and Russia is, implicitly or explicitly, envisaged as a privileged relationship.[3] Relations should presumably thus not just be 'close' (and moving closer) in terms of more or less objective criteria, but also comparatively, as in 'closer' than their relationships with other international actors.

The aim of this chapter is therefore to view the bilateral relationship between the EU and Russia in a comparative perspective. Two caveats are in order. First, in order for such a comparative analysis to be com-prehensive, it should ideally include both Russian and EU foreign policy. This chapter limits itself to the latter. Secondly, Russia is, in this context, in a unique position vis-à-vis the EU, as the only major global actor that is also a direct neighbour. While this chapter focuses on EU–Russia relations in the context of EU neighbourhood policy, this unique dual position of Russia in EU foreign policy should not be forgotten.

The EU and its neighbours: the priority of the CFSP

The European Economic Community (EEC) developed relations with non-member states from its establishment in the late 1950s. The process of establishing close institutionalized relationships moving from more traditional forms of international cooperation towards deeper integra-tion, is however mainly a post-Cold War phenomenon. Although this development has been global in scope, it has been particularly intense with countries in the Union's geographical proximity. Since the late 1980s, the EU deepened and widened its relations successively with the Western European countries of the European Free Trade Association (EFTA), the countries in Central and Eastern Europe, the former Soviet

Union, the Southern Mediterranean, and the Western Balkans, creating a complex set of contractual agreements across an ever broader range of policy areas, supported by large programmes of economic assistance.[4]

Within these broader frameworks, relations were primarily conducted on a bilateral basis, providing preferential trading arrangements and liberalization of the movement of persons, partial inclusion in major EU policies such as the free trade area, the customs union, the single market, and the Schengen regime, participation in the numerous EU programmes (on research, education, culture and such), and association with the growing number of EU agencies (environment, food safety, Europol and so on). While closer relations with the EU initially entailed primarily economic cooperation, the growth of EU competences in other fields has broadened the scope of the relationships through an increasingly extensive political dialogue and a multitude of agreements of cooperation and integration also in the fields of justice and home affairs, and foreign, security and defence policies.

Russia and the former Soviet Union were designated as one of main priorities for the Common Foreign and Security Policy by the Lisbon European Council in June 1992. Among these priorities – the others were Central and Eastern Europe, the Balkans, the Maghreb and the Middle East – the EU's overall relations have arguably been the least developed with respect to Russia and its partners in the CIS.

The principal priority has, of course, been the enlargement process to North, Central and Eastern Europe and now South Eastern Europe. Since the break-up of the Soviet Union, 13 new members have joined the EU: three EFTA countries acceded in 1995 and eight Central and Eastern European countries and two Mediterranean countries joined in 2004. An additional eight countries, two of which are expected to enter in 2007, are currently acknowledged by the EU as potential members. As part of the pre-accession process, the candidates were gradually integrated with the EU economy following their adoption of EU rules and standards, the (in)famous *acquis communautaire*, participated in EU programmes and agencies as associates or observers, and engaged in an extensive multilateral and bilateral political dialogue. The movement of persons was facilitated through the lifting of visa requirements, and they were represented alongside the EU member states in the Convention on the future of Europe in 2001–03 leading to the draft Treaty on a Constitution for Europe.

Relations have, in many respects, developed further also with the countries of the Maghreb and the Middle East, the two Southern Mediterranean priorities of the CFSP in 1992. This has, since 1995, taken place through the Euro-Mediterranean Partnership, also known as the Barcelona process, which is now to be further enhanced and subsumed within the framework of the ENP. As part of this process, the EU has entered into preferential trading relationships and more comprehensive association agreements with its Southern Mediterranean partners than with Russia.[5]

These developments are, to a considerable extent, a consequence of the fact that Russia and the other CIS countries remain, more than a decade after the dissolution of the Soviet Union, only partially integrated into the wider European and global economic and political system of international organizations, treaties, conventions and regimes. This is a prerequisite for most, if not all of the officially stated long-term objectives for EU–Russia relations. Russia and most of the countries of the CIS are, for instance, among a dwindling number of EU neighbouring countries that are not members of the WTO, which is a prerequisite for preferential trade agreements with the EU. Only four countries in the current EU neighbourhood were among the founding members of the WTO in January 1995. By 2005, the number had risen to 18.[6]

The EU regime for entry of non-EU citizens to the EU is in general more restrictive vis-à-vis its neighbours than its trade policy, and citizens of most neighbouring countries require visas to enter the EU. The EU currently has visa waiver arrangements with 12 neighbours.[7] The citizens of the other 12 European countries that are not EU member states, including Russia and the European states of the CIS, as well as nine of the 10 Southern Mediterranean partners, require visas to enter the EU.

The EU's priorities are also reflected in the relative amounts of economic assistance provided to neighbouring countries. In the 1995–2002 period, EU aid commitments to the countries of the Balkans were on average 246 euros per capita, to the Mediterranean partners 23 euro on average. Russia was allocated 7 euro per capita, slightly below the CIS average of 8 euro per capita. In the EU's financial perspective for 2000–06, the enlargement candidates (from 2004 full EU members) receive almost 1200 euro per capita on average, Western Balkan countries in excess of 200 euro per capita, the Mediterranean partners 31 euro per capita. Russia and the other New Independent States were allocated only 13 euro per capita.

A notable exception to the relative underprivileged state of relations with Russia compared with other EU neighbours is the political dialogue. Russia is the only country with which the EU has regular biannual summits, in addition to the more typical annual foreign ministers meetings and *ad hoc* ministerial meetings. Twice in recent years, at the European Council in Stockholm in March 2001, and in connection with the St Petersburg tercentenary in May 2003, the EU has been represented by all its Heads of State and Government at EU–Russia summits, an honour seldom accorded to other than the US president. The recently upgraded institutional framework of EU–Russia relations – the Permanent Partnership Council – is the first of its kind in EU external relations. While it retains EU representation by the troika, as in the previous PCA Cooperation Council and which is typical of other EU third country agreements, it is the only cooperation council with third countries that can – as the EU's own Council of Ministers – meet in different formations.

The EU and the CIS: the 'Russia first' strategy

While the EU's relations with Russia and its CIS partners are less developed than with the EU's other neighbours, relations with Russia have arguably developed faster and become more substantial than EU relations with the other former Soviet republics. This 'Russia first' strategy has been criticized by some analysts and CIS diplomats as being based more on old-fashioned *realpolitik* than a sobre assessment of the relative progress of the transition process in Russia and other CIS states and their respective aspirations vis-à-vis the EU. Relations with CIS countries other than Russia are thus seen as a function of policy towards Russia, rather than being developed on their own merit.

Differentiation between the countries of the CIS was initiated in the early 1990s, evident initially in the scope and timing of the bilateral PCAs negotiated with all the former Soviet Republics. The PCAs with Russia, Ukraine and Moldova were in particular more extensive than the PCAs with the countries of the South Caucasus and Central Asia.[8] The PCA with Russia in December 1997 was also the first PCA to enter into force, followed by similar agreements with Ukraine and Moldova in 1998.

The process of differentiation in EU policy towards the CIS members continued in the second half of the 1990s, with relations with Russia developing faster and more extensively than with countries, such as Ukraine and Moldova. Russia was the subject of the first Common Strategy in June 1999, followed by Ukraine later in 1999. No Common Strategies were developed for the other CIS countries. A series of policy 'dialogues' were initiated from 2000 onwards with Russia, on energy, foreign, security and defence policy and most recently transport, and have led to the conclusion of a number of bilateral agreements and common projects. As part of the Northern Dimension initiative, in 2001

Russia became the first CIS country in which the European Investment Bank (EIB) was allowed to operate. In 2002, Russia was accorded so-called market economy status, which as of 2005 has not yet been accorded to Ukraine. Russia was among the first countries in the world with an agreement with Europol, with which no other CIS countries currently have contractual arrangements for cooperation. In November 2003, Russia became the first country of the CIS to join the Bologna process on higher education.[9] In Autumn 2005, Russia became the first CIS country with which the EU had concluded agreements on visa facilitation and readmission after several years of negotiations, following the successful conclusion of bilateral visa facilitation agreements with certain EU member states.[10] The Commission received its mandate to negotiate a similar visa facilitation agreement with Ukraine in late 2005. The institutionalized political dialogue is also more extensive with Russia, notably at the highest level. Biannual summits take place between the EU and Russia, yearly summits with Ukraine, while the other CIS states do not meet with the EU at the highest political level. The one-of-a-kind Permanent Partnership Council (PPC), which replaced the foreign minister level Cooperation Council in 2004, has already been mentioned.

There are some exceptions to this 'Russia first' strategy. In the field of justice and home affairs, for instance, arguably relations have been developed further in certain areas with Ukraine than with Russia. Ukraine has an extensive Action Plan on cooperation in the field of justice and home affairs with the EU, while the parallel agreement with Russia is limited to combating organized crime. Furthermore, Russia does not participate in EU initiatives in energy and transport such as the INOGATE and TRACECA programmes created in the early- to mid-1990s, both of which include most other CIS states. This was however due to Russia's unwillingness to join, and does not detract substantially from the overall assessment that whereas relations with Russia and the CIS are the least developed relations in EU neighbourhood policy, Russia has so far been the privileged partner of the EU in the former Soviet Union.

The decoupling of Russia: the ENP and the four 'common spaces'

EU policy towards the 'post-Soviet space' has undergone an overhaul in recent years through the creation of the ENP (see also Moroff on EU *Ostpolitik*, pp. 100–2). First known as the 'New Neighbours' initiative in early 2002, it was primarily focused on Ukraine, Moldova and Belarus. Its geographic scope was broadened in late 2002 to include Russia and the Southern Mediterranean and renamed the 'Wider Europe' initiative. The first detailed proposals were released in March 2003 followed by consultations on future bilateral Action Plans – the principal instrument of the ENP – from late 2003, a second report from the European Commission in early 2004 and the conclusion of negotiations on the first Action Plans in late 2004.

Early on, Russia was sceptical of the ENP, preferring instead to develop bilaterally the four common spaces.[11] According to Special Representative of Russia to the EU Sergei Yastrzhembsky, the ENP was inappropriate for EU–Russia relations since 'no other EU neighbour had relations as intense as Russia'.[12]

This decoupling of EU policy towards Russia from its policy towards the Western members of the CIS has been accompanied by a growing EU engagement with the CIS members now covered by the ENP. Over the last few years, the EU has launched a series of initiatives in Moldova, particularly related to the frozen conflict in Transnistria. Although less conspicuously than in Moldova, EU engagement with the ENP partners in the South Caucasus has also increased in recent times, most significantly through the inclusion of the three countries of the region in the ENP in June 2004. Most recently, the EU looks set to get further engaged also in Belarus, providing support for independent radio broadcasting from autumn 2005.

The end of the 'Russia first' strategy?: action plans and road maps

EU neighbourhood policy currently consists of three main strategies: the enlargement process, the European Neighbourhood Policy and the four 'common spaces' with Russia (see Moroff on the structure of the EU–Russian dialogue, pp. 108–13). The EU's principal priority in its neighbourhood policy remains enlargement, even after the accession of ten new members in May 2004 and two in January 2007. There are now six acknowledged candidates for EU membership at different stages in the process. As in previous EU enlargements, the pre-accession phase will include the gradual integration of the candidates with the EU as these countries adopt EU rules and policies.

The second EU neighbourhood strategy – the ENP – is also likely to receive considerable attention and resources in the coming years. The process is already well underway. The first seven bilateral Action Plans were adopted in the first half of 2005, while preparations for Action Plans with a further five ENP partners, including the three countries of

South Caucasus was initiated in the second half of 2005. Five of the first seven Action Plans are with Southern Mediterranean partners.[13] More importantly for Russia, the ENP is also progressing with the Eastern CIS neighbours. The first ENP Action Plans to be adopted in February 2005 were those with Ukraine and Moldova. In early 2005, the EU showed its readiness to continue to accelerate EU engagement with these countries, through a 10-point plan of 'additional measures to further develop and enrich' the Action Plan with Ukraine following the Orange Revolution, and the decision to appoint an EU Special Representative to Moldova as well as to establish a Commission delegation in Moldova.

The ENP Action Plans are similar in structure, and in many cases also substance, to the Road Maps for the four common spaces. There are however, important differences. A first is the relative absence of political conditionality in the Road Maps. The ENP Action Plans contain long detailed lists of political criteria on issues such as democracy, rule of law and human rights, to be fulfilled in order to move 'from cooperation to integration' and further deepen bilateral relations. Apart from the brief preamble in the Road Map on the Common Space of Freedom, Security and Justice there are only scattered references to 'common values' in the other Road Maps. In contrast to the ENP Action Plans, where there are numerous references to upcoming elections in Moldova and Ukraine, upcoming parliamentary and presidential elections in Russia in late 2007 and early 2008 are not mentioned in the Road Maps.

The Action Plans and the Road Maps also differ on economic issues. First, the PCAs with all of these three states call for eventual free trade. This goal is reiterated in the Action Plans, but is not mentioned at all in the Road Maps. Implementation of PCA provisions features prominently in the economic sections in the Action Plans with Moldova and Ukraine. There are only two references to the PCA in the entire 18-page Road Map for the Common Economic Space.[14] Legislative approximation and regulatory convergence are also prominent in both the Action Plans and the Road Maps. But whereas it is explicitly stated in the Action Plans that this entails convergence towards EU rules and standards and/or international standards, the Road Maps are not clear on this. While there are a few references to international standards and agreements, EU rules and standards – the *acquis communautaire* – are not mentioned at all. Thus is the notion of a partnership 'on the basis of equality' maintained, as repeatedly called for by Russian officials and experts.

The question of the fate of the three PCAs upon their expiry in 2007–08 is addressed in the Action Plans with Ukraine and Moldova, reinforced in the former by the 'additional measures' adopted in

February 2005, which call for a new upgraded agreement to replace the PCA in 2008. The PCA between the EU and Russia is sparsely noted in the Road Maps, and the question of its expiry in December 2007 is not mentioned at all. While experts have called for the future of EU–Russian contractual relations to be addressed for some time, the issue was not raised at the highest level until the May 2005 summit.

To sum up, the Road Maps are less ambitious, less easily translated into concrete action, with fewer conditions attached to further cooperation, and do not address the key question of the future of the contractual framework of the bilateral relationship. In short, the Road Maps for the four common spaces are indeed a 'weaker and fuzzier' derivative of the ENP Action Plans.

The changes in EU priorities vis-à-vis the former Soviet Union implied by the differences between the Road Maps and the Action Plans – away from a 'Russia first' strategy towards equidistance in the short term followed by closer relations between the EU and Europeanizing states such as Ukraine, Moldova and Georgia in the medium term – have been apparent in the allocation of EU economic assistance for some time. Russia's share of TACIS funding has been gradually reduced during the Putin presidency, to a large extent due to increased aid to Ukraine and other Western NIS (see Figure 6.1).

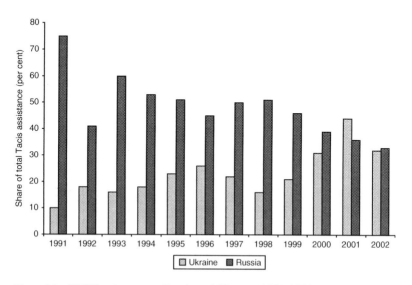

Figure 6.1   TACIS assistance to Russia and Ukraine, 1991–2002

It is also seen in the EU Council decision in February to allocate up to 50 per cent of the total loans made available from the European Investment Bank (EIB) to the CIS to Ukraine, as one of the 'additional measures' adopted together with the EU–Ukraine Action Plan in response to the Orange Revolution. Until now, Russia has been the only CIS country to which the EIB was allowed to provide loans.

This is a reflection of what appears to be a more fundamental change in EU policy towards the entire 'post-Soviet space'. EU policy is gradually shifting in line with domestic changes in the CIS, developing closer relations with those CIS countries that are Europeanizing through political and economic reform than with those moving in towards more authoritarian political and economic systems.

There is a notable correlation between the state of political and economic freedom and amounts of EU aid in per capita terms to the CIS. The most 'free' countries, such as Moldova, Ukraine, Armenia and Georgia, received significantly greater amounts than the authoritarian regimes in Central Asia and Belarus (see Figures 6.2 and 6.3, and Annex). The latter were indeed the only countries to receive less EU assistance than Russia.

This trend is likely to continue as the EU member states (eventually) agree on the next EU budget, the Financial Perspective for 2007–13.

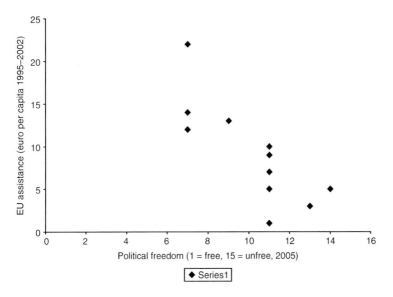

Figure 6.2 Political freedom and EU aid

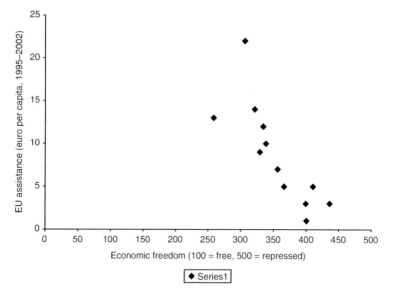

Figure 6.3 Economic freedom and EU assistance

The EU has promised significant increases in economic assistance under the ENP, and the Commission initially proposed that the assistance provided to the ENP partners be doubled over the term of the financial perspective. A fierce battle among the member states – between net contributors and net recipients, and between new and old member states – over the budget is underway. In the initial proposals from the Commission, the overall spending on external action would remain roughly stable over the period, a figure that was subsequently reduced significantly during the aborted negotiations among the member states in June 2005. Unless the EU is to considerably reduce its assistance to developing countries and to the enlargement process, both of which seem unlikely, this makes it highly probable that Russia will receive less assistance from the EU for the foreseeable future, surely in relative terms as a share of the total EU external action budget, but most likely also in absolute terms.[15]

Beyond the European Neighbourhood Policy?

The long-term objectives of the CIS countries vis-à-vis the EU have diverged over the course of the last decade. A number of CIS countries, such as Moldova, Ukraine and Georgia, now seek association with the EU on the road towards full membership, while Russia seeks neither association nor membership. This difference in strategic aims is increasingly correlated with the state of political reform, as these three countries become more democratic while Russia and other CIS states not seeking membership become more authoritarian. Many of the EU actors that favour a tougher line vis-à-vis Russia would also like to be more accommodating with CIS countries converging towards European norms and standards, in particular those seeking EU membership.

The Orange Revolution brought the question of Ukrainian membership in the EU to the top of the political agenda. While there is broad support in the EU behind the ENP generally, as well as greater EU engagement with Ukraine in response to the Orange Revolution specifically, there is considerable disagreement within the Union on whether or not to acknowledge Ukraine as a prospective member of the EU. The European Parliament did not receive support from either the Council or the Commission on its January 2005 Declaration on Ukraine calling on the EU to provide a membership perspective for Ukraine. Although a number of (mainly new) member states support this position, there is a clear majority among the member states against acknowledging Ukraine, or other CIS countries such as Moldova and Georgia, as potential candidates, in the foreseeable future.

Nonetheless, governments in countries such as Ukraine, Moldova and Georgia insist that EU membership remain their long-term objectives. If the current movement of Ukraine and other CIS members on the 'pre-pre-accession' road of the ENP is sustained, even if eventual membership remains highly uncertain and is in any case more than a decade away, Russia is faced with a situation where much of the political energy among key neighbouring states will be directed towards the EU. A by-product of this is likely to be that relations with Russia become less of a priority for the countries concerned.

It would also, eventually, clash with Russian plans to develop deeper economic integration in the CIS that involve countries seeking EU membership. The plan for a Single Economic Space (SES) between Russia, Ukraine, Belarus and Kazakhstan is currently a key issue. Agreed in principle by the four parties in September 2003, this envisages the creation of an economic union in stages, starting with a free trade area, then a customs union followed in the end by 'full' economic union, with common rules and standards and common economic policies. While the first stage of the SES – a free trade area – could be compatible with a pre-accession process, it would have to be abandoned upon accession to the EU, unless the EU has, by then, free trade agreements with Russia and the other countries of the CIS. The later stages envisaged – a customs union followed by an economic union – are simply incompatible with EU membership, unless of course all relevant CIS members join the EU. The latest development is indeed that Russia, Kazakhstan and Belarus plan to go ahead on the SES without Ukraine, which is unwilling to take part as it could endanger its prospects of eventual EU membership.

If Ukraine were eventually to join the EU, perhaps together with Moldova and also other CIS members, this could lead to a Union of 35 or more member states with a total population of 600 or even 650 million, almost five times greater than the population in Russia. There are currently more than 8 million ethnic Russians in Ukraine, and more than half a million in Moldova, including some 100,000 Russian citizens in Transnistria. Added to the more than half a million Russian speakers currently living in the EU, a large majority of whom reside in Estonia, Latvia and Lithuania, there would be around 10 million Russians residing in the EU. Less than half of the 20 official languages in the EU are spoken as a first language by as many people. While this would constitute less than 2 per cent of the total population of the EU, it would also be more than one third of all Russians living outside Russia, equal to 7 per cent of the population of Russia.[16]

Further EU enlargement to include 35 or more member states would increase the economic asymmetries between Russia and the EU. The 2004 EU enlargement increased the size of the EU economy by approximately 350 billion USD (or less than 5 per cent) to 8500 billion USD. While modest compared with the total EU economy, the addition to the EU economy was more than twice the size of the 145 billion USD Russian economy. Although most of the putative EU candidates in South Eastern and Eastern are much poorer than the current members of the EU, their accession would further increase the size and, more importantly, the potential of the EU economy.

The economic significance of such a long-term expansion of the EU for Russia is however more significant than this only slightly increased economic asymmetry implies, due to the considerable economic interdependence between Russia and the relevant CIS states. The 2004 EU enlargement increased the importance of the EU as a trading partner of Russia, with the EU's share of Russian total trade increased from 35–40 per cent to 50–55 per cent. Current EU candidates, notably Turkey, are becoming increasingly important trading partners of Russia. Were Ukraine and some other former Soviet states also to join the EU, the share of EU in Russia's overall trade would of course increase further.

Trade with the CIS constitutes approximately 15 per cent of Russia's overall trade, much of it with the CIS members seeking EU membership. Conversely, and given the significant role of trade with Russia for the putative EU members in the CIS, Russia would become a more important trading partner for the EU, although much less dramatically than in the case of EU as a trading partner of Russia. Any predictions on EU membership in 2020 or so are highly uncertain, but an EU of 35 or more member states could be responsible for two thirds, or even three quarters of Russia's overall trade.

Furthermore, Russian business is even more heavily involved in the Ukrainian economy than in the new EU member states in Central and Eastern Europe. As Ukraine adopts EU standards, Russian business in Ukraine will be forced to become 'EU compatible', creating a growing Russian constituency in favour of EU harmonization. This may have consequences in favour of Russia adopting EU rules and standards. Since Ukraine receives most of its energy from Russia, Ukrainian EU membership would also make the EU even more dependent on Russian energy supplies, although its eventual inclusion into the EU's internal energy market would enhance security of transit of Russian energy to European markets, 80–90 per cent of which currently passes through the territory of Ukraine.

In geopolitical terms, the Black Sea would become dominated by the EU to an extent comparable with the current situation in the Baltic Sea. Ukrainian EU membership would almost double the length of the EU–Russian border, from 2200 km to more than 3750 km. If the countries of the South Caucasus were also to join the EU some day, this would further expand the EU–Russian border by almost 1000 km. The Russian–Ukrainian border regime is currently very liberal, where Ukrainian and Russian travellers are not required to hold passports to cross the border. This would eventually have to change on the Ukrainian side to comply with the Schengen *acquis*, unless of course the EU and Russia have by then established a genuine 'common space of freedom, security and justice'.

It may seem fanciful to discuss this as a credible scenario, even in the long-term. The current difficulties of the reform process in many 'post-revolutionary' CIS countries, the unwillingness of the EU to acknowledge Ukraine and other EU membership aspirants as potential candidates for accession, and, perhaps most importantly, the current crisis in the EU following the 'no' vote on the Constitutional Treaty in France and the Netherlands in May and June 2005, all can be said to weaken this scenario. The votes against the Constitutional Treaty were interpreted by many experts and political leaders as a vote against EU enlargements, be it to Central and Eastern Europe, Turkey or in general. Furthermore, changes to the French constitution adopted in March 2005 entail that any future enlargements after the accession of Romania, Bulgaria and Croatia will be determined by a referendum in France. Other EU member states have indicated that they too will have to approve future EU accessions by referendum.

Past experience indicates, however, that countries that are sufficiently determined in their European aspirations eventually join the Union. The ENP is not the first attempt by the EU to develop alternatives to EU membership for neighbouring countries. The original rationale behind the European Economic Area – incidentally known initially as the 'common European economic space' – was to pre-empt membership applications from the EFTA countries. In the early 1990s, the EU flirted with ideas to create a European Confederation or a 'European Political Area' as an alternative to full membership for the newly liberated countries of Central and Eastern Europe. A number of European leaders have called for the creation of a 'privileged partnership' with Turkey as an alternative to full membership. All of these efforts have, with minor exceptions in the case of some EFTA countries, failed in the end, as the neighbours in question opted instead for full membership.

Conclusion: two strategies, one partnership

Returning to the bilateral EU–Russian relationship, a key issue is the apparent inability of the two parties to develop the substantive and privileged strategic partnership both sides repeatedly claim as a common goal. The large number of major policy initiatives in EU–Russia relations testifies to an ambition to be pro-active. But important developments in the bilateral relations, positive or negative, have largely been an unintended consequence of events and developments elsewhere. The liberalization of the EU–Russia trading regime was, for instance, a result of the completion of the Uruguay Round, a process in which Russia played no role, rather than a result of a specific rapprochement between the EU and Russia in the context of the plans to develop free trade bilaterally. Likewise, the reintroduction of a visa regime between Russia and its neighbours in Central and Eastern Europe resulted specifically from the accession of the latter to the EU, and more generally as enlargement took precedence over EU relations with Russia among the EU's foreign policy priorities, and not from any conscious decision to tighten the regime for the movement for persons with Russia *per se*.

It has become commonplace to attribute this discrepancy between rhetoric and reality to a lack of 'common values' between the EU and Russia. Whereas Russia is seen as a de-democratizing state imbued by realist geopolitical zero-sum game perceptions of international relations, the EU is regarded as an incoherent 'post-modern' idealist soft power. But this does not explain the fact that the EU's relations with other neighbours – for instance, most of the Southern Mediterranean partners, with whom the 'values gap' is as wide or arguably even wider than it is vis-à-vis Russia – have been developed further in key areas such as trade and economic integration than has been the case with Russia. This can, however, be accounted for by Russia's limited integration into the international economy and participation in key international economic regimes such as the WTO, due to some extent to the relatively underdeveloped state of economic governance in Russia compared with other EU neighbours. The EU appears unable to develop relations on terms that are favourable to partners bilaterally, notably concerning economic integration, but also in the domains of justice and home affairs and foreign and security policy, where integration with and in the EU is premised on participation in, and adherence to, international organizations and regimes.

But it is also a matter of strategic choice. While the EU and Russia both agree in principle on the need for a close and privileged strategic partnership, there appear to be fundamental differences between the two parties as to what such a strategic partnership would entail in policy operational terms.

Russia seems to envisage the strategic partnership in terms of traditional modes of international cooperation, akin to the great power relationships familiar from the so-called Westphalian states system. This would be a partnership of equals in which cooperation would primarily be limited to the traditional domains of foreign policy. There would thus be geostrategic alignment and considerable cooperation on global security issues. In extension of the sharp distinction made between domestic and foreign policy, the two sides would adhere to the principle of non-interference in each others domestic affairs.

Such a conception of the strategic partnership significantly curtails the prospects of a privileged partnership with an entity such as the EU. First, and in spite of the development of the CFSP and the ESDP, the EU as such has limited competences and discretionary power in the traditional areas of foreign and security policy. While a deepening trade relationship could certainly be envisaged once Russia eventually joins the WTO, it would hardly be privileged compared with the EU's other neighbours, most of which have moved or are moving beyond traditional free trade towards deep economic integration with the Union. This is however dependent on the neighbours adapting to EU rules and standards, which Russia appears to be unwilling to contemplate. Indeed, more generally domains traditionally considered domestic policy constitute an important element in EU foreign policy in general, and its neighbourhood policies in particular.

The divisions within the EU on its policy towards Russia have increased in recent years, and it is more difficult to speak of a common EU conception of the 'strategic partnership'. Indeed, there is considerable sympathy within the EU, most notably among the leaders of some of the larger member states, for the Russian conception of the 'strategic partnership.' But although there are different views on the extent to which domestic developments in Russia should affect the relationship, it should be emphasized that there is at the same time a broad consensus on the basic approach the EU should take in developing relations with third countries. Indeed, this was determined as early as 1987, when the Commission laid down the so-called Interlaken principles for the association of EFTA with the EC.

First, the EC would give priority to its own integration. Second, the autonomy of the EC's own decision making should not be threatened, and third, there should be a fair balance of rights and obligations. Although various models for the participation of representatives of non-member states in the decision-shaping process exist in the EU, for instance the EEA and Schengen, the EU draws a clear line in defending its decision-making autonomy.

In the specific context of EU–Russian relations, it is clear that the only conceivable outcome of the 'regulatory convergence', 'harmonization' and 'legislative convergence' at the heart of the planned Common Economic Space would be through an alignment of Russian domestic policies and laws to EU standards. Enhanced economic cooperation largely depends upon Russia's accession to the WTO. Further liberalization of trade would inevitably entail greater changes and concessions on the Russian side, as its tariffs remain overall more than ten times higher than those of the EU. The development of the bilateral relationship in other areas (such as justice and home affairs and foreign, security and defence policy) depends upon Russian adoption and implementation of a number of international treaties and conventions, as well as its fulfilment of international commitments already made (such as the 1999 OSCE commitment to withdraw Russian forces from Georgia and Moldova). While the political dialogue would be more extensive with Russia, given its seat in the UN Security Council, its nuclear weapons and, perhaps most importantly, its size and location being by geographic default an actor in a number of key regions in the world, the regimes governing the bilateral relationship will be essentially on the EU's terms. The further development of the bilateral relationship would be a fundamentally asymmetric process, with Russia converging on the higher standards of the EU. In some areas, this is due to the EU's broader commitments – for instance, in the WTO – which prevents it from developing the bilateral relationship with non-member Russia. In other cases – for instance, on the ESDP – the EU has simply decided to construct itself as being unable to cooperate on equal terms with its neighbours.

The strategic choice seems sharp: either an equal but underprivileged relationship in line with a 'Russian style' strategic partnership, or a privileged but asymmetrical relationship in accordance with a European conception of a strategic partnership. If the currently dominant paradigms hold sway in both the EU and Russia, the creation of an equal and privileged partnership seems, at this stage, like mission impossible. Determining the extent of overlap among these two diverging visions of the strategic partnership thus becomes a first challenge for the further development of EU–Russian relations. In the longer-term, an important issue becomes the malleability of these diverging conceptions; that is, the extent to which Russia could accept an asymmetric relationship, the extent to which the EU are willing to make a special case of Russia in terms of the existing methods of cooperation with neighbouring countries, and whether the EU or Russia or both could conceivably change their basic positions on the nature of the strategic partnership. This seems to be a basic requirement for the translation from the rhetoric of partnership to a real strategic partnership between the EU and Russia.

Indeed, the two sides had better start searching for a durable model for EU–Russia relations that could combine the two conceptions of a strategic partnership. This is likely to be necessary to avoid a situation that neither side currently want; namely, that Russia aspires to become a member of the EU. In the absence of a viable long-term model of a strategic partnership, and as long as the only countries treated by the EU as equals are the member states themselves, the logical change in Russian strategy vis-à-vis the EU would be to demand to be acknowledged as a candidate for full membership. But it is difficult, to say the least, to envisage Russia accepting to be a pupil of the EU for a generation, while the prospect of Russian membership could, in the current climate in the EU, become the famous straw that broke the camel's back. While this may be exaggerated, it augments those arguing in favour of the fundamental importance of the bilateral EU–Russian relationship, both for the future of the EU and of Russia.

Annex 6.A1   Political and economic freedom and EU aid to the CIS

	EU aid per capita 1995–2002 (€)	Political rights*	Civil liberties*	Economic freedom†
Partly free				
Moldova	22	3	4	3.06
Ukraine	14	4	3	3,21
Armenia	13	5	4	2,58
Georgia	12	3	4	3,34
Not free				
Azerbaijan	10	6	5	3,38
Kyrgyzstan	9	6	5	3,29
Russia	7	6	5	3,56
Kazakhstan	5	6	5	3,66
Turkmenistan	5	7	7	4,36
Belarus	3	7	6	3,99
Uzbekistan	3	7	6	4,10
Tadjikistan	1	6	5	4.00

*Political rights, and civil liberties: 1=Free, 7=Not free.
† Economic freedom: 1=Free, 7=Repressed.

Sources: Freedom House, Heritage Foundation/Wall Street Journal and European Commission, 2003.

Notes

1 It was, for instance, expected that Russia would accede to the WTO in 1998 or 1999 when the PCA was concluded in 1994, see Arts 3, 4 and 5(2) of the PCA. Also, actual negotiations on emerging issues were arguably started far later than necessary on important issues such as Kaliningrad (2002), nuclear safety (1998), and EU enlargement (2004).

2 According to Sergey Yastrzhembskiy, Special Representative of President Putin for relations with the EU Interview on RTR Russian TV, 3 December 2004, downloaded from http://www.gateway2russia.com/art.p hp?artid=258999& rubid=496&parent=Interview+and+Opinion& grandparent= on 20 July 2005.

3 See, for example, statement by Jacques Chirac at St Petersburg Summit, 31 May 2003, 'French president speaks for Russia–EU privileged partnership', retrieved from www.Pravda.ru; comment by former Commission President Jacques Santer in F. Bolkestein, *The Limits of Europe* (Brussels: Lannoo Press, 2004): 243; J. Gower, 'Russia and the European Union,' in Mark Webber (ed.), *Russia and Europe: Conflict or Cooperation?*, (London: Macmillan 2000) 66–98 (77); A. Pushkov, 'Putin at the helm', in Dov Lynch (ed.), *What Russia Sees*, Chaillot Paper 74 (Paris: European Union Institute for Security Studies, January 2005): 45–60 (49).

4 The European Economic Area with the EFTA states, Europe Agreements and PHARE with Central and Eastern Europe, PCA's and TACIS with the former Soviet Union, Euro-Mediterranean Association Agreements and MEDA with the Mediterranean neighbours and Stability and Association Agreements and CARDS with the Western Balkans.

5 As noted by the Commission, 'in contrast to contractual relations with all the EU's other neighbouring countries, the PCA's in force with Russia, Ukraine, and Moldova grant neither preferential treatment for trade, nor a timetable for regulatory approximation' (Commission, 2003): 5. This is part of a global trend of a growing number of bilateral and regional trade agreements, which have effectively 'degenerated the MFN principle to Least Favoured Nation'. See *Future of WTO Report*, retrieved from www.wto.org, and Peter Sutherland in the *Financial Times*, 18 January 2005. The quote is from an editorial in the FT that same day.

6 The four were Iceland, Morocco, Norway and Romania. In addition to the current 4 EU accession candidates (Bulgaria, Romania, Turkey and Croatia) and the 4 EFTA countries, this list includes 5 (of 10) Mediterranean partners, 2 (of the 4) countries in the Western Balkans, and 3 (of the 7) European countries in the CIS (Armenia, Georgia and Moldova). The WTO has, as of 2006, 149 members.

7 These are the EU candidates Bulgaria, Romania and Croatia, the four EFTA states and the four micro states (Andorra, Monaco, San Marino, and the Holy See). The other 25 non-visa countries are in the Americas (17), Oceania (2), Asia (5), in addition to Israel. The 12 with visa requirements are seven CIS members, four countries of the Western Balkans and Turkey.

8 Only the PCAs in the former group include the prospect of a free trade agreement. See D. Tirr, 'The Contractual Framework for Trade between the European Community and the Independent States of the Former Soviet Union, and the Prospects for the Future Development of the Frameworks,' in *Free Trade Agreements and Customs Unions – Experiences, Challenges and Constraints* (Maastricht: European Institute for Public Administration, 1997).

9 The Bologna process was initiated in 1999, and now includes 40 countries (25 EU member states, the 8 current and prospective EU candidates in South East Europe, 6 EFTA and very small European states, and Russia).

10 Agreements on simplified visa procedures for selected groups for longer-term stays were signed with Germany in December 2003, with Italy and France in June 2004, and with Cyprus in 2005.

11 See, for example, statement by Russian Deputy Foreign Minister Chizov, 'Mission of RF to the EU', Press Release No 32/03, November 11, 2003.

12 Quoted in *International Herald Tribune*, 10 November 2004.

13 Israel, Jordan, Morocco, the Palestinian Authority and Tunisia.

14 The first reference calls for harmonization of competition legislation and refers to the relevant PCA Article (53.2.2.), see section 1.4: 5 of the first *Road Map*. The second reference calls for the establishment of a mechanism for cooperation on space issues 'in the framework of the PCA institutions,' see *ibid.*, section 5: 17.

15 Russia is set, however, to benefit from the ENP economic assistance through the new European Neighbourhood and Partnership Instrument.

16 '20 million Russians Reside in the CIS', *Pravda.ru*, 5 February 2005.

Part III
Patterns of Integration

7
Parallels and Divergences of Integration in Ukraine and Belarus

Lien Verpoest

> 'When we blindly adopt a religion, a political system, a literary dogma, we become automatons. We cease to grow.'
>
> (Anaïs Nin)

The past century was in many respects an exceptional one for the European continent. Not only was it scarred by two World Wars, but it was at the same time marked by several economic and political integration processes. Some of these processes were democratic and economically motivated, whereas others were considered totalitarian and ideologically motivated. The twenty-first century is seeing a continuation of integrational processes. The EU's most recent enlargement has both strengthened and weakened the European Union. In Eastern Europe, the Commonwealth of Independent States persists as a looser structure of post-Soviet states. It is often claimed that CIS integration mirrors the EU example. It is therefore interesting to look whether 'parallels of integration' really exist between the European Union and the integration initiatives among the members of the Commonwealth of Independent States. Second, the countries 'in between' deserve some attention as well. Both members of the CIS, Belarus and Ukraine simultaneously find themselves at the border of an enlarged Europe, and are often labelled 'outsider states'. This chapter intends to assess divergent institutional developments and parallels of integration in Ukraine and Belarus after 1991.

The chapter is structured as follows; first, a comparison of possible divergences in the institutional development of Ukraine and Belarus towards the European Union and the CIS will be made. Second, in order to detect parallels of integration, I will briefly look into sub-regional integration initiatives. The Union between Russia and Belarus will be used as a case study here. Third, special attention will be paid to the rationale behind aiming for parallel integration. Exploring the causal mechanisms that steer these tendencies to parallels and divergence might lead to some interesting insights and contrasts.

Ukraine and Belarus between the EU and CIS: divergent integration objectives

The post-communist transition led to a significantly heterogeneous political landscape in the post-Soviet space. In late 1997, Zatulin and Migranian recognized in an article that geopolitical pluralism had arrived in the former USSR.[1] Geopolitical pluralism can be observed in different levels of state and society: the divergent policy preferences of the former Soviet states, in different political models on which these states based themselves during transition or diversity in economic transition and trade links. Also, the divergent foreign policy preferences epitomize the path of development these countries have embarked upon.[2] It is interesting to see how this geopolitical pluralism is reflected in the institutional change of Ukraine and Belarus. Disparate developments and apparent divergence in the foreign policy preferences of Ukraine and Belarus can lead to the question as to whether the formal institutions in these countries were being redrafted to fit the EU or CIS cooperation structures. Nevertheless, when one looks more in general at the European Union and the CIS as 'organizational fields',[3] institutional parallels between these fields might be detected as well. For example, both the institutionalization of the Belarusian–Russian Union State, as well as Putin's repeated statements that Belarusian–Russian integration should evolve along the lines of EU integration appear to be a case of institutional mirroring.

Ukraine: institutional confusion and European illusion

In Ukraine, the main factors complicating institutional reforms were its Soviet legacy and the chaos surrounding independence. The precipitation of the Soviet implosion left Ukraine institutionally unprepared. In the subsequent institutional confusion, a logical action for Ukrainian policymakers seemed to be to resort to old Soviet institutions for inspiration. D'Anieri noted that 'the government consisted of a mix of institutions that were held over from the communist era (such as the *Verkhovna Rada*) because there was no time to create new ones, and of institutions that had to be devised in great haste (such as the presidency and cabinet system) without sufficient consideration of how they might work'.[4] This ambiguous attitude towards institutional reform did not bode well for Ukraine's future development. Because Ukraine's institutions did not break with their Soviet past, to a certain extent they inherited the Soviet inertia, a factor that contributed to institutional confusion and fragmentation. So, although Ukrainian parliament strove to adopt the function of a Western legislature, it continued to work in its previous form.[5]

Ukrainian officials failed to validate the opportunity for institutional redesigning and settled for a political system that combined the old and the new; a hybrid of old (Soviet) and new (more Western inspired) elements.[6]

On the other hand, a parliamentary constitutional commission that was established to draft a new Constitution led to more widespread discussion between the different 'camps' in the Ukrainian political elite. The Constitution of 1996 was the result of a protracted and laborious process that took Ukrainian law makers more than five years. This process was intertwined with the laggard institutional reform in post-communist Ukraine. Marc Nordberg mentions that Gerald Caiden's list of administrative problems facing states made newly independent by 'decolonization' is applicable to post-Soviet Ukraine. It is a pertinent remark in this context. Caiden enumerates problems that arise when a country becomes independent, such as 'lack of experienced administrators, the need for systemic reform, transition pains, an increase in corruption, and the need for international aid'.[7] These are the shortcomings that Ukraine had to deal with in the beginning of 1992. Caiden also remarks that 'these new states attempted to cram hundreds of years of Western development and experience into less than a decade of reform', and that 'in this, most were doomed to failure. They attempted too much too quickly and fell victim to their own maladministration'.[8] This is what happened during the first years of transition. Despite all these complicating factors, the constitutional process continued, albeit slowly. Every time a new draft was presented in parliament, the constitutional commission consultations turned out to be a discussion forum par excellence. In this respect, the 1990–96 constitutional process can be identified as a critical juncture for institutional change in Ukraine. It delineated the main institutional design for the new state structure of independent Ukraine and triggered discussion among the political elite on foreign and domestic policy issues. Thus, the presence of discussion indicated a certain dynamism that was also reflected in Ukraine's foreign policy, which demonstrated more dynamism than Belarusian foreign policy, especially vis-à-vis the European Union.

Belarus: institutional stagnation

Although Belarus and Ukraine are generally thought to have evolved along similar lines in the first years of their independence (both countries knew a certain degree of popular mobilization and a reluctant nomenklatura), certain divergences can be observed, especially on the level of institutional reforms. This disparity became much more apparent in the years that followed. The 1991–94 period in Belarus was predominantly marked by institutional paralysis. However similar to Ukraine, the reasons for this stagnation differed. The Belarusian Popular Front (*Belaruski Narodny Front*)[9] failed politically to validate its popularity (unlike Rukh in Ukraine, which enjoyed immense popularity and translated this into votes). Internal quarrelling and the relative political inexperience among the leaders weakened the BPF to the advantage of the 'old guard', led by Viacheslav Kebich and his cronies, who became known as the 'Party of Power'. Along the traditional lines of patrimonial communism, Kebich was supported by a network of the old nomenklatura who had managed to maintain key positions all through the first years of transition.

The limited political success of the BNF combined with the rise of Kebich and his Party of Power eventually resulted in institutional stagnation in Belarus. The absence of reforms also implied the absence of discussion in the compliant parliament, which differs significantly from the situation in Ukraine, where discussion caused some dynamism in the early post-Soviet politics of the country.

Moreover, the unanticipated election of Aleksandr Lukashenka as President of Belarus further radicalized the situation.[10] Lukashenka introduced institutional reforms, yet the way he did this (through rigged referenda) was deemed unconstitutional and illegitimate. Moreover, the goal of Lukashenka's reforms was not so much to enhance the level of democracy in Belarus, but was aimed more at strengthening the institution of presidency – to the detriment of other institutions – especially that of the Supreme Soviet. These 1995 and 1996 referenda turned out to be critical junctures for Belarus; they 'legitimized' Lukashenka's power grab and his undemocratic institutional reforms, which significantly determined the country's domestic and foreign policy, and alienated Belarus from the West for years to come, since the European Union, the Council of Europe and the OSCE all condemned Lukashenka's actions.

The countries compared: similar starting position, divergent development

Although it seems that Ukraine and Belarus developed along the same lines in the first years of their independence, the mid-1990s signalled a double divergence; in the countries' domestic institutional development and in their foreign policy orientation.

First divergence: domestic political developments

In Belarus, Lukashenka orchestrated the institutional reforms in order to strengthen his power base by eliminating the pro-reform, pro-Western opposition through the dissolution of parliament and hand picking the members of the new parliament. As mentioned earlier, his actions were considered unconstitutional.

In Ukraine, on the other hand, it was exactly the 1996 Constitution that limited the president. The Constitution did not give the president as much power as in Russia or Belarus. Unlike in Belarus, the president was accountable to the *Verkhovna Rada* for his policy decisions. In Belarus, the President deprived the opposition of a voice by replacing them with less critical deputies, which gave him a free hand in decision making without being amenable to another institution. So, in comparison to Belarus the institutional structures in Ukraine tend to be more proportioned. The country managed to score a better balance between legislative and executive institutions. Although relations have been strained and dissenting opinions will always remain, since the 1996 Constitution the president and parliament in Ukraine have more mutual checks and balances on each other than their Belarusian counterparts will ever have.

Second divergence: foreign policy orientation

Over the past decade, new sections have been added to existing government institutions as a consequence of Belarus and Ukraine's foreign policy priorities. Special sections and departments were added to the MFAs and new parliamentary committees were launched according to the countries' 'Western' (EU) or 'Eastern' (CIS) orientation. Moreover, specific interinstitutional cooperation structures were created between Ukraine and Belarus, and the EU and the CIS respectively.[11] One of the reasons behind Ukraine's and Belarus's institutional adaptation and the emergence of interinstitutional cooperation mechanisms is their goal to gain legitimacy. Powell and DiMaggio enumerate four organizational characteristics that might indicate a certain institutional adaptation:

(1) An increased interaction among organizations;
(2) The emergence of interorganizational structures;
(3) An increase in information load;
(4) The development of a mutual awareness of being involved in a common enterprise.[12]

I will use these organizational characteristics to assess briefly the institutional adaptation and foreign policy initiatives of Ukraine (Table 7.1) and Belarus (Table 7.2) towards the EU and the CIS. In doing so, certain

Table 7.1 Institutional adaptation and foreign policy initiatives of Ukraine towards EU and CIS

Organizational characteristics	Ukraine	
	EU	CIS
Increased interaction among organizations in the field	Declared intention of becoming (associate) member of EU Institutional definition: – MFA: Department for European Integration, Section for EU Affairs – Verkhovna Rada: Committee on issues of European Integration-now: Vice-Prime Minister for Issues of European Integration National Agency for Development and European Integration	Reluctant member of CIS, yet participation in CIS integration process and some subregional initiatives (EvrAzES, SES) Institutional definition: – MFA: NR, no specific departments for CIS – Verkhovna Rada: NR, no specific committees
Emergence of inter-organizational structures	PCA 1994, into force 1998 Cooperation Council Cooperation Committee Parliamentary Cooperation Committee Subcommittees ENP 2004 – Action plan	Participation in CIS instit. structures: Council of Heads of States/governments Council of Ministers (Foreign Affairs, Defence, ...) Interparliamentary Assembly CIS
Increase in information load	Official documents and speeches: • 'Strategy for the Integration of Ukraine into the European Union's numerous documents, speeches and reports asserting European ambitions of Ukraine' • EU–Ukraine Action plan 2005–07 (ENP)	Official documents: NR No specific strategies towards CIS, only treaties: Belavezha Treaty (1991), Yalta Charter of GUUAM (1997), Treaty founding Eurasian Economic Community (2000), Pact on Common Economic Space (Sept 2003)
Development of mutual awareness of being involved in a common enterprise	Intention of becoming member state of EU, initiatives from EU side: Common Strategy, participates in European Neighbourhood Policy	NR; Reluctant CIS member, limited participation Founding member of GUUAM

Note: NR = Not relevant.

Table 7.2 Institutional adaptation and foreign policy initiatives of Belarus towards EU and CIS

Organizational characteristics	Belarus	
	EU	CIS
Increased interaction among organizations in the field	Until 1996: developing relations with EU: PCA and temporary trade agreement concluded Since 1996: NR – MFA: NR, no specific department for EU integration[13]	Participation in CIS integration process and most sub-regional initiatives (EvrAzES, CES, Alma-Aty Declaration) Institutional definition: – MFA: Department for Russia and the Union State, Department for CIS and EvrAzES, Department for countries of CIS – Palata Predstaviteley: permanent commission for international affairs and relations with the CIS
Emergence of interorganizational structures	Until 1996: PCA and Interim trade agreement concluded Since 1996: NR; PCA not ratified, sanctions. ENP on hold.	Participation in CIS instit. structures: Council of Heads of States/Governments Council of Ministers (Foreign Affairs, Defence, ...) Interparliamentary Assembly CIS Belarus–Russia Union State: Supreme State Council Permanent Committee Council of Ministers Parliamentary Assembly, ...
Increase in information load	No specific strategies, some official documents and speeches: – 'The Enlargement of the EU and possible consequences for Belarusian foreign trade interests' – 'Current Requirements of the EU-Belarus Relation' – 'On the Relations with the European Union'	Official Documents and publications: – 'Foreign Policy and economic priorities of Belarus in the light of the Union State with the Russian Federation' – 'Cooperation in the Framework of the CIS' – 'The Union State: Today, Yesterday, and Tomorrow', ...
Development of mutual awareness of being involved in a common enterprise	NR	Zealous member of CIS, integration efforts with Russia

Note: NR = Not relevant.

divergences in foreign policy priorities and subsequent institutional development might be detected.

Ukraine demonstrates active institutional dynamism towards EU integration. Specific institutions were established over the years that focus on EU integration. Apart from the specific parliamentary committee for European Integration, a specific section on the EU reported alternately under the Ministry of Economy and later under the MFA, until a special vice-prime minister for European Integration was named in Yushchenko's first cabinet. After the dismissal of this cabinet in September 2005, the vice-prime minister for European Integration was appointed Secretary of State by President Yushchenko. He immediately announced dynamic plans to form a Committee for European Integration directly reporting under the cabinet, based on the Polish model of European integration. As Table 7.1 shows, the many strategies, as well as interinstitutional mechanisms such as the EU–Ukraine Cooperation Council and Parliamentary Cooperation Committee clearly illustrate Ukraine's consistently European ambitions. Therefore, since increased interaction has been taking place between Ukraine and the European Union, since there is a clear emergence of interorganizational structures, since there is a significant increase in information load by means of numerous official documents describing Ukraine's strategy of integration into the EU and, last but not least, since there appears to be development of a certain mutual awareness of being involved in a common enterprise, one can say that Ukraine fulfils the basic conditions of institutional approximation vis-à-vis the EU. Whether Ukraine's European ambitions are a realistic aim for now, is a different story.

The foreign policy initiatives in Belarus on the other hand, or the lack thereof, gives us a rather different picture.

It is clear from the data provided in Table 7.2 that Belarus lacks Ukraine's institutional dynamism vis-à-vis the European Union. Although increased interaction and the emergence of interorganizational structures could be observed during the first years of Belarusian independence, most of these processes were reversed after Lukashenka came to power. The information load was limited and mostly stressed the negative aspects of relations with the EU and the negative consequences of EU enlargement. Moreover, there was absolutely no mutual awareness of being involved in a common enterprise, especially since the EU declared sanctions after the rigged referenda and did not recognize Lukashenka as the legitimate leader after his original term expired in 1999. The Belarusian government reacted defiantly to the European criticism and relations soured even further.

The dynamism that is missing in Belarus's European policy is, however, all the more present in its relations with the Commonwealth of Independent States (CIS). Since its very foundation, Belarus has maintained a consistently open policy towards the CIS. As early as the spring of 1993, Kebich and his Party of Power expressed the will to give up Belarusian neutrality in favour of an economic union and military alliance with the CIS states. This policy eventually materialized when Lukashenka became president. A Union between Belarus and Russia developed along several stages (cfr infra).

Lukashenka's anti-Western stance went hand in hand with a neo-Soviet attitude that is also reflected in Belarusian foreign policy. From 1994 onwards, there was an even stronger interaction with the CIS. The fact that the Belarus–Russia Union served as an example of 'the highest form of integration' within the CIS only intensified Lukashenka's Eastern drive. Elaborate interinstitutional structures were created on the national (sections for CIS and Union affairs in the MFA, a commission for CIS in parliament) and interinstitutional level (summits, inter-parliamentary assembly, executive committee and so on). Numerous official documents illustrate the Belarusian orientation towards the Commonwealth of Independent States. The documents as well as all the interinstitutional mechanisms signal a mutual awareness of being involved in building an integrational structure (CIS) in the post-Soviet region, of which the Union State serves as model for closer integration.

In stark contrast to this, Ukraine's relations with the CIS clearly lack the momentum of the Belarus-CIS/Russia cooperation. Although Ukraine's eastward policy is by far not as strained as Belarus's relations with the EU, it is clear that Ukraine limits its political involvement in CIS institutions to a minimum. As one can see in Table 7.1, inter-organizational structures between Ukraine and the CIS are present, yet no particular official documents delineate a specific strategy towards the CIS. There is no mentionable increased interaction between Ukraine and the CIS as an organization. Ukraine has continually limited its participation in the few tangible initiatives that the CIS has taken, such as the Collective Security Treaty, by using the argument that its participation in CIS structures or agreements cannot contradict the Constitution, which prohibits any supranational body to be allowed to impose its rule over Ukraine. Moreover, Ukraine's official policy over the last years has tended to non-participation in any CIS integration initiatives that are not in line with Ukraine's official state policy of integration into the EU. Therefore, Ukraine's reputation as a distinctly unenthusiastic member of CIS, combined with its European ambitions, implies that the level of mutual awareness to be involved in a common enterprise is low as well.

Causal mechanisms behind the foreign policy divergences

To summarize, we can state that Ukraine shows institutional dynamism towards EU integration, whereas Belarus clearly lacks this European vigour. On the other hand, Belarus has displayed a consistently open policy towards the Commonwealth of Independent States, whereas Ukraine's relations with the CIS lack momentum and its political engagement in the CIS institutions is limited. A clear divergence can be observed in the policy choices of Ukraine and Belarus. This can be considered surprising, even more so because these countries have a markedly similar history and background. Some reasons behind these choices however might explain this disparity.

History/socio-cultural factors   Historical and cultural factors always play a significant role in the policy preferences of political actors, more than one usually gathers. In this case, Belarusian history shows that, over the course of the centuries, the country has almost never been an independent state. On the contrary, the Belarusian lands were practically continually part of a greater dominion, either the Great Duchy of Lithuania or the Russian Empire.[14] Hence, it is not very surprising that the Belarusian people have a limited national consciousness. This weak national identity was also apparent in the late 1980s and early 1990s, when the Belarusian Popular Front – although causing mass protests – failed to catch on like the Ukrainian Rukh.

Ukraine on the other hand has a stronger national identity, not only because Western Ukraine had been part of the Habsburg Empire, which – according to many Ukrainians – gave ground to Ukraine's strive for European integration, but most probably also because of the presence (up until this day) of a considerable Russian minority to which Western Ukrainians have reacted by asserting their identity even more strongly.

Leadership   The role of leadership in Ukraine and Belarus is perceived relatively differently. Whereas Ukraine is not confronted with an extremely predominant leadership, and the president – although constantly attempting to increase his power vis-à-vis parliament – is basically one part of the whole, Belarus is faced with a strong leader who predominates in every aspect of Belarusian politics. Lukashenka's omnipresent influence permeates, in true Soviet style, all government levels and policy fields. It is therefore only logical that it is the president who has mainly determined (and continues to determine) Belarus's Eastern orientation.

Civil society The development of civil society in Ukraine and Belarus may have seemed similar at first, with the BPF organizing mass protests demanding to look into the Kurapaty issue and the Chernobyl fallout, and the Ukrainian Rukh bringing about popular mobilization and political awareness. But eventually, the Belarusian BPF failed to appeal to the wider public because of its increasingly outspoken anti-Russian stance. The rise of civil society in Ukraine was more successful. Rukh played a pioneering role in this in the early 1990s, and set the basis for grassroots organizations. And although the Ukrainian public was generally perceived to be too passive and indifferent to take to the streets over the government corruption over the years to come, civil society played an (albeit limited) role when the people finally took to the streets in the winter of 2004 and procured the power switch from Maidan Square.[15]

Foreign interests A last and very obvious reason that explains the disparity in foreign policy choices between Ukraine and Belarus is strategic interests. The West (both the European Union and the United States) has an economic strategic-interest in Ukraine.[16] This became all too clear during the Orange Revolution, which was sponsored both morally and (indirectly) financially. The West however has little economic or political strategic interest in Belarus. Although grassroots organizations are sponsored to procure democratization and maintain somewhat of a critical voice against the president in the country, Belarus is largely perceived as and left in the Russian sphere of influence. Because of this, closer integration between Russia and Belarus became a real option.

The state of the Russia–Belarus Union: parallels of integration?

In this last section, the Russian–Belarusian integration will serve as a case study to illustrate that the post-Soviet space is not only an arena of divergent policies, but is also aiming for parallels of integration, looking for inspiration at other integration initiatives on the European continent. The Belarusian–Russian Union State is often claimed (even by its founders) to be mirroring the example of European integration.

Although Viacheslau Kebich already made plans for a Russian–Belarusian rapprochement earlier on in the 1990s, the real integration process only started under Lukashenka, when Belarus became more isolated in the international arena. Both now and then, enthusiasm from the Russian side was relatively high. They considered integration with Belarus a good way to counter the waning influence of the former superpower that was Russia. Table 7.3 gives an overview of the different steps of integration.

Table 7.3   Russia–Belarus integration: official agreements and treaties

12 April 1994	Monetary Union between Russian and Belarus (abandoned by Russia later that year)
6 January 1995	Customs Union between Russian and Belarus
26 May 1995	Agreement on Friendship, Goodneighbourly Relations and Cooperation between Russian and Belarus
2 April 1996	Creation of a Community of Sovereign Republics (*Soobshchestvo*)
5 December 1996	Declaration of further unification between Russia and Belarus, Treaty on equal rights for citizens
2 April 1997	Creation of a Union (*Soyuz*) between Russia and Belarus
8 December 1999	Treaty on the formation of a Union State (*Soiuznoe Gosudarstvo*) between Russia and Belarus

As mentioned earlier, President Vladimir Putin has more than once declared that the Belarusian–Russian Union State should follow the path of European integration in its rapprochement. Different Russian prime ministers and senior officials have eagerly endorsed this discourse and consistently mentioned the EU model of integration as an example for Russia–Belarus integration in their speeches and during press conferences.

However, by assessing the levels of integration and looking into the actual institutional set-up of the Union State, one cannot but come to the conclusion that mirroring – let alone following the EU model of integration – is relatively limited here. As for the different levels of integration, not every aspect of integration in the framework of the Union State has been equally successful. In order to assess the extent of integration between Russia and Belarus, and to check whether integration actually follows the oft-mentioned European model, I will briefly go into the economic, military, political and institutional level of integration.

Economic integration

Many specific agreements have been concluded on economic integration, mainly focusing on the harmonization of tariffs and the creation of a free market.[17] Moreover, Belarus has received considerable loans and energy subsidies from Russia over the years, a support without which the Belarusian economy would not have been able to exist, and for which Russia receives cheap transit rates for gas and oil. Belarus never made a secret of its goal to secure as many subsidies and loans as possible – even President Lukashenka stated at one point that 'we should squeeze out as much as possible from the Union treaty currently into force'.[18] The Belarusian opposition leaders have hence repeatedly labelled the economic relations between Russia and Belarus as 'Russian oil for Belarusian kisses'.[19] Nevertheless, ever since President Lukashenka started backtracking on his earlier promise to give Gazprom a controlling stake in the Belarusian Beltranshaz company, this path of cooperation has been strewn with obstacles. Both in 2002 and 2004, incidents[20] have occurred in which the Belarusian side narrowly avoided Gazprom's threats to raise energy prices (which are now at 46.68USD per 1000 cubic meters) to European prices (appr. 230USD), and further troubles are brewing.[21]

Apart from these problems, one of the key aspects of Russian–Belarusian economic integration, its monetary policy, is still not effectively coordinated. Announced as one of the pinpoints from the very start of the integration, a combined monetary policy through the introduction of a single currency has gradually turned into a big failure. In early 2002, both Russian and Belarusian sides still agreed on the need to create a single currency before proceeding to political integration, but when President Putin started pressing his Belarusian colleague towards concrete action, it was again Lukashenka who started backtracking on his promises and stressed the need for political integration first (by means of a joint constitution). From August 2002 onwards, both sides' opinion on the single currency diverged. Putin had already taken up the proposal to introduce the single currency on 1 January 2004, one year ahead of the term stipulated by the union treaty (1 January 2005). Lukashenka on the other hand opposed the predominance of the Russian Central Bank in the process and maintained that the switchover to the Russian ruble as the new single currency should close both countries' integration, rather than being introduced at the start. The clashing opinions soon led to a deadlock and further delayed the process. In September 2003, then Russian Prime Minister Kasyanov announced that that no agreement to introduce the Russian ruble as the single currency of Russia and Belarus would be signed in the near future, because of Minsk's insistence that Russia adopt a constitutional act on the formation of a union state before a common currency could be introduced.[22] Further delays followed in 2004. Both states failed to meet the 1 January 2005 deadline, and in April of that year, Lukashenka and Putin jointly declared at a meeting that they decided to delay the introduction of a single currency and declined to set a new date.[23] The latest reports speak of 2008 as the earliest date for introducing the single currency. As for the oft-repeated claims of basing the Belarus–Russia integration on the European model, especially on the economic level, it is rather telling that of all things, monetary integration, which has been one of the more successful aspects of European economic integration, has turned out to be such a failure in the Belarusian–Russian integration process.

Military integration

Cooperation in the military field started early on in the integration process and can be considered the most successful aspect of Belarusian–Russian integration. As early as in 1995, agreements were concluded on Russia's free use of the Vileika communications facilities and Baranovichi missile warning station in Belarus.[24] Apart from the mutual use of infrastructure,[25] an intensive cooperation between border troops arose from the mid-1990s onwards in which Russia and Belarus combined efforts in guarding the borders between their countries and Poland and the Baltic States respectively. Moreover, plans to develop joint rapid reaction forces are on the table, joint air force and other military exercises take place on a regular basis.[26] Maybe even more impressively, both countries' Ministries of Defence initiated joint collegial sessions at the end of the 1990s and took up the plan of drafting a common defence policy. Early drafts were published in 1998 and 1999, and the year 2000 even saw the first common defence orders of Russia and Belarus.[27]

All this and more can lead us to the conclude that military integration is developing at a much faster pace and is therefore much more successful than the other aspects of Russian–Belarusian integration. However, two remarks should be made here. First, the military aspect of integration may have developed more easily and quickly because it is grounded in existing CIS cooperation structures – the central CIS air defence administration, for example, is located in the Baranovichi station, and many of the cooperation agreements and joint military exercises can be situated in the wider CIS military cooperation framework as foreseen and elaborated under the 1992 Tashkent Collective Security Treaty. In this sense, the aspect of military integration might considered successful not so much due to the exclusive merits of Russian–Belarusian integration, but rather because it is a sort of 'enhanced cooperation' embedded in existing CIS structures. This enhanced cooperation entails some mutual privileges for Russia and Belarus; for example, the rent free use of infrastructures, or the training of Belarusian officers in Russian military academies on the same programmes as their Russian colleagues. Second, this type of 'enhanced cooperation' hardly follows the EU model, where soft security issues currently prevail over hard security issues, and where military integration is still one of the 'weakest links' in the overall European integration process.[28] Here also, it goes to show that the more elaborate or successful aspects of Russian–Belarusian integration do not correspond with those of the EU.

Institutional integration

As the Russia–Belarus Union took shape from the mid-1990s onwards, different Union institutions were established. The 1996 treaty on the formation of a Community (*Soobshchestvo*)[29] established the Supreme Council (*Vysshiy Sovet*, Art. 9) and the Parliamentary Assembly of the Union (*Parlamentskoe Sobranie*, Art. 10), as well as the Executive Committee (*Ispolnitelnyi Komitet*, Art. 11). The Supreme Council clearly was considered to have authority over the latter two institutions, and was the highest power organ of the Russia–Belarus Union. On 8 December 1999, the signing of the Union State treaty (*Dogovor o Sozdanii Soiuznogo Gosudarstva*) drew the definitive institutional lines along which the Russia–Belarus integration was supposed to develop. The Executive Committee was transformed into a Permanent Committee (*Postoiannyi Komitet*), the Supreme Council was strengthened, and the Council of Ministers gained importance. The competences of the Union State Parliament were also further specified by dividing it into a Chamber of the Union (*Palata Soiuza*) and a Chamber of Representatives (*Palata Predstaviteley*).[30] Other institutions like an Accounts Chamber and Court were planned in the Union State Treaty, but as yet have not materialized. Without going too deeply into specifics, one could say that relations between the two countries' Heads of State and their further plans is a dominant factor in the successful development of the Union State institutional framework. The past six years have demonstrated that progress in integration greatly depends on what is being discussed at the relatively regular meetings of the Presidents in Sochi. The fact that relations between Lukashenka and Putin are precarious, to say the least, might partly explain a certain absence of momentum in institutional integration. A second factor that might explain the slow development of the Union State institutional framework is the protracted process of constitution making which is supposed to delineate the competencies of these institutions once and for all in a mutually agreed document, but has become one of the stumbling blocks in the countries' political integration.

As for basing institutional integration on the European model, a double picture emerges here. On the one hand, the institutions established by the different integration treaties seem to a certain extent parallel to their European counterparts, at least in name and structure. One might compare the Parliamentary Assembly (*Parlamentskoe Sobranie*) and the Executive Committee (*Ispolnitelnyi Komitet*) as described in the 1996 Community Treaty to the European Parliament and the European Commission. On the other hand, the institutions might seem similar, but their competences and procedures diverge. First, apart from the fact that these institutions represent only two countries instead of many (as in the EU) these institutions were also 'clearly subordinated to the authority of the Supreme Council, which was initially made up of the heads of state, the heads of government, the chairs of national parliaments ... and the Chairman of the Executive Committee. The Presidents of Russia and Belarus rotate in the office of Supreme Council Chair'.[31] This powerful institution was unprecedented up until now; it does not have a European counterpart and significantly shifted the institutional balance in the Union State.[32]

The fact that the 1999 Union State Treaty considerably diminished the powers of the Executive Committee (then renamed the Permanent Committee) to the advantage of the Council of Ministers only underlines the different balances of power present among the Union State institutions and the EU institutions respectively. Unlike the European Commission, the Permanent Committee was left after 1999 with a mainly coordinating role. Through the inclusion of the Union State Secretary Borodin and Union State Agencies, the Council of Ministers ceased being intergovernmental, as was its European equivalent (Council of the European Union).[33]

Political integration

Up until 1999, political integration between Russia and Belarus seemed rather promising. A certain goodwill was shared by both President Lukashenka and President Yeltsin not only to focus on military or economic aspects of integration but also to take the Union one step further and develop an integration mechanism that entailed aspects of supranationality. The 1999 Union State Treaty, for example, delineated a list of exclusive Union State competencies (*k iskliuchitelnomu vedeniiu Soiuznogo Gosudarstva*, section II, Art. 17) which, among others, entailed the creation of a common economic space, the unification of transport and energy systems, the coordination of border polices of the Union State and so on.[34]

However, much of this goodwill vanished when Putin succeeded Yeltsin as President of the Russian Federation. He quickly replaced Russia's general benevolence towards Belarus with clear pragmatism. Apart from the energy conflicts in 2002 and 2004, divergent opinions soon surfaced concerning the further path of political integration that the countries should follow. In June 2002, the new Russian president expressed irritation over Lukashenka's approach to the integration. He publicly reproved Lukashenka for his eagerness to 'make something resembling the former Soviet Union' and pointed out that the Belarusian economy only amounts to 3 per cent of the Russian economy, and Belarus should therefore not demand equal veto rights in the future union.[35]

A second and more serious incident occurred only two months later. Putin's blatant pragmatism once again shone through in a proposal he made at the joint press conference in Moscow on 14 August that shocked President Lukashenka to the core. The Russian President proposed two scenarios for integration. One of them was to follow the path of 'ultimate integration', which would mainly imply Belarus becoming a 90th subject of the Russian Federation.[36] In that case, a referendum on this topic could take place in May 2003, followed by elections for a joint parliament in December 2003, the introduction of the Russian ruble as the Union State's single currency in January 2004, and the election of a Union president in March 2004. If the Belarusian leadership was not ready to move so rapidly however, Putin added, a second scenario entailed that unification could be 'modelled on the European Union'. In that case, the integration process should be taken up by the Union's parliament.[37]

Analysts at that time labelled Putin's move as calling Lukashenka's bluff.[38] Shaken by Putin's proposal, Lukashenka refused to discuss the incorporation option by expressing his love for and adherence to Belarus's sovereignty as never before.[39] A couple of months later, the Belarusian president offered a third option – maintaining the status quo on the basis of the Union State Treaty. 'Let us not destroy what we have today', he urged.[40]

It seems that a status quo is what eventually developed over the years that followed. Russian–Belarusian integration gradually lost momentum and no major high-level agreements were concluded beyond 1999. Belarus kept on stressing the importance of a joint constitution as it was foreseen in the Union State Treaty, and once in a while forwarded a draft constitutional act, which was invariably labelled preposterous by Russian senior officials or the Union State secretary.[41] They claimed the drafts were invariably based on Belarus maintaining its state sovereignty, territorial integrity and veto rights, which according to the Russians did not reflect the real balance of power.[42] Although the process of constitutional drafting was recently taken up again in 2005, no Constitution has been signed so far. Ironically, this might be the biggest parallel between Belarusian–Russian integration and European integration to this date: the failure to adopt a joint constitution.

The claims of following the European model for this aspect of integration as yet do not seem to have materialized. On the one hand, the political discourse does mirror EU examples: in the agreements and legal

documents up to 1999, 'the objectives declared in the integration agreements have mirrored the achievements of the European Community/
Union to a considerable extent'.[43] However, objectives were mirrored,
not actions. Because the mirroring remained limited to the discourse of
officials, parallels between the Union State and European integration are
meager to say the least. Yet, one aspect in the field of political integration was successful: the harmonization of foreign policy. Since 1998,
both the Russian and Belarusian Ministries of Foreign Affairs initiated
'Programmes of Coordinated Actions in the Field of Foreign Policy',
which included joint collegial sessions from February 2000 onward.
Moreover, Belarusian diplomats have received training at the Diplomatic
Academy of Russian MFA and MGIMO. Yet again, given the fact that
coordinating foreign policy among member states is one of the weaker
points of European integration, this can not be considered a successful
example of mirroring the European model. The successful harmonization of both countries' foreign policies (and some of their joint stances
on defence) rather originate in an 'us and them' reasoning, incited by
the international situation, in which both countries feel the need for
coordinated actions and an ally.

Causal mechanisms behind parallel integration

In sum, it seems that the very process of integration lost it momentum
almost immediately after the signing of the 1999 agreement on the formation of the Union State. Not surprisingly, this deceleration in the
integration process coincided with the advent of a new Russian
President; Vladimir Putin. This fact actually sheds a light on the causal
mechanisms behind the Belarus–Russia integration project. It is clear
that the institutional, economic, military and, most importantly, political achievements of this 'protracted integration process' are limited.
Integration has been going on since 1994, and the results – apart from
bilateral relations and specific agreements that could have just as well
been concluded outside the Union state (in a CIS context) – are trifling.
Apart from interparliamentary cooperation, all the aspects that are
exclusive to Belarus–Russia integration – first and foremost the development of functioning Union State institutions, a joint Constitutional Act,
a single currency and a clear agreement on where this Union State is
developing towards – have stalled. Why then do the leaders of both
countries still hold on to the existence of this Union State? Moreover,
why would some leaders of the Belarus–Russia integration aim for a
parallel integration following the European model, and declare it so
intentionally?

The Belarusian reasons to stick with this Union have been clear from the start: Belarus has a lot to gain from the economic advantages that the Union with Russia provides.[44] Many observers say that Belarus has become so dependent on the Russian economy over the years that it cannot survive without the support of Russian energy subsidies and loans. Second, Lukashenka's Pan-Slavic neo-Sovietism, as well as his increasing position of isolation on the European continent give him all the more reason to concentrate on rapprochement with Russia.

Whereas Belarusian motives to hold on the Union State integration are mainly economic-strategic, Russia's motives are political-strategic. Not to say that Russia does not enjoy any economic privileges as a consequence of the integration; the transport of Russian gas and oil to Europe runs through Belarus at very cheap rates. Yet, Russia does not need these economic advantages half as much as Belarus does. Russia's underlying motives for integration are clearly more political-strategic, every step of integration coincided with the need for a political boost for the Russian president.[45]

Both President Yeltsin and President Lukashenka pretended a preference for integration not only to increase their popularity when needed, but also to bolster their country's geopolitical or economic position. However, when the time came for serious reforms (such as executing the goals of the Union State Treaty), the integration process slowed down. As mentioned, a chill in Belarus–Russia relations occurred from 2001 onwards. The loss of momentum in the relations, the 2002 and 2004 gas conflicts, the failure of the Constitutional act and the Single Currency cannot solely be contributed to the clashing personalities of Lukashenka and Putin. Another significant factor here turned out to be Russia's improved relations with the West after the 2001 September 11 tragedy. The surge in cooperation with the West made holding on to faithful ally Belarus somewhat redundant. A couple of years later however, the coloured revolutions in Ukraine and Georgia coincided with a renewed impetus in Belarus–Russia integration. The idea of a joint Constitutional Act was taken up again months after the Orange Revolution of December 2004, four draft versions are up for discussion, and word is that the joint constitutional act might soon be signed. Suddenly, the faithful ally became necessary again.

This whole process gives the impression of being an integration game rather than a serious strategy for unification. Integration in itself does not seem to be the main goal of the game. Other motives are clearly at play here. First, the idea of integration has proven to be a convenient and effective tool for political manoeuvre. Second, it has served Russia's pragmatic goal of keeping Belarus in the Russian sphere of influence, and it has equally served Belarus's economic strategic purposes. Third, it has led to considerable discourse mentioning parallel integration with the European Union, a discourse that one also finds in the context of CIS integration.[46] Fourth, and most importantly, the timing of the Belarus–Russia integration was not accidental. It occurred simultaneously with the Central European states filing for accession to the European Union and NATO structures.[47] The peak of Belarusian–Russian integration, the Union State agreement, was concluded in the same year of the NATO strikes on Serbia that were widely contested both in Russia and Belarus.

On the other hand, the appeal of the EU as an institutional model is at least partly due to the high prestige of the EU as an integration mechanism on the European continent and in the eyes of the Russian and Belarusian elites; they associate the EU model with the growing prosperity of the member states.[48] Although all these developments in the 1990s led to a growing fear of isolation and encirclement, it did not however prompt Russia or Belarus to opt for EU membership. On the contrary, Clelia Rontoyanni very rightly points out that

> the complexity of the EU enlargement process appears to have led Belarusian & Russian elites to the conclusion that the capacity of the existing supranational structures could not be stretched to geographical or cultural limits of European continent – at least in the foreseeable future. The concurrent realization of the need for Russia, Belarus and the rest of the CIS to become an integral part of broader economic and political processes inevitably – for the time being – centered around the EU and NATO, has prompted a strategy of parallel integrative processes combined with growing interaction with the European core.[49]

Nevertheless, this chapter has illustrated that the actual 'mirroring' of EU integration remains very limited. Analysis has shown that some of the most successful aspects of EU integration (such as a single currency) have failed to catch on or, at least, have encountered problems (energy rates and so on). The most successful aspects of the Belarusian–Russian Union State (military cooperation, harmonization of foreign policy) on the other hand actually turn out to be the weaker aspects of European integration. This constatation shows that the motives behind both integration initiatives are very different. Whereas the European Union started out as an economic organization, the Belarus–Russia unification process draws upon geostrategic motives that have at least to some extent originated in a perceived common threat; the geopolitical changes that have been going on since the 1990s.

Conclusion: parallels and divergences of integration

In this chapter, I looked at two countries which started their postcommunist transition from very similar backgrounds and have developed in very divergent directions. This was illustrated by gauging the presence of four organizational characteristics in the institutional reforms and foreign policy orientations of the two countries. After an initial phase of balancing, Ukraine seems (even more so since the December 2004 Orange Revolution) to be staunchly heading for European integration. Yet, both its energy dependence on Russia as well as the persistently lukewarm reaction of the European Union might keep these ambitions in check. The fact that the SES initiative is not completely written off altogether, even by the Yushchenko administration, illustrates Ukraine's occasional reality check. The integration initiatives in which Ukraine is involved, mentioned by Dragneva and Dimitrova in Chapter 9, might not prove incompatible for the time being, but it remains to be seen how these initiatives – and, more importantly, the CIS as a regional organization of which Ukraine still is a member – will develop in the future.

In the same CIS context, Belarus on the other hand has from the start abstained from the balancing option occasionally taken up by Ukraine. As one of the most enthusiastic CIS member states, Belarus became Russia's partner in what is known as the 'highest form of integration' within the CIS. Especially given the economic advantages that have become indispensable for its economy, Belarus will keep on free-riding as long as it can. However, as Vinokurov points out very rightly in Chapter 2, Russia has taken up the policy of reasserting its zone of influence since Putin's second presidential term. For Belarus, this implies on the one hand that certain integration initiatives, such as the Joint Constitutional Act, have acquired a new lease of life. On the other hand, it also implies that Russia might not only use 'friendly' carrots, but also more coercive sticks in its relations with other CIS states, such as energy prices as a tool for political maneuvering. This Russian fickleness sheds some light on the main difference between the EU and CIS integration initiatives. Unlike the European Union, the Commonwealth is dominated by one state – Russia. This mars the stability of the integration process, since it becomes much more dependent on the political, economic and strategic whims of this country.

Nevertheless, these two parallel integration initiatives coexist on the European continent. As for the mirroring of integration models; the example of the Belarusian–Russian Union has shown that the level of this mirroring should not be overrated. To a certain extent, looking across the borders for inspiration is a natural process, even a historical tradition in the East–West context. The same applies for the EU and CIS 'parallel' integration; a certain influence of integration initiatives in its periphery can be considered normal. Nominally, the formal structures and institutions of EU and CIS might seem similar, but (1) the level of integration, and (2) the reasons for integration differ substantially. First, the different level of integration is manifested among others by the major time disparity between both organizations. The CIS is a loose construction that has been 'developing' only since 1991, and is already gradually being outpaced by sub-regional initiatives that gain importance. The lifespan of the EU on the other hand exceeds the CIS fivefold; the EU has developed at a steadier rate, with an initially limited focus both in content and geography, before gradually venturing into other areas. Second, the reasons for integration also differ. European integration was initiated by idealistic-economic reasons after the Second World War, when all European countries were economically (and ideologically) drained. In this light, the foundation of the CIS on 8 December 1991, several weeks before the official end of the Soviet Union, more resembles a move of damage control triggered by pragmatic–economic considerations. The idea of the CIS looking at the more experienced and longer lasting EU model seems very natural in this light. Moreover, there is no reason why these two integration initiatives cannot coexist on the European continent. The only countries who might suffer some collateral damage from this are the countries that are stuck inbetween the EU and the CIS. The situation of Ukraine and Belarus, both in and between these two integration mechanisms, is not an easy, yet it is a challenging one. Looking at the bright side of things, one could say that one day, good governance in Ukraine and Belarus might just be able to steer this intermediate position into an advantageous one of bringing the countries the best of both worlds.

Notes

1 The term was first asserted by Brzezinski in 1994, and was purposefully supported by the West, with the objective of weakening Russia's leading role in the CIS. K. Zatulin and A. Migranian, 'SNG Posle Kishineva: Nachalo Kontsa Istorii', *Sodruzhestvo NG*, 1 (1997): 1–2; P. Kubicek, 'End of the Line for the Commonwealth of Independent States', *Problems of Post-Communism*, 46 (1999): 15–24.

2 Three different trajectories pointed out by Taras Kuzio (European, Westernizing, and Russophile) also illustrate these different paths, in T. Kuzio, 'Promoting Geopolitical Pluralism in the CIS: GUUAM and Western Foreign Policy', *Problems of Post-Communism*, 47 (2000): 25–35.

3 W. Powell and P.J. DiMaggio, *The New Institutionalism in Organizational Analysis* (Illinois: University of Chicago Press, 1991).

4 D'Anieri, R. Kravchuk and T. Kuzio, *Politics and Society in Ukraine* (Boulder: Westview, 1999): 86.

5 Since, initially, there was no clear demarcation of the Rada's authority and duties, it often became involved in day-to-day affairs of the government.

6 As a consequence, institutional continuity actually outpaced institutional change in Ukraine.

7 Caiden, in M. Nordberg, 'State and Institution Building in Ukraine', in T. Kuzio (ed.), *Contemporary Ukraine: Dynamics of Post-Soviet Transformation* (London/NY: M.E. Sharpe, 1998): 41.

8 *Ibid.*

9 The BPF came into the picture in the late 1980s when one of its main leaders, Zianon Pazniak, called for inquiries into the Kurapaty forest that turned to be a Soviet mass execution place. The organization also put the Chernobyl fallout and the Belarusian language question on the political agenda.

10 In Belarus, the legislature was overall weak and compliant. When reform minded Stanislau Shushkevich was, moreover, ousted from the Supreme Soviet chairmanship on claims of corruption, Kebich was in pole position for the 1994 presidential elections. Olga Belova rightly remarks that the situation in Russia, Belarus and Ukraine required a similar presidential model: 'a famous Soviet administrative manager, who had been in charge of some high offices in the Communist Party apparatus and in central executive bodies, organizes the transfer of his position of power in the next presidential institution', in O. Belova-Gille, 'The Difficulties of Elite Formation in Belarus after 1991', in E. Korosteleva, C. Lawson and R. Marsh (eds), *Contemporary Belarus: Between Democracy and Dictatorship* (London: Curzon Press, 2003): 57. This trajectory was most obvious in Belarus, since the institution of presidency was tailored to fit then Prime Minister Viacheslau Kebich.

11 See L. Verpoest, *Institutional Isomorphism in the Slavic Core of the CIS: Towards a Theoretical Framework for Institutional Change*, http://www.essex.ac.uk/ecpr/events/jointsessions/paperarchive/uppsala/ws18/Verpoest.pdf (2004).

12 W. Powell and P.J. DiMaggio, 'The Iron Cage Revisited: Institutional Isomorphism and Collective Rationality in Organizational Fields', in *American Sociological Review*, 48 (1983): 147–60.

13 There is a *Departament Evropy*, but this department focuses on bilateral relations with European Countries.

14 After the First World War, Belarus enjoyed a short period of independence. Independence was declared on 25 March 1918 (on the initiative of the Socialist Hramada in Belarus, but the state was formed under the occupation of the Central powers) and ended on 1 January 1919 when the Soviet Regime was proclaimed in Smolensk. So, independent Belarus only lasted for 9 months. After a brief period of joint Lithuanian–Belarusian Soviet regime, Belarus joined the USSR on 30 December 1922 and became the BSSR (*Belarusskaia Sovietskaia Sotsialisticheskaia Respublika* or the Belarusian Soviet Socialist Republic).

15 The fact that any grass roots organizations and NGOs in Belarus that defend a critical point of view toward the government are either swiftly closed down or constantly harassed by overly thorough tax controls or given exuberantly high fines since Lukashenka has become president illustrates that the chance for Belarusian civil society to further develop is virtually nonexistent.

16 And to a lesser extent, the West also has a geopolitical interest in keeping Ukraine outside Russia's sphere of influence.

17 For an overview of these agreements, check http://www.mid.ru/ns-rsng.nsf/sngintegr or http://www.soyuzinfo.ru/

18 RFE/RL NEWSLINE, 6, 153, Part II, 15 August 2002.

19 Mikalay Statkevich, leader of the Belarusian Social Democratic Party, as quoted by Belapan on 13 June, 2002.

20 In November 2002, just before winter, Gazprom reduced the gas supplies to Belarus because of outstanding energy bills. In November 2004, again before winter, another crisis occurred in which Gazprom even shut down Belarus' gas flow for one day. In autumn 2005, Lukashenka managed to secure a one-year contract with Gazprom in which it would provide gas at the 46.86USD price.

21 On 30 March 2006, Gazprom CEO Aleksey Miller met with Belarusian Energy Minister Aliaksandr Ageev and Dimitry Kazakov, the head of Beltranshaz, and announced that in 2007 Belarus will be charged European rates for Russian gas deliveries. In January 2007, a new gas row erupted.

22 Newsru.com, 7 September 2003.

23 A couple of months later, the head of the Belarusian National bank, Piotr Prakapovich, stressed that Putin and Lukashenka did not agree upon introduction of the single currency on 1 January 2006, and cited the above mentioned differences as the reason for it.

24 The agreements foresaw rent and tax-free use for Russia over a period of 25 years. See *Biulleten Mezhdunarodnykh Dogovorov*, November 1996: 48–55.

25 This was further elaborated in the 1998 agreement 'On the Joint Use of Military Infrastructure Objects', according to which 'the Russian and Belarusian militaries may use all kinds of installations (e.g. command and communications centres, aerodromes, air-defence facilities, bases and depots) in the two countries' border regions for training purposes or on a temporary basis.' For more information on this agreement, cfr Clelia Rontoyanni's excellent paper on 'The Union of Belarus and Russia: The Role of NATO and the EU', Paper presented at the conference 'European Security and the post-Soviet Space, Integration or Isolation', University of Aberdeen, 26–7 November 2000: 16–17.

26 The most notable were the 'West 99' joint exercises of June 1999, in which Russian and Belarusian armed forces combined a joint strategic exercise which included a possible attack from the West on their lands similar to the NATO strikes on Yugoslavia.

27 C. Rontoyanni, 'The Union of Belarus and Russia: the Role of NATO and the EU', Paper presented at the conference 'European Security and the post-Soviet Space, Integration or Isolation', University of Aberdeen, 26–7 November 2000; C. Rontoyanni, 'A Russo–Belarusian "Union State": A Defensive Response to Western Enlargement?', One Europe or Several? Working Paper, 10, 2000, http://www.one europe.ac.uk/pdf/W10Clelia.PDF

28   One can rather compare this successful aspect of integration to the Western example of NATO cooperation than to EU integration.

29   'Dogovor ob Obrazovanii Soobshchestva Rossii i Belarusi ot 2 Aprelia 1996 goda' http://www.soyuzinfo.ru/ru/juridical_library/statutory_acts

30   'Dogovor o Sozdanii Soyuznogo Gosudarstva ot 8 dekabrya 1999', statya 38–43, http://www.soyuzinfo.ru/ru/juridical_library/statutory_acts

31   Rontoyanni, *op. cit.*: 12.

32   The Union State Treaty significantly increased the powers of the Supreme State Council (the former Supreme Council); Council decisions could from then onwards issues decrees, resolutions and directives (Art. 35).

33   Rontoyanni, *op. cit.*

34   Article 18, moreover, enumerates competences not exclusive to but shared by both countries of the Union State. The most important shared competences here are the coordination of foreign and defence policy.

35   Never before had a Russian president shown Lukashenka his place in such clear terms, and the Belarusian president expressed shock, yet only half-heartedly denied Putin's reproaches: 'Lukashenka ... denied Putin's implication that the Belarusian side has proposed resurrecting "something like the Soviet Union." He admitted, however, that he advised Putin to use the experience of the USSR rather than that of the European Union in modelling the Belarusian-Russian state. "We lived together in the Russian Empire for more than a century. Subsequently, we were together in the Soviet Union. Let us use our own experience, from our history. This was the only sense of my referring to the Soviet Union in our conversation. And am I not right? Why should we reject the experience of the Soviet Union?" Lukashenka asked' (*RFE/RL NEWSLINE*, 6, 114, Part II, 19 June 2002).

36   Possible implications of this option are elaborated by Prof. K. Malfliet and G. Kurdiukov in Chapter 9.

37   Yet, the countries of the EU have similar economies, while Russia and Belarus have very different ones (alluding to Belarus's state-led economy as opposed to Russia's market economy), and these differences 'might create problems'. Putin as quoted in *Gazeta.ru*, 14 August 2002.

38   Andrey Riabov of the Carnegie Moscow Centre commented that 'Putin is using Belarus's isolated international and political situation to force Lukashenka to agree to a rigid unification model on Russia's terms. In doing so, Putin transformed himself into the driving force of integration and Lukashenka into the main dis-integrator' (Andrey Riabov quoted in *Izvestiia*, 14 August 2002).

39   Lukashenka moreover accused Putin of treating Belarus worse than Lenin or Stalin ever did, and refused to discuss the issue any further.

40   *UPI*, 26 August 2002.

41   On 16 June 2002, Union State Secretary Pavel Borodin called Belarus's latest draft proposal 'nonsense' and a 'simply foolish document', in *RFE/RL NEWSLINE*, 6, 113, Part II, 18 June 2002.

42   After the August rift, an intergovernmental commission was appointed in December 2002 which was assigned to draft a joint constitution, a process that they finalized in March 2003, but again turned out not to be acceptable to Russia, which in October of that year described the constitutional process to be in a stalemate.

43   Rontoyanni, *op. cit.*: 11.

44   Among these advantages are, for example, the cancellation of Belarusian debt to Russia in 1996, cheap energy from Russia, and the sale of Russian weaponry. Lukashenka moreover avoids adopting laws that allow Russian industrialists to privatize Belarusian enterprises, publicly remarking that 'property means power'.

45   The 2 April 1996 Agreement on the Formation of a Community (*Soobshchestvo*) of Belarus and Russia came at a time when President Yeltsin sought to use the unification process for political purpose: first, to compensate for Russia's failures during the Chechen war and, second, and more importantly, to increase his chances for re-election, which were considered minimal at that point. Unification with Belarus turned out to be convenient means to achieve his goal: the President was re-elected in June 1996. Some observers saw the hand of Yeltsin's top foreign policy advisers (such as Primakov) in the signing of the 2 April Agreement on a Union between Belarus and Russia in 1997 (A. Stanley in the *New York Times*, 3 April 1997). They saw a need to speed up integration as a symbolical political response to the Western plans for NATO's eastward expansion. Although 1998 initially saw a lull in integration efforts, the August 1998 economic crisis and the ensuing uncertainty in the Russian political climate triggered the need to take up the integration process again. Moreover, Yeltsin wanted a new Treaty before the end of his Presidency in December 1999 as his own political legacy. The Agreement on the formation of a Union State was signed on 8 December 1999.

46   Since both processes of integration are dominated by Russia, this parallel is an evident one.

47   Rontoyanni, *op. cit.*: 16.

48   *Ibid.*

49   *Ibid.*: 17.

8
Patterns of Integration and Regime Compatibility: Ukraine Between the CIS and the EU

Rilka Dragneva and Antoaneta Dimitrova

Introduction

Ukraine's history and geopolitical position seem to define its destiny of a state that needs to maintain a difficult balancing act between Russia and the West. Yet, after the Orange revolution in 2004, the possibility of European Union membership for Ukraine has emerged. While in the past Ukraine's European choice has been more of a declared, symbolic wish of the Ukrainian authorities counterweighted by the hard reality of the country's close proximity and ties with Moscow, the new impetus for democratic reforms provided by the election of President Viktor Yushchenko could potentially change the precarious balance of Ukraine's foreign relations and economic orientation. Since his election in December 2004, President Yushchenko has made numerous moves towards a rapid start of negotiations with the EU. Leaving aside how realistic such a scenario is given the EU's new cautious stance on enlargement, we anticipate that any progress towards starting enlargement negotiations would put Ukraine into a different regime, that of adopting the rules of a closely-knit multilevel system of governance, such as the EU. This change to a different type of governance has serious potential to create incompatibilities with existing regimes with Russia at the centre, in which Ukraine participates. Indeed, perceptions of incompatibility between a pro-Russian and pro-Western orientation of Ukraine in general, and its membership (or other form of enhanced cooperation) in the EU as well as in the Commonwealth of Independent States (hereinafter, 'the CIS'), in particular, have already been revealed by policy makers both in the East and in the West.

In this work, we focus on the problem of compatibility of the two regimes in which Ukraine participates as they develop. More specifically, we examine when and what kind of incompatibility is likely to arise and what its implications are. A discussion of the nature and dimensions of incompatibility is important for several reasons. First, it allows differentiation between actual, 'hard' law incompatibility and the perceptions of its existence. Second, it shows the limitations of future policy choices. Third, it highlights the requirements for adaptation, renegotiation or sequencing of measures.

Ukraine in the context of several international regimes

In addressing the main puzzle of this chapter, we conceptualize Ukraine's relations with the EU and the CIS as international regimes. Regimes are defined here following Krasner as 'principles, norms, rules, and decision making procedures around which actor expectations converge in a given issue area'.[1] We find this broad definition helpful as it specifies the elements of a regime but also stresses the importance of actors' expectations.

In this spirit, if regime incompatibility is to arise, its foundations are to be sought in two primary directions. The first relates to the institutions that make up these two regimes. We include here the system of relations structured through 'hard' or highly legalized institutions (that is, existing treaty obligations and other legal rules and disciplinary mechanisms) as well as 'soft' institutions or informal rules, norms and principles with low level of legalization (that is, political dialogue, diplomacy, meeting forums and procedures).[2] It is important to include both so as to encompass the different forms of cooperation and the intricate interplay between legal and political elements that characterize regional integration in the EU and the CIS today.

Incompatibility would be easiest to detect at the level of 'hard' law in the form of legal obstacles such as conflicting obligations, exclusivity clauses or the inability to respond to conditionality. It may entail a default in respective obligations and, hence, the activation of certain legal remedies. At the level of political practices and routines, incompatibility may not be always so explicitly revealed; similarly, there may be no clearly enforceable penalties attached to it. Yet, in the sphere of international relations 'soft' incompatibility can be equally problematic as it can lead to reputational damage and reciprocal action, and strongly affects strategic policy formulation.

Second, following from this, perceptions of incompatibility are also important as they shape the choices of actors and their understandings as to the 'rules of the game' in which they might be engaged. Perceptions of incompatibility are closely related to the familiar concepts of 'frames'. In public policy, the way key actors frame a policy has consequences for the policy options that policy makers think they have at their disposal.[3] Similarly, when elites perceive (unconsciously) or frame (consciously) Ukraine's closer integration into the CIS as incompatible with its pro-EU orientation, this will affect the country's future choices, even if no legal or economic obstacles exist. Thus, we will examine the rules making up the main part of relations between Ukraine and the EU and the CIS, but also recognize the expectations and perceptions associated with them. The latter will be derived from political discourses and will be taken as an indication of the actors expectations.

This chapter will proceed as follows. Having defined our question and the conceptual framework, the second part of the chapter will focus on the actual comparison of the institutions of the EU–Ukraine and Ukraine–CIS regimes. We are aware that it is difficult to conceive of Ukraine–CIS regime as a single, coherent relationship. Indeed, several sub-regional groupings within the CIS have been formed, which have their own dynamics. Similarly, one cannot neglect the pivotal role of Russia in the CIS and the importance of the bilateral relations established with it. Yet, the general institutional features of the CIS determine the shape of the sub-CIS regimes. Thus, we review the general CIS framework as well as one sub-regional regime; namely, the Single Economic Space (hereinafter, 'SES'), which has the potential to lead to the deeper integration of its members and, thus, create most serious incompatibility problems for Ukraine.[4]

As noted above, we examine the legal rules and organizational structures set up in pursuit of cooperation in terms of the degree of their institutionalization and mutual compatibility. In addition, we find it important to deepen the analysis of the general institutional framework in the direction of two specific areas of relations; namely, trade and legal harmonization. We choose trade as it is the key form of economic cooperation with both the EU and the CIS at present. It is also the area where traditionally economic concerns mingle with sovereignty sensitivities, directly affecting perceptions and expectations. The harmonization of legal systems also puts significant demands on domestic legal systems and is crucial in ensuring the long-term compatibility of regimes. We proceed, then, by discussing the current perceptions of Ukraine's elites suggestive of actors' expectations for the future. Last, we discuss this juxtaposition of the various regimes in the context of the most likely scenarios for Ukraine's relations with the EU and offer some conclusions.

Comparing general regime institutions

Ukraine–CIS

The CIS, the organization that succeeded the USSR, has been of key importance to Ukraine post-1991. Similarly, Ukraine has been a major force in shaping (at least, initially) the features of the institutional regime of the CIS.[5] Several general characteristics of this regime need to be mentioned here.[6]

As in other regional groupings, political dialogue and cooperation within the CIS are structured through a system of organs. Specifically for the CIS, however, the formation of these organs reflected the high sovereignty sensitivities of its member states, the rejection of the centralizing tendencies of the past, and the differing perceptions of the CIS member states as to the tasks of the organization.[7] Three main characteristics of CIS institutional rules and organizational structures should be noted. First, in comparison to other organizations such as the EU, CIS institutions were set up some time after the signing of the founding treaties, and very gradually. At the emergence of the CIS no common organs were agreed upon, except for the Councils of Heads of State and Government, defined as 'the coordinating institutions' of the Commonwealth.[8] Gradually, a number of other bodies was created; namely, a general executive, a parliamentary body and a dispute-resolution body, as Table 8.1 shows. Today, incremental innovation remains a constant feature of the institutional landscape of the CIS, but it has more often than not led to confusion and uncertainty, and lack of coherence between the operation of the different CIS organs.[9]

Second, while the CIS moved to strengthen the institutional foundations of the organization and make them a suitable vehicle for reintegration, it remained rooted in international law, avoiding any confederative or constitutionalizing solutions. This feature is revealed in the following elements of the regime:

- Inter-state cooperation is pursued through a system of multi-lateral and bilateral international agreements.[10]
- Any Council's decisions with normative content have the status of international agreements, and are adopted by consensus.
- The executive bodies set up (permanent general or specialized) have no or limited decision-making powers of their own but only implement the decisions of the Councils.[11]
- Any acts adopted by the parliamentary body (the Inter-Parliamentary Assembly) and the judicial body (the Economic Court) have the power of recommended acts.[12]

Table 8.1   Participation of Ukraine in CIS organs

Type	Institution (found)	Participation of Ukraine	Note/importance of institution
General congress	Council of Heads of State and Government (1991)	Yes	Purely intergovernmental, interested party principle
Parliamentary organ	Interparliamentary Assembly (1993)	Yes, since 1999	Recommended acts (model laws), broad inter-parliamentary cooperation
General executive	Coordination and Consultative Committee (1993)	Yes, with reservation	Ceased to exist
	Executive Committee (1999)	Yes, with 'notes'	
Specialized executive/ congress	Inter-State Economic Committee (1994)	Yes	Possibility for qualified and weighed qualified majority with regard to some questions; ceased to exist
	Economic Council (1999)	Yes, with reservation	Purely intergovernmental.
Judicial organ	Economic Court (1992)	No	Non-binding decisions

- Finally, as the CIS Charter provides, inter-state disputes are ultimately resolved through the political vehicle of the Council of Heads of State, rather than through a legal procedure.[13]

Third, the CIS is a multiple speed community in the sense that its member states do not participate equally in the above mentioned organs. Given that organs were created incrementally and on the basis of separate agreements, the member states could apply one of the founding principles of the organization (namely, the interested party principle) in shaping their participation in the CIS.[14]

Ukraine has been particularly keen to use this flexibility. After its initial reluctance to agree to any common institution, it later supported the formation of a general executive. Yet, in most cases, it signed the agreements creating permanent executives with a note of reservation in an effort to minimize as far as possible any deviation from intergovernmental principles.[15] As far as the Inter-Parliamentary Assembly is concerned, Ukraine did not sign the original 1992 agreement setting it up as a vehicle of inter-parliamentary cooperation of the member-states, neither did Ukraine sign the 1995 Convention incorporating the Assembly into the systems of organs of the CIS. It joined in 1999, as a part of a package deal with Russia. Very importantly, Ukraine does not participate in the CIS Economic Court, set up in 1992. In principle, the Court's competence with regard to particular states can be extended to states that did not sign its founding documents, if individual agreements provide that 'other disputes' between such states can be submitted to it.[16] The 1994 FTA agreement, which was signed by Ukraine, envisaged a dispute resolution sequence of measures including resort to the Economic Court. Yet, such a provision is more the exception rather than the rule,[17] and there is no evidence that Ukraine has been involved in a dispute in front of the Economic Court.[18] This confirms Ukraine's cautious stand with regard to any potentially 'hard' law disciplines within the CIS.

Given the above mentioned characteristics, the system of organs set up in the CIS has served two primary functions. The first is to represent a vehicle for a structured political dialogue. Indeed, despite the numerous trials and tribulations and crisis points within the organization, a regular political dialogue has been maintained. Moreover, it can be argued that participation in the CIS framework has been of primary political importance to former USSR states, including Ukraine. Ukraine has indeed regularly taken part in the meetings of the Council of Heads of State and Government. Further, even when it has eventually decided not to sign a certain decision or an agreement, it has frequently taken part in the process of its preparation.[19]

The key importance of the political role of the CIS, especially as far as Ukraine is concerned, is particularly well illustrated if we consider the question about its very membership in the CIS. In legal terms, 'membership' in the organization was defined in its Charter adopted in January 1993 as determined by the participation in the founding agreements of December 1991 (which Ukraine did) as well as 'assuming the obligations under the Charter' within a year of its adoption (which Ukraine did not).[20] Yet, despite this questionable in legal terms membership, Ukraine continued participating fully in summit meetings and signed a number of important agreements open only to members of the CIS.[21] Indeed, there is no doubt whether Ukraine is formally a member of the CIS or not.

The second function relates to the CIS as a medium for cooperation in specific areas of common interest through the conclusion of international agreements, subject to the interested party principle. Despite the ambitious range of areas of cooperation and the numerous agreements signed for their pursuit, the effects of those agreements have remained shallow.

To illustrate this, in the section below we examine the agreements concluded in the area of trade. At this point, it suffices to note that, as with other CIS member states, Ukraine has frequently used a number of devices to mitigate the legal effects of the commitments made in international agreements.[22] For example, reservations have been extensively used.[23] Where multilateral agreements have been concluded, the rules have been kept vague and general, leaving more precise undertakings to bilateral negotiations. The binding effect of many agreements has been further neutralized by their late ratification or lack thereof. Ultimately, the commitments undertaken have remained 'soft' as evidenced by the lack of a binding dispute resolution mechanism. Furthermore, what seems to have become the troubleshooting methodology of the CIS (namely, resolving the problems of existing agreements (or institutions) by the conclusion of even more agreements (or founding new institutions)) has created its own problems of conflict of rules, uncertainty and lack of coherence.

This brief summary of Ukraine's role in the CIS suggests that Ukraine has aimed for flexibility in its participation in the CIS institutions and agreements. Despite the intended international law form of this participation (as opposed to a constitutional or confederative one, on the one hand, or a purely political one, on the other), it rarely amounts to 'hard' legal commitments: legal effects tend to be 'softened', and ultimately no effective regional legal remedies are provided. There exists, however, a clear political, 'soft' law engagement through a structured and regular dialogue, and the (often little more than) political symbolism of participating in an international law-making process.

Ukraine–SES

The Single Economic Space is the arrangement that causes most concerns in view of the compatibility of the commitments undertaken by Ukraine and those undertaken towards the EU. These concerns stem, to start with, from the institutional structure of the SES.

In addition to the Council of Heads of State, in which states are to be represented on strict intergovernmental basis, the Agreement provides for a 'single regulating organ' (*edinyi reguliruiushchii organ*) to which participating states will delegate some competences on the basis of international agreements.[24] Further to the delegation of competences, the Agreement provides for the following principles of operation of this organ: it will decide not by consensus but by weighted (according to economic power) voting and its decisions will be obligatory for implementation in the participating states. Thus, the Agreement provides for some supranational elements in the governance of the single economic space. Importantly, however, no special dispute resolution mechanism is created apart from resorting to negotiations.[25]

It has to be noted, nonetheless, that the founding 2003 Agreement sets up a very minimal and general regime for the SES. Its provisions are more like statements of intent rather than a basis for credible legal obligations. The Concept on the Formation of the SES contains some more information on the design of the SES; it also represents an inseparable part of the Agreement, yet it is ultimately a political document in nature and style.

At this stage, it is not clear how realistic the setting up of such a system of organs is, given the CIS tradition and the diverging views of the SES members on this matter. While President Kuchma signed the 2003 Agreement without any of the reservations suggested by members of his government,[26] there has clearly been a change of attitude under the new administration.[27] Moreover, it should be remembered that one of the main principles of the SES, similar to the CIS, is 'variable-level and variable-speed integration' (*raznourovnevaia i raznoskorostnaia integratsiia*),[28] where countries determine for themselves to what extent and in what frameworks to participate. It is yet to be seen what the effects of this formula will be on institution building in the SES.

Despite the differing views on the SES institutions or its economic objectives, it is clear that the SES is another political cooperation forum, where high-level dialogue takes place on a regular basis. It has also become obvious that Ukraine will not be pulling out of it; on the contrary, there have been indications that it might play an active role in shaping its future.[29] Official statements discussed below, declaring incompatibility of the country's wish to join the EU with the SES commitments, however, make the country's stance ambiguous at the least. The question as to whether this ambiguity reflects a continuation of an ingenuous balancing act or uncoordinated foreign policy stance, may remain open for some time.

Ukraine–EU

Ukraine and the European Union's relations have come through several phases in the post-Soviet period. The most important determinants of the existing regime are the Partnership and Cooperation Agreement (PCA), the 1999 EU Common Strategy for Ukraine and the recently adopted EU Action Plan (hereinafter, 'AP').[30] Other important priority areas for cooperation for both sides are covered by the separate agreements, some of which we now discuss.

The PCA between Ukraine and the EU was signed in June 1994 and entered into force in March 1998. It constitutes the legal basis of EU–Ukraine relations and creates several bilateral organs which, as with other EU agreements with third countries (and especially the EU's Association Agreements with Central and Eastern Europe), have the potential to take a life of their own in shaping the common regime. It contains legally binding commitments with some important internal implications for both sides, but in contrast to the Association Agreements with the countries of CEE, the PCA does not, as such, constitute a step on the road to membership.[31] The formulation of the objectives of the political dialogue of the PCA (strengthening links, convergence of positions, stability and security in Europe) as well as the differences with the Association Agreements,[32] suggests that the EU saw Ukraine early on mostly as a neighbour and not as a candidate for membership.[33]

The institutions set up with the PCA create conditions for EU–Ukraine political and expert dialogue and the institutional framework that structures this dialogue. Furthermore, as other EU agreements with third countries, the PCA contains provisions aiming to encourage Ukraine's respect for democratic principles and human rights.[34] Art. 2 of the PCA defines respect for the principles of market economy also as an essential element of the EU–Ukraine partnership. Importantly, these provisions introduce EU conditionality in the bilateral relations defined by the PCA. The consensus is that the 'essential element clause' of Art. 2 of the PCA when read in combination with the suspension clause of Art. 102 ('The Bulgaria clause')[35] and the 'material breach' requirement of Art. 60 (3) (b) of the Vienna Convention on Law of Treaties, amounts to a complex suspension procedure in case of a failure to comply with democratic principles and market mechanisms.[36] Thus, violations of human rights or disrespect for the principles of market economy, would amount to a case of 'special urgency' under Art. 102, whereby the EU will be able to suspend the implementation of the PCA unilaterally.[37]

The institutional rules and organizational structures of the EU–Ukraine relationship defined by the PCA are summarized in Table 8.2.

The regular meetings of the various institutions created by the PCA create openings for the adjustment of mutual relations under the new Ukrainian administration in 2005. The ministerial level meeting between the EU troika and the Ukrainian minister Tarasyuk of March 2005, for example, discussed cooperation in the area of CFSP and the implementation of the EU–Ukraine Action Plan, but also Ukraine's EU aspirations. It is important to note, however, that unlike their Association Agreements counterpart, the Cooperation Council's decisions do not have a binding force. Thus, any advancements of the regime have to be undertaken through the conclusion of

Table 8.2 Political and expert dialogue institutions between the EU and Ukraine established with the PCA

Institutional		Participation		
Level	Function	EU	Ukraine	Frequency
Summit level Bilateral summit meetings since 1997	Provides direction	EU Presidency, Commission President, EU High Representative	President	Annually
Ministerial level cooperation Cooperation Council (1998)	Can settle disputes on interpretation of the agreement Troika meetings	Members of the Council of the EU, Members of the European Commission; Ministers	Members of the Government Ministers	Once a year and 'when circumstances require' regularly once a year
Senior civil servant level	Cooperation Committee (1998)	Council of the EU and European Commission members representatives	Representatives of the Government	Determined by the Cooperation Council
Parliamentary level, Interparliamentary Cooperation Committee (1998)[38]		Members of the European Parliament	Members of the Ukrainian Parliament	Determined by the Committee itself annually
Experts level, sub-committees		Experts		
Working group		Experts		

Sources: Joint Report on the Implementation of the Partnership and Cooperation Agreement between the EU and Ukraine; http://europa.eu.int/comm/external_relations/ukraine/intro/index.htm from 11.04.2005; http://www.ukraine-eu.mfa.gov.ua/cgi-bin/valmenu_miss.sh?1p0401.html

new agreements, rather than through the partnership institutions decision-making.[39]

On the whole, the regime between the EU and Ukraine established by the PCA is a 'soft' regime in the political sphere. There are, however, commitments in the sphere of goods, services, labour and capital movement which, in the words of the European Commission, 'introduce extensive, legally binding commitments with considerable implications for the domestic legislation of Ukraine'.[40] How binding these commitments are, however, varies between the specific provisions. The trade provisions of Title III, as will be discussed below, are fairly precise and impose clear, enforceable obligations. Other provisions, however, (for example, in the area of labour cooperation), amount to no more than 'best endeavour' clauses.[41]

Another important aspect of the PCA regime relates to its dispute resolution provisions. The PCA envisages a special dispute-resolution procedure, whereby parties submit disputes to the Cooperation Council or, in case of its failure to do so, to a number of conciliators.[42] Similarly, under Art. 102, parties are allowed to take 'appropriate measures' in case of a failure of the other party to fulfil an obligation. Such measures, except in 'special urgency' situations as discussed above, also require the notification of the Cooperation Council. The decisions of the Council or the mediator, however, have only the power of recommendations. Nonetheless, their political importance and the potential reputational damage given the broad ramifications of the European project are undoubtedly high.

The other most important determinants of the EU–Ukraine regime are the EU Common Strategy for Ukraine adopted in 1999 and the EU Action Plan, part of the European Neighbourhood Policy adopted in February 2005. The AP was developed and prepared in the period before the last elections in Ukraine and it reflects an EU desire to create a framework of relations suitable to the changed circumstances of an enlarged Union.[43] Thus, the document places the cooperation process in the new policy situation of neighbourhood and envisages a number of priorities for its strengthening. The PCA still remains the legal basis on which relations are build, yet, according to some, the AP appears to harden some of the PCA commitments.[44] It proposes a number of reforms to be undertaken by Ukraine but also offers an increase in funding from the EU for the support of these reforms.

Importantly, neither the Strategy Paper nor the AP go as far as a membership offer, yet they contain a new promise: that of new Neighbourhood Agreements to supplement the existing contractual framework, which would provide for 'new entitlements and obligations' when the current potential is exhausted.[45] The contents of the AP was approved by the EU–Ukraine Cooperation Council in December 2004, but the EU waited till the free and fair elections were held to give its final seal of approval. Ironically, at this new stage, with EU membership a policy goal for Yushchenko's presidency, the plan seemed to go less far than Ukraine wanted. The election results and the spirit of the Orange revolution prompted the European Parliament in January 2005 to urge for the revision of the framework of the European Neighbourhood Action Plan to offer a 'clear European perspective' and the consideration of 'other forms of association ... possibly leading ultimately to the country's accession to the EU'.[46] The drive of the European Parliament, however, was neutralized by the undoubtedly positive, but less committing statement of Commissioner Benita Ferrero-Waldner of February 2005 that, 'this is a plan to bring Ukraine closer to Europe, not hold it in any way at arms length'.[47] Similarly, the decision of the EU–Ukraine Cooperation Council of 21 February 2005 on initiating 'early' consultations on an 'enhanced agreement' to replace the PCA at the end of its initial ten-year period subject to certain conditions, remains within the bounds drawn in the Strategy Paper.

While the PCA and the AP are (in effect) EU instruments, the Ukrainian side has also been active in trying to determine the unwritten rules of the common regime and to shift expectations towards membership of Ukraine in the EU. This had already been achieved in the Kuchma period, by adopting the so called European Choice strategy, which declared the preparation of the country for EU membership in 2011 as Ukraine's main policy priority.[48] Kuchma's Presidential address to the Parliament (the *Verkhovna Rada*) in 2002 singled out European integration as the focal point of Ukrainian reform efforts and development in the period until 2011.

While the European choice strategy may have been formally adopted by the government and President Kuchma, the rules-in-practice and elite attitudes changed significantly in the direction of real steps towards EU membership after the 'Orange revolution' and the installation of Yushchenko as President. Already as presidential candidate and opposition leader, Viktor Yushchenko gave strong signals that he was expecting more than the current relations defined by the PCA, Common Strategy and Action Plan. In a December 2004 interview with the *Financial Times*, for example, he suggested that Ukraine was hoping for concrete steps from the EU as a response to the democratic changes in Ukraine. Furthermore, he suggested a four-point plan for integration of

Ukraine into the EU: recognition of Ukraine as a market economy, joining WTO, Associate membership of the EU and finally joining the EU.[49] Upon taking office in January 2005, Yushchenko declared that, 'Our place is in the European Union. My goal is Ukraine in a united Europe'.[50] He reiterated this goal when he addressed a parliamentary session of the European Parliament on 27 January 2005. In Strasbourg, Yushchenko even went as far as to name strategically a concrete date, 2007, for the conclusion of an Association Agreement with the EU, which as discussed above, can be seen as a precursor to EU membership. However, despite his numerous efforts to change mutual expectations through a number of statements and actions, so far the EU has been firm on its position that membership is not on the agenda yet for Ukraine.

Trade regimes

Ukraine–CIS/SES

One of the legacies of the USSR was the high level of economic interdependence between its former republics. This interdependence still holds true, despite the trade reorientation that has taken place. As Table 8.3 shows, the share of CIS trade has decreased significantly. Yet, Russia has remained a key trade partner of Ukraine, certainly the major one within the CIS, followed by Turkmenistan, Kazakhstan, Belarus and Moldova. Ukraine is particularly dependent on energy imports from these countries. It also still exports significantly to the CIS, despite the growing importance of the EU as an export partner.[51] These realities may underpin an argument that Ukraine's ties to its former USSR family would make a radical political and economic reorientation detrimental.

Table 8.3   Trade balance (exports and imports) of Ukraine in 1990–2003 (per cent)

	1990	1993	1996	1999	2003
Exports	100	100	100	100	100
RF	54.6	34.8	38.7	20.4	18.7
Rest of CIS	26.6	11.5	12.7	7.3	7.5
EU	5.6	6.4	11.1	20.5	19.8
Baltics	1.7	1.1	1.8	1.5	3.8
Imports	100	100	100	100	100
RF	58.0	45.1	50.1	48.0	37.6
Rest of CIS	20.3	19.0	13.4	9.8	12.4
EU	5.3	8.2	15.4	23.1	25.2
Baltics	2.3	2.1	1.6	1.6	1.1

Source: World Bank Trade Policy Study, November 2004.

The trade regime of Ukraine with the rest of the CIS is structured through a complex web of overlapping international agreements:

- Bilateral free-trade agreements (hereinafter, 'FTA') with all other CIS countries, supplemented by annual protocols on exemptions.[52]
- CIS-wide multilateral agreements on free trade[53] as well as selected trade related issues, such as customs procedures, transit, rules of origin and standards (see Table 8.4).
- Bilateral agreements on selected trade related issues, such as transit, customs cooperation and indirect taxation.

Table 8.4 Ukraine's participation in CIS multilateral agreements related to FT

CIS Multilateral FTA regime	Ukraine's position	Note
FTA Agreement 1994	Signed and ratified	Not ratified by RU among others
FTA Protocol 1999	Signed and ratified	Not ratified by RU
On the Re-export of Goods 1994	Not ratified	
On Cooperation in Customs Affairs 1994	Signed and ratified	
On the Payment Union 1994	Not signed	
On the Foundations of Customs Legislation 1995	Not ratified	
On the Formation of a Common Transport Space 1997	Signed and ratified	Not ratified by RU
On Indirect Taxation 1998	Not signed	Not ratified by RU among others
On Rules of Transit 1999	Signed and ratified	
On the Procedure for Customs Treatment and Customs Control of Goods 1999	Signed and ratified	
On Technical Barriers 2000	Not signed	Not ratified by RU among others
On Rules of Origin 2000	Signed and ratified	

Sources: Own compilation on the basis of *Garant* database and the *Rada* website.

Pursuant to these agreements, Ukraine operates a free-trade regime with the CIS, covering a large number of commodities. Ukraine has negotiated exemptions with regard to a number of 'sensitive' goods, primarily agricultural commodities.[54] Such 'exempted' products are traded subject to tariffs and quotas on a most-favoured nation (hereinafter, 'MFN') basis.

We would also mention here a few of the other important elements of the trade regime. First, according to the FTAs, countries can apply unilateral contingent protection measures (imposing temporary import or export quotas, or anti-dumping or safeguard measures). The agreements and domestic legislation provide for certain conditions under which such measures can be applied, which increasingly comply with WTO requirements. Yet, as observers note, the application of such measures is ultimately unilateral and there are no means of solving potential disputes other than diplomacy and the adoption of reciprocal measures.[55] Indeed, many examples can be given of the imposition of such measures in the relations between Russia and Ukraine, especially after 1999. The exemptions and the possibility for trade protection measures result in uncertainty and 'trade wars'. It has been argued that they affect only a limited number of products and amount to minor losses. Yet, such measures clearly have a high symbolic effect. Indeed, the Ukrainian government has declared that their goal in the SES still remains free trade with no exemptions.[56]

Second, the free trade provisions are supplemented by provisions on free transit. This is a particularly sensitive issue for exporting nations (such as Russia) and transit nations (such as Ukraine) particularly in the area of energy. Yet, despite the large number of agreements (multi- and bilateral, general FTAs and specific ones) concluded since the early days of the CIS, *de facto* free transit has not been achieved. There is abundant evidence that Ukraine, for example, continues restricting transit and/or applying discriminatory treatment with regard to its neighbours.[57]

Third, despite the substantial removal of trade barriers, trade itself has been plagued by many administrative and other non-tariff barriers. A number of measures have been undertaken to improve customs cooperation and harmonize customs forms and procedures. Yet, these agreements have not made a significant difference to traders so far.

Finally, the FTAs also contain a standard clause whereby their provisions do not preclude participation in other organizations or agreements, which do not contradict the objectives and terms of the FTAs.[58]

Even this brief review, however, shows that despite the willingness of the CIS to enter into (legally binding) free-trade arrangements, the regime rules remain insufficiently effective. To mention but a few of the problems, legal rules in the various agreements fall short of a coherent regime; unilateral measures are applied with no resort to a binding regional dispute resolution mechanism; and compliance with the obligations undertaken remains low. Thus, the CIS FTAs lag behind the institutional robustness of other FTA regimes.

It is important also to consider the question about the possible development of the FTA regime into a more advanced form of economic integration. Within the CIS, free trade was initially conceived as a first stage in the progressive achievement of an economic union.[59] By 1999, however, despite the occasional contradictory messages, it became accepted that free trade as such is what the CIS as a whole can strive for, leaving more advanced forms of integration to smaller sub-regional formations, such as the SES.

The SES's founding documents referred to the creation of an economic union as its objective. There are number of factors, however, that throw doubt on the achievement of this goal. As developments have already shown, the countries participating in SES have differing views on the level of economic integration they are willing to pursue with it. Ukraine has most recently shown that its primary interest within the SES is free trade without exemptions, as mentioned above.[60] Furthermore, the experience of the CIS and the groupings within it over the last decade does not lend any extra confidence in the success of this initiative in the short- or medium-term.[61] For the time being, there are few signs that Ukraine will be prepared to engage in any specific measures in pursuit of advanced forms of integration beyond those amounting to general statements.

Ukraine–EU

In terms of volumes of trade, post enlargement, the EU became the largest foreign trade partner of Ukraine, with the EU share of foreign trade reaching, according to different estimates, between 33 and 35 per cent of Ukraine's total trade in 2004 (see also Table 8.3). If we consider the determinants of the common regime to be driven by domestic economic interests, this can be interpreted an important sign of shifting Ukrainian priorities.

The trade relations between the EU and Ukraine are governed by Title III of the PCA and a number of specific sectoral agreements.[62] The relations have been given a boost and prioritized more specifically with the adoption of the Ukraine–EU Action Plan of 2004.[63]

In essence, the regime set up provides for a MFN treatment of products within the framework of GATT. The PCA excludes only textiles,[64] steel,[65] and nuclear materials,[66] which have been regulated separately. It is important to note that the PCA builds on the generalized system of preferences (GSP) of the EU which was extended to Ukraine in 1993, whereby certain products are granted preferential treatment (that is, lower duties than the MFN duties), subject to the fulfilment of a number of conditions. In this sense, the PCA arguably does not grant any new advantages, except for the certainty of the MFN access to non-exempted commodities.[67]

Several other elements of the trade regime need to be mentioned here. First, the regime allows for the imposition of special protection measures. Indeed, such measures have been used extensively both by the EU and Ukraine. Importantly, it was in October 2000 that the EU Council of Ministers granted Ukraine the status of an economy in transition. This means that Ukrainian companies are given the opportunity to show in anti-dumping proceedings that they operate under market economy conditions with the effect of receiving the more beneficial 'market economy' treatment. Despite this positive step, however, there still remains a great deal of uncertainty in anti-dumping proceedings with the burden of proof (and cost) placed on Ukrainian businesses. The intensification of relations in the post-Presidential election period, however, suggests that the granting of a 'market economy' status is not far off.[68]

Second, the PCA contains provisions in relation to free transit of goods. As is the case with Russia, free transit through Ukraine is of great significance to the EU.

Third, the PCA regime makes an allowance for any free-trade or customs union arrangements (including such on free transit) made by Ukraine with its CIS partners.[69] Indeed, regional cooperation within the CIS has been one of the important premises of the PCA framework.

Fourth, the PCA contains an evolutionary clause for the establishment of a FTA subject to the advancement of economic reform in Ukraine and the development of the PCA trade regime.[70] This clause does not introduce a hard obligation, yet it is indicative in terms of the long-term intentions of the parties. Currently, an important element of the Action Plan is the revision of the feasibility study on the establishment of a FTA with the intention of starting negotiations upon Ukraine's accession to the WTO.[71]

Finally, as mentioned above, the EU–Ukraine trade regime is grounded within the GATT/WTO framework. Indeed, the support for Ukraine's WTO accession has been an important aspect of the bilateral relations with the EU: Ukraine and EU completed their market access negotiations in 2003, and the EU is assisting in the multilateral working group negotiations on the incorporation of the WTO legal regime. The implications of the WTO accession for the EU–Ukraine bilateral relations are expected to be quite significant. The speeding up of the prospective formation of the FTA is one example; another relates to the changes the EU will need to effect in order to annul or replace some of its non-WTO compliant trade barriers (that is, import quotas on steel) with less harmful ones.

Legal harmonization

Ukraine–CIS

It can be argued that harmonization was attributed a particularly important role within the CIS – in the context of regional integration and as an aid to domestic legal reform in the transition to a market economy.[72] Similarly, for some, it had the important symbolic role of preserving aspects of the common legal space inherited from the USSR.

In view of sensitivities to the centralizing tendencies of the past, however, the primary mechanism used has been voluntary harmonization through the medium of model legislation adopted by the CIS Inter-Parliamentary Assembly. We take the example of one of the most important documents passed within this framework, the CIS Model Civil Code.[73] Civil Codes in Eastern Europe have often been termed 'the economic constitution' of a country. The Model Civil Code, in particular, has been one of the successes of harmonization within the CIS, used as a drafting source in most CIS countries. As mentioned above, Ukraine did not become a member of the IPA until 1999. It did, however, participate in the drafting process of the Model Civil Code and other model legislation.[74] Yet, while undoubtedly taking into account the solutions of the Model Civil Code, the drafters of the Ukrainian Civil Code adopted in 2003 made a number of departures from it. Some of these departures were connected to the specificity of legal reform in Ukraine (for example, the Economic versus Civil Code debate), learning from experience of the other CIS states, but also the conscious attempt to incorporate more closely some of the provisions of European (EC as well as domestic) legislation.[75]

In terms of 'hard' law instruments for harmonization, the experience of the CIS has not been very successful.[76] A number of international agreements have been signed in relation to economic integration, as noted above. Yet, given the general problems of cooperation through international agreements in the CIS, it is difficult to gauge their effect. In addition, the analysis above and the summary in Table 8.4 indicate that Ukraine has been selective when incorporating substantive law agreements into its domestic legal order.[77]

Ukraine–EU

Approximation of Ukrainian legislation to the EU is among the main priorities and determinant features of the PCA regime. Art. 51 contains a list of areas which are to be included in the approximation process; such as, customs law, company law, competition, intellectual property and consumer protection. As formulated, the article provides for a voluntary endeavour on the part of Ukraine to make its legislation compatible with that of the EU. Thus, it remains short of taking a 'hard' obligation for harmonization or adoption of the *acquis*, requirements that would come up should Ukraine become a candidate for membership.

The Ukrainian authorities, however, have clearly recognized the importance of legislative approximation and have been supported by technical assistance facilities set up by the EU. Indeed, several initiatives have been undertaken since 1998 and have gradually intensified with the growing involvement of all state institutions with an input in law-making.[78] These initiatives have been focused and prioritized within the framework of the 2005 Action Plan. Thus, a process has been set in motion which already has contributed to legislative harmonization in a number of key areas of legislation. This development suggests that Ukraine may be coming closer to the EU's regulatory system, thus increasingly diverging from what was the common legal heritage of the USSR and from its current CIS partners.

From 'hard' and 'soft' rules toward perceptions of incompatibility

As discussed earlier, regimes can be seen to include not only 'soft' and 'hard' rules but also elites' perceptions which shape mutual expectations. In terms of perceptions of Ukrainian elites regarding the compatibility of its regime memberships, the picture is more complicated than in the case of 'hard' and 'soft' rules. There is some evidence that the views of important actors are changing on issues of incompatibility. In the first place, Russia's government. Led by president Putin, the Russian administration has, in the last decade or so, been reframing Russia's foreign policy position towards something that can be called a 'return to the great Russia' model. As part of this process, Russia has made material and symbolic claims to regaining its influence in the CIS and the so-called 'near abroad'. In terms of relations with Ukraine, this has been most evident in Putin's support for Viktor Yanukovich, the failed pro-Russian presidential candidate during the last Presidential elections. The elections in December 2004 and the loss by the Moscow supported candidate Yanukovich have been regarded by analysts as one of Putin's most important foreign policy failures. His attitude to the strong pro-Western aspirations of Ukraine remains, as a result, ambivalent. We can expect this ambivalence to continue for some time and, as Brzezinski has argued, to be a litmus test for Russia's future course of development.[79]

More importantly for Ukraine, the perceptions and expectations of its current leaders play an important role in deciding its future course. An examination of Ukraine's post-Soviet history shows that, Ukrainian leaders have tried to balance their country's position between Russia and Europe to match the country's geographical position and its regional and social diversity. Kuchma's administration developed the policy doctrine of Russia's European choice as a way to get closer to the European Union, while Yushchenko made a symbolic visit to Putin at the start of his presidency to signal the importance of Russia. These actions indicate that Ukrainian leaders are well aware of the precariousness of the balancing act between Russia and the EU, the only policy that can ensure Ukraine's current economic growth and future prospects. But recently, some indications of change have become apparent.

It is quite clear that, under President Kuchma, Ukraine's balancing act was tipping in the direction of Russia and President Yushchenko's preferences lean in the direction of the EU. In this context, some members of the new administration have declared that they will be revising plans for closer cooperation with Russia. In February 2005, Ukraine's new Justice Minister Zvarich was quoted as saying that the country was reconsidering plans to join the SES. 'It won't do to flip back and forth between the West and East – that's nonsense', he added.[80]

On the EU side, the statement of EU Commissioner Verheugen, where he warned that a Customs Union with the EU would not be compatible with the foreseen obligations under the SES indicates an increasing perception of incompatibility.[81] This indication of potential incompatibility of participation in the two regimes suggests the limitations to the country's future choices, which will be discussed in the last part of this chapter.

From current compatibility to future incompatibility?

Our examination of the development of the regimes between Ukraine and the EU, and Ukraine and the CIS/SES until now, as well as their potential as revealed so far, are summarized in Table 8.5.

Based on this picture, a number of conclusions can be drawn about the current and future compatibility of Ukraine–EU and Ukraine–CIS regimes.

Table 8.5 Current and potential stages of development of Ukraine–EU and Ukraine–CIS regimes

	Ukraine–EU	Ukraine–CIS/SES
General framework		
Current	• Partnership (PCA) • Neighbourhood (AP plus)	• Flexible, 'soft' membership
Potential	• Enhanced agreement • EU membership	• Strengthened institutions • Confederative regime (SES)
Trade provisions		
Current	• MFN (PCA plus)	• Weak FTA
Potential	• MFN (WTO regime) • FTA • Customs Union plus	• Strengthened FTA • Customs Union plus (SES)

No current 'hard' incompatibility

To start with, the analysis reveals few current incompatibilities. As we have shown briefly above, the EU and Ukraine especially took care to recognize and encourage Ukraine's cooperation with former USSR states in the PCA. At the same time, Ukraine has maintained a position within the CIS that allows it a great deal of flexibility in its participation. Similarly, despite the SES ambitious goals, its institutional set up allows for a multi-speed participation, and is at this stage too general to lead to enforceable commitments or ceding of sovereignty. Thus, no 'hard' law problems are presented by coexistence of the general institutions for cooperation and political dialogue within these frameworks.

The review of trade arrangements shows that in legal terms the PCA MFN regime is also compatible with the FTA arrangements within the CIS. Currently, the arrangements within the SES do not pose a problem either, having as their focus the creation of a FTA.

Furthermore, we argue that legal incompatibilities are unlikely to arise in the short term either, leaving Ukraine the opportunity to continue its balancing policy. Both regimes reveal an institutional flexibility which allows for adjustments. For example, the decisions of the EU–Ukraine Cooperation Council are not binding, nor is the outcome of any dispute resolution. The short-term economic goals of the two regimes are not conflicting either. Neither a WTO accession of Ukraine nor a free-trade area with the EU will create 'hard' incompatibilities with the participation of

Ukraine in CIS economic arrangements, even if they develop in a most optimistic fashion.

In the area of legal harmonization, despite the common USSR legal heritage and the participation in the CIS model law process, Ukraine has made efforts to progressively align its legislation with that of the EU. Some may argue that, in doing so, Ukraine has steered too far from its CIS partners. It is with harmonization of regulatory regimes that the most serious incompatibilities may arise. Yet, we believe potential incompatibilities at this stage are mitigated by a number of factors, which stem from international processes of diffusion of norms between different regimes. Among these very important factors, we can list the adoption of best practices, the CIS region's adjustment to the EU as a large trading bloc and the worldwide influence of the WTO.

First, taking the example of the adoption of the CIS Civil Codes, ultimately all Codes rely on common legal sources; namely, the domestic codes of the West European countries and other 'best practice' modern legislative acts.[82]

Second, Ukraine is not the only CIS country participating in a partnership regime with the EU. While the degree to which voluntary harmonization is taken seriously differs from a country to country, it can be argued that the PCAs with other CIS states, such as Russia, create similar pressures for convergence. Most importantly, Russia has been going through a somewhat parallel process of intensified relationships with the EU through the framework of the 'common spaces'.

Finally, all CIS countries (except Turkmenistan) have applied for a WTO membership. Despite the differences in their accession progress, the process contributes to the incorporation of a common set of legal rules related primarily to trade liberalization, but also reaching further.

Future incompatibility

The situation described above changes, however, if Ukraine makes a step in the direction of becoming an EU member or even adopting a large part of the EU *acquis* in preparation for membership and accession negotiations. Even before membership, complications may arise related to the still unclear idea concerning a new 'enhanced agreement' to substitute the PCA. Incompatibility may be expected given that the current Action Plan seeks a 'closer integration into the EU's Single Market'. At the same time, similar incompatibility effects may be caused by Ukraine moving in the direction of the formation of a customs union within the Single Economic Space. Not only political statements, but also the logic of customs union itself suggests that being a member of two customs unions would be impossible. When a customs union is created, by definition, it entails the adoption of a common external customs tariff and the close coordination of foreign economic policy. Furthermore, countries cede sovereignty to a common institution, charged with commercial relations with third countries. Thus, provided Ukraine enters into a customs union with its SES partners (or another CIS constellation), it will be the customs union states and institutions, not Ukraine, that will have to renegotiate current (or pending) FTA arrangements with the EU, and vice versa, in the case of membership into the EU.[83] Given the complex political landscape and economic interdependence, however, such a renegotiation would not be an easy feat.[84] Furthermore, a World Bank study suggests that entering into a customs union within the SES has the potential to lead to real adverse effects for Ukraine if Russia uses its superior bargaining power in imposing its tariff structure as the SES common external tariff.[85] Thus, participation in both an EU and a SES customs union, and even the credible preparation for such participation, will not be possible.

Last, but not least, being a candidate for EU membership, as we have witnessed in the cases of new member states from CEE, requires tremendous internal transformations. Sooner or later, in the course of this transformation, perceived incompatibilities with membership in the CIS, closer ties with Russia and joining the SES will grow. This transformation requires real reforms and domestic adjustments, among which is a whole array of difficult measures; such as reforming the administration, limiting the role of the state, regulating state aids and many more. These reforms will be the real test of Yushchenko's ability to deliver on his membership promise.

Importance of 'slow' and 'fast' scenarios

Our expectations of incompatibility come into focus when looking at two scenarios for the EU–Ukraine relations – those of a slow and a fast accession. We argue that, not only has Ukraine's wish to join the EU sooner rather than later created a dilemma for the European Union, but it can also present some difficulties for Ukraine. Even if the EU manages to overcome its present Euroscepticism and open the prospects for enlargement in the longer term, enlargement governance,[86] as it has evolved in the last enlargement, requires extensive efforts in reform from both elites and the public against the promise of future membership. This is a long process, in which elites use their political capital to make changes in the expectation that joining the EU will bring more benefits (material and immaterial in terms of reputation) in the future than the costs incurred at present. This process is sustainable only with relatively secure membership prospects and few other alternatives. When it stretches over a longer period, it is possible that the well known decline in public support for membership, which occurs as a reaction against the loss of sovereignty and the costs of adjustment, could combine with pre-existing pro-Russian attitudes to make the task of elites in Ukraine near impossible. This expectation is supported by several sources, from opinion polls to elites' statements. First, evidence from a 2000 survey conducted by White, McAllister and Light,[87] suggests that even though 35 per cent of those surveyed in Ukraine had fairly positive impressions of the EU and 25 per cent were strongly in favour of joining (with 36 per cent somewhat in favour),[88] focus group respondents had some reservations. In particular, Ukrainian students expressed concerns about the implications of changes in tax policy, budgetary requirements and other external 'conditions' for the country's independence.[89] Even though students have been one of the main driving forces of the Orange revolution in Ukraine and have sought the EU option as an alternative to the country's former direction of support for Russia and limited reforms, they and others are likely to balk at the EU's extensive requirements for adjustment if the prospect of membership is delayed ten years and more. This is confirmed by statements from 2005 in which Ukrainian politicians have expressed to their European Parliament colleagues their belief that the lack of a clear prospect of EU membership reduces the effects of the EU Action Plan. Thus, according to this scenario, long and laborious adjustment to the EU demands would make the domestic balancing act unsustainable and incompatibilities would come to the fore.

Given the considerations above, rapid enlargement seems more beneficial to Ukraine. The reason for this is that the costs of adjustment to the EU, not only in terms of trade but in all areas affected by the *acquis* harmonization, would be balanced by the benefits of joining, material and symbolic. However, this scenario seems unlikely in the current post-enlargement, post-constitutional referenda climate inside the EU.

Rapid enlargement, even though beneficial for reforms domestically, would bring incompatibility with Russia in the form of an EU Customs Union, which would set new barriers for Russian goods. A number of agreements with Russia may have to be renegotiated, as this as been the case with the Baltic states, and Russia may find itself unwillingly negotiating with the whole European Union to settle relations with Ukraine. Even if this scenario is not very likely to materialize, it highlights the potential problems if Ukraine were to succeed quickly in its bid for EU membership.

Conclusion

The analysis in this chapter shows that at present there are few real incompatibilities between Ukraine's legal obligations, institutional arrangements and 'soft' rules in the context of the two regimes discussed here. Obligations under the CIS remain 'soft' and Ukraine remains able to pick and choose the institutions it participates in. Obligations under the PCA with the EU take into account CIS obligations, so no real incompatibilities exist there.

In terms of both regimes, however, Ukraine is in a kind of halfway house in more ways than one. Both the SES and the EU application lead to customs union arrangements which, as discussed above, are incompatible. A second way to look at this is to note the incompatibilities in perceptions and statements of members of the Yushchenko (and before that the Yushchenko–Timoshenko) administration. The administration is in a halfway house in terms of coordinating its message as to its intentions for deepening participation in one or other regime.

Furthermore, there are a number of developments that suggest potential changes to the middle of the road position Ukraine has held so far. The presence of the European Union as Ukraine's new neighbour and biggest trade partner is one. The Orange revolution of December 2004, with its drive not only to remove the previous corrupt leadership and hold free and fair elections, but also to join the West, the European Union, is another. Post-Orange revolution, the wish to join the EU has been reframed by President Yushchenko as Ukraine's civilizational choice. This gives Ukraine's bid to accede to the EU a new dimension, that of domestic mobilization for modernization and Europeanization, and may lead to changes that go beyond the mixed foreign policy messages which have maintained Ukraine's balancing act so far.

Notes

1 S.D. Krasner, 'Structural Causes and Regime Consequences: Regimes as Intervening Variables', *International Organization*, 36 (2) (1982): 185.
2 We use the terms 'hard' and 'soft', 'legal' and 'political' as interpreted in the literature on legalization of international relations, see K. Abbott *et al.*, 'The Concept of Legalization', *International Organization*, 3 (2000): 401–19.
3 D. Schoen and M. Rein, *Frame Reflection* (New York: Basic Books, 1994).
4 Other sub-regional regimes that need to be mentioned are: (1) GUUAM formed in October 1997 between Ukraine, Uzbekistan, Azerbaijan and Moldova. The GUUAM member states signed a free trade agreement in July 2002; (2) the Euro-Asian Community formed in October 2000 on the basis of earlier agreements between Russia, Belarus, Kazakhstan, Kyrgyzstan and

Tajikistan. Ukraine acquired an observer status to the organization and even briefly entertained the possibility of joining the Euro–Asian Community.

5   Indeed, it has been argued that the CIS emerged because it was the only post-USSR framework within which Ukraine (having rejected the draft Union Treaty) was prepared to participate. Russia, in particular, which was otherwise prepared to sign the Union Treaty, was reluctant to create a post-USSR formation without Ukraine. For more, see F. Feldbrugge, 'The CIS: Legal and Political Re-Integration of Eastern Europe', in W.J.M van Genugten *et al.* (eds); *Realism and Moralism in International Relations* (Den Haag: Martinus Nijhoff, 1999; R. Solchanyk, 'Ukraine: A Year of Transition', in V. Tolz and I. Elliot (eds), *The Demise of the USSR* (London: Macmillan, 1995) E. Walker, *Dissolution* (Oxford: Rowman & Littlefield, 2003).

6   For more, see K. Malfliet, 'The Commonwealth of Independent States: Towards Supranationalism?', in F. Feldbrugge (ed.), *Law in Transition* (Den Haag: Martinus Nijhoff, 2002); R. Dragneva, 'Is "Soft" Beautiful? Another Perspective on Law, Institutions, and Integration in the CIS', *RCEEL*, 3 (2004): 279–324.

7   For some ('the minimalists'), the CIS was only the 'executor' of the will of the USSR; for others ('the maximalists'), it has important tasks in fostering the reintegration of the post-Soviet space. The distinction is not necessarily a neat one, however: for example, while some countries (that is, Georgia and Kazakhstan) remained fairly consistent in their stance, others changed their position over time (that is, Ukraine and Moldova).

8   Art. 7 of the Minsk Agreement of 8 December 1991, Agreement on the Coordinating Institutions of the CIS of 21 December 1991. Indeed, on account of this as well as other aspects of the CIS initially, there was a great deal of uncertainty as to the legal nature of the new formation (a regional international organization, a confederation or an amorphous organization), see V. Pustogartov, 'Mezhdunarodno-pravovoi Status SNG', *Gosudarstvo I Pravo*, 2 (1993): 27–36; V. Fisenko and I. Fisenko, 'Khartiia sotrudnichestva v ramkakh SNG', *Moskovskii zhurnal mezhdunarodnogo prava*, 3 (1993): 36–62.

9   This is particularly true with regard to the so-called 'branch coordination' organs of the CIS, which we leave out of the scope of this review.

10   Art. 5 of the CIS Charter.

11   An exception represented the Inter-State Economic Committee which was set up in 1994, see Table 8.1.

12   For more, see R. Dragneva, *op.cit.*, note 6.

13   Arts 10, 17 and 18 of the Charter. For more on the relations between these provisions and the mandate of the Economic Court, see M. Kleandrov, 'Economicheskii Sud SNG: Chto eto takoe?', *Khoziaistvo i pravo*, 7 (1993): 60–9.

14   The principle was inherited from the CMEA framework and provided that a member state can choose not to participate in a decision or an agreement in which it is not interested. Art. 3 of the Temporary Agreement of 30 December 1991, incorporated later in Art. 23 of the CIS Charter.

15   See, for example, Decision on the Coordination Consultative Committee of 14 May 1993, Decision on the Executive Secretariat of the CIS of 14 May 1993, Protocol Approving the Statute of the Executive Committee of the CIS of 21 June 2000. The only document in this category, which was signed without a note or reservation was the Agreement setting up the Inter-State

Economic Committee of April 1994. This is a significant exception given that important departures from the principle of intergovernmentalism were allowed in this agreement.

16   Art. 3 of the Statute of the Economic Court, Art. 32 of the CIS Charter. For more, R. Dragneva, *op. cit.*

17   Furthermore, it was amended in the 1999 Protocol on the FTA to exclude a specific mention of the Economic Court. Some other agreements provide for a choice between the Economic Court and 'other competent international judicial bodies'; for example, the 1999 Agreement on the Procedure for Customs Treatment and Customs Control (signed by Ukraine) and the 2000 Agreement on the Technical Barriers in the FTA (not signed by Ukraine).

18   Some rulings of the Economic Court, nonetheless, mention agreements concluded by Ukraine; for example, 1996 Advisory Opinion on the use of reservations.

19   One clear example is the adoption of the CIS Charter in January 1993: Ukraine participated in the process of its negotiation, it shaped the draft which was eventually adopted by the other member states, yet it decided not to sign it.

20   Art. 7 of the CIS Charter. For more on the issue of membership, see V. Fisenko and I. Fisenko, *op.cit.*, note 8.

21   The perceptions on the issue were perhaps best expressed by the then President of Ukraine Leonid Kravchuk at the press conference after the signing of the 1993 Charter: 'The States, both those who signed and those who did not, are not burdened by any kind of consequences; that is, the CIS works and we all are members of the CIS, actively participating in its improvement. This is very important, I would like you to pay attention to this, because many thought that those who did not sign are already outside the CIS and in such a way are not affected by any political, economic or other factors', *Diplomaticheskii Vestnik*, 3–4 (1993): 42, authors' translation.

22   For more, see R. Dragneva, *op. cit.*

23   For example, one telling example is Ukraine's reservation to Art. 22 Para. 2 of the Decision to approve the draft 1994 FTA ('Reservations to this agreement are not allowed'), which states 'Except for Paragraph 2 Article 22'.

24   Art. 4 of the SES Agreement.

25   Art. 7 of the SES Agreement.

26   As reported by T. Silina, 'The SES Choice', *Zerkalo Nedeli*, 20–26 September 2003, www.mirror-weekly.com/ie/print/42213

27   See Yushchenko's statement reported on 31 May 2005, 'Yushchenko: Sozdanie nadnatsional'nykh organov v ramkakh EEP prezhdevremenno', www.newsukraina.ru/news.html?nws_id+402535

28   Art. 5 of the 2003 Agreement.

29   See Timoshenko's statements reported on 16 April 2005, 'Timoshenko: Ukraina Stala Liderom v formirovanii kontseptsii EEP', www.rian.ru; that of the Ukrainian Economy Minister S. Terekhin, reported on 8 April 2005, 'Terehin: Ukraina namerena razshiriat' stepen' integratsii v EEP', www.rian.ru; or the adoption of a decree by Yushchenko of 16 June 2005 on 'Urgent Measures for Activisation of Ukraine's Participation in the Formation of SES'.

30   A number of other documents preceded the 1999 Strategy Paper; namely, the Common Position of the EU (1994) and the Action Plan for Ukraine (1996),

which we leave out as they do not introduce key advancements to the PCA regime.

31 Neither did the Association Agreements, in strictly legal terms, but, they were, to a greater extent, created with the expectation they would prepare the CEE candidates for membership.

32 For more on the differences with the Association Agreements, see C. Hillion, *The Evolving System of the EU External Relations as Evidenced in the EU Partnerships with Russia and Ukraine* (Leiden, 2005).

33 PCA Title II, Art. 6.

34 PCA, Art. 2.

35 First introduced in the EU's Association Agreement with Bulgaria.

36 The PCA also incorporates a Declaration concerning Art. 102, which clarifies 'special urgency' as meaning cases of 'material breach' (that is, 'violation of a provision essential to the accomplishment of the object or the purpose of the treaty') under the 1969 Vienna Convention. For more, see P. Eekhout, *External Relations of the EU. Legal and Constitutional Foundations* (Oxford: Oxford University Press, 2004); C. Hillion, *op.cit.*, note 32.

37 It is another question, however, who and under what criteria would activate this clause, making it a very ambiguous and complex process certainly on side of the EU, see C. Hillion, *op. cit.*

38 Report on the Implementation of the Partnership and Cooperation Agreement between the EU and Ukraine (2002) – according to the report the committee had met 5 times until 2002 since the entry into force of the PCA, therefore it should be considered as functioning since 1998: 7.

39 See C. Hillion, *op. cit.*

40 European Commission, at http://europa.eu.int/comm/external_relations/ukraine/intro/index.htm#pol

41 An example is the provision of Art. 24 PCA: 'the Community ... shall endeavour to ensure that the treatment accorded to Ukrainian nationals ... shall be free from any discrimination'.

42 Art. 96, PCA.

43 And a Union in which the last enlargement still needs to be absorbed by the public and enthusiasm for a next enlargement is completely lacking at present.

44 Hillion, *op. cit.*, at 219.

45 http://europa.eu.int/eur-lex/en/com/cnc/2003/com2003_0104en01.pdf, at 17. For a brief discussion of the possible nature of such an agreement, see Hillion, *op. cit.*, at 220.

46 See European Parliament Resolution on the results of Ukraine elections of 13 January 2005, P6_TA(2005)0009, particularly items 14 and 16.

47 Commissioner Ferrero-Waldner in *Zerkalo nedeli*, 19 February 2005.

48 Evropeiiskii Vybor, 'Kontseptualnyuie osnovyi strategii ikonomocheskogo i sotsyyalnogo razvitia Ukrainyi na 2002–2011 godyi'.

49 Cited by *Euroactiv*, 13 December 2004, at www.euroactiv.com, consulted 17 January 2005.

50 At www2. europarl.eu.int, consulted 26 January 2005.

51 This will be even more so in view of the latest enlargement including the Baltic states. As of the entry into the EU, Ukraine and Latvia, Lithuania and Estonia do not operate a free-trade regime anymore, yet it is expected that trade links will be preserved.

52 Belarus (1992), Russia (1993), Armenia (1994), Turkmenistan (1994), Uzbekistan (1994), Kazakhstan (1994), Azerbaijan (1995), Kyrgyz Republic (1995), Georgia (1995), Tajikistan (2001), Moldova (1995, 2003).

53 Ukraine signed both the 1994 FTA and the 1999 Protocol amending it. Despite the fact that the agreements have entered into legal force (determined by the fact that they have been signed by at least three countries), *de facto* the regime they set up has been blocked by Russia's lack of ratification of these agreements.

54 Most specifically, with Belarus, Georgia, Kazakhstan, Moldova, Russia and Uzbekistan.

55 World Bank Ukraine Trade Policy Study 2004. As mentioned above, the multilateral FTAs contained some reference to a dispute resolution procedure, including a resort to the Economic Court. The bilateral FT agreements, however, refer only to settling disputes through negotiations. Entry into WTO will mean applying the WTO disciplining mechanism in this respect.

56 For example, see www.rian.ru, 8 April 2005.

57 World Bank, *op.cit.*, note 55.

58 For example, Art. 13 Ukraine–Russia FTA, Art. 20 of the 1994 FTA. The only duty imposed to the country which enters another preferential or integration agreement, then, is to notify its partners of the terms of its participation.

59 See the 1993 Treaty on the Economic Union. Ukraine took part in the negotiations on the Treaty, yet it chose to remain an associated (rather than a full) member of the Union. The (legal and political) meaning and relevance of this 'associated' membership is difficult to judge given that the 1994 Agreement of Ukraine's joining as an associated member never entered into force and that the whole Economic Union project was compromised arguably as early as 1994. At the same time, as mentioned above, Ukraine signed the 1994 FTA which referred to an FTA as a first step to achieving a customs union.

60 As reports show, currently, Ukraine is even reluctant to include transit in the SES as going beyond the FT essentials www.rian.ru

61 For example, ten years after its formation the customs union between Russia and Kazakhstan, now within the framework of the Eurasian Community, is still a long way off being completed.

62 The trade provisions were activated before the entry into force of the PCA through the 1995 Interim Agreement.

63 See, for example, Decision 117-r of Ukraine's Cabinet of Ministers of 22 April 2005 on Measures to Implement the Ukraine–EU Action Plan in 2005.

64 Art. 21 PCA, Sectoral Agreement of March 2005.

65 Art. 22 PCA, Sectoral Agreement of December 2004.

66 Art. 23 PCA, Sectoral Agreement of July 1999.

67 World Bank, *op. cit.*

68 See Decision of Cooperation Council of 25 February 2005, 'as soon as the limited remaining issues have been satisfactorily resolved'; also RFE/RL, 30.11.2005, 'European Commission: It will Propose Ukraine Get a Market Economy Status'.

69 Arts 3, 11 and 12, PCA, and Annex I.

70 Art. 4, PCA.

71 Such a feasibility study was conducted in 1999. See Cooperation Council Decision of 25 February 2005.

72 For more on the general aspects of the process and on the key area of contract law, see R. Dragneva and E. Ioriatti Ferrari, 'Contract Law Harmonization and Regional Integration: Can the CIS Learn From the EU?', *RCEEL*, pp. 1–43; (2006), vol. 31; W. Simons, 'The CIS and Legal Reform: The Harmonization of Private Law', *Law in Transition* (2000).

73 For the other model laws adopted, see www.iacis.ru

74 The drafting of model legislation was initially commissioned to the Scientific-Consultative Centre for Private Law created by a decision of the CIS Council of Heads of State. Ukraine took part in the respective drafting groups within the thus created Centre. The model laws were then approved through the IPA process.

75 For more, see N. Kuznetsova, 'Concept and Structure of the Draft Civil Code of Ukraine', Paper at the Conference 'Results and Perspectives of Civil Law Codification in the CIS Member- States', held on 24–25 February 1997 in St Petersburg; A. Dovgert, 'The New Civil Code of Ukraine 2003: Main Features, Role in the Market Economy and Current Difficulties in Implementation', Paper presented at a conference at the University of Illinois, 8–9 April 2005, http://www.reec.uiuc.edu/events/Conference/lawconf_paper/dovgert.pdf

76 For examples, see Dragneva and Ioriatti, *op.cit.*, note 72.

77 For example, Foundations of Customs Legislation, which in effect is an uniform Customs Code.

78 For example, an Interagency Coordination Council for approximation of legislation was established in 1998, a National Council on Approximation of Legislation under the President of Ukraine – in 2000, a law On the Concept of the National Programme for Approximation of the Legislation of Ukraine to the Legislation of the EU was adopted by the *Rada* on 21 November 2002.

79 *Washington Post*, 1 March 1992.

80 M. Ruuda, 'Ukraine repeats membership calls' 09 February 2005, EU observer at http://www.euobserver.com/

81 Delegation of the European Commission to Ukraine. 'Towards a new era in EU-Ukraine relations'. Press release 2411, Kyiv, 12 September 2003.

82 On the sources and input into the Ukrainian Civil Code, see A. Dovgert, *op.cit.*, note 75; P. Maggs, 'The Civil Codes of Central Eurasia – A Comparison', available at http://home.law.uiuc.edu/~pmaggs/codes.htm

83 For example, the Baltics' FTAs with Ukraine were terminated upon their entry into the EU, and now the EU negotiates with Russia.

84 Indeed, a number of potential problems are revealed when examining the example of the Euro–Asian Community, which has aimed at the creation of a customs union. Even though the common customs tariff of the EAC has only been completed at about 60–70 per cent (according to different sources), relations have been complicated by the 1998 accession of Kyrgyzstan into the WTO. The Customs Union, as well provided by Art. XXIV GATT, can participate in the WTO, yet a completion of a customs union after the accession into WTO may involve renegotiation of the commitments already undertaken.

85 See World Bank, *op. cit.* The recommendation is for the short- and medium-term for Ukraine to sequence its steps: strengthening the CIS FTA, pushing for a EU FTA (and de-linking it from the EU membership issue), investing in

the WTO accession process, and refraining from steps to commit itself to a SES customs union. EU membership, according to the Bank should be viewed only as long-term anchor for institutional and structural reforms.

86   A. Dimitrova (ed.), *Driven to Change: Enlargement Viewed From the East* (Manchester: Manchester University Press, 2004).

87   S. White, I. McAllister and M. Light, 'Enlargement and the New Outsiders', *Journal of Common Market Studies*, 40: 1 (2002): 135–53.

88   *Ibid.*: 143.

89   *Ibid.*: 145.

9
Integration by Absorption: New Subjects for the Russian Federation

Gennadi Kurdiukov and Katlijn Malfliet

Introduction

After the demise of the Soviet Union, its former Union republics started a difficult process of state building. The new states in the post-Soviet space, however, are not immutable as political and legal entities. Their interdependence is often underestimated. 'Frozen conflicts' create tensions not only within the country but also in the country's relations with Russia and with the European and international communities. Also, the relatively powerful position of Russia has to be taken into account.

This chapter discusses only one aspect of the rapidly changing situation in CIS territory. The Russian Federation's domestic law provides for admitting states or parts of states into the Russian Federation as new subjects. In this way, the thesis of a possible absorption of FSU states – or parts of them – into the Russian Federation has lost its purely hypothetical character. This law, a Russian federal constitutional law of 17 December 2001, did not appear coincidentally; it allowed Russia to profile itself as a multi-tier governance structure and as an actor of 'modernized Russification'.

Multi-tier governance structures on the territory of the former Soviet Union

Russia as a 'core state successor' to the Soviet Union

The unstable situation created by the implosion of the Soviet Union at the end of 1991 remains extremely fragile and insecure. Legal uncertainty related to the founding documents of the Commonwealth of Independent States (CIS) should at least partially account for this. The preamble of the Minsk Declaration of 8 December 1991 expressed the political positioning of the three Slavic Union Republics: they established 'as a fact' (*konstatiruem*) that the USSR ceased to exist 'as a subject of international law and as a political reality'.[1] The resulting status of the Union republics as independent states was resumed in Art. 1 of the agreement, which provided that the high contracting parties founded a Commonwealth of Independent States. The Minsk agreement was vulnerable to criticism, as it was established without the involvement of the other members of the Soviet Federation (Union republics outside the Slavic core). Nevertheless, the Minsk Declaration was approved on 21 December by the leaders of 11 Union republics (the Baltic republics had previously declared their independence and had no intention to join; Georgia joined later in 1993) by the Declaration and the Protocol of Alma-Ata.[2] The Protocol of Alma-Ata corrects the absence of eight Union Republics in Minsk, and confirms their status as Newly Independent States. Further CIS documents endorse the sovereignty of the member states: the CIS charter of 1993 underscores the CIS as neither a state nor a supranational (*nadgosudarstvennyi*) entity.[3]

Subsequently, there has been substantial scholarly debate concerning the legal nature of the CIS: is this international cooperation structure to be considered a confederation, an international inter-state organization or a regional organization under Art. 52 of the UN Charter? The fundamental problem was, and remains, the lack of deep consensus about the aims of the organization: it means quite different things to the various participants. Feldbrugge compares the CIS to 'an amorphous lump of potter's clay which is being molded by several artists simultaneously'.[4] The international community hesitated, but finally agreed that the implosion of the Soviet Union could be considered as a case of succession, involving the 'core state' as a successor to the previous federal union. Upon the demise of the USSR, the Russian Federation indeed took the position of the successor of the Soviet state. On 21 December 1991, the CIS's Heads of State Council supported Russia's continuance of the USSR membership in the United Nations, including permanent membership of the Security Council and other international organizations.[5] The European Union also endorsed this qualification of the Russian Federation as the core state successor of the former Soviet Union.[6]

This attitude of the international community deserves some explanation: the potentially disruptive effect of creating new states needed to be minimized, especially with regard to arms control treaties, in which the Soviet Union had been a part. However, this presumption of continuity, although legitimized by a concern for controlling nuclear and other weapons that are subject to treaty regulations, equally implied an assumption of continuity of Russia's 'core state status' as related to the Newly Independent States. With the break-up of the Soviet Union, the confusion between Russia as a state or the centre of an empire was extended or transplanted to the new CIS framework. In this way, the international community reiterated the acceptance of a long-standing entanglement between Russia representing the empire and Russia as a state.[7] Paradoxically, international practice did not accept the surviving Federal Republic of Yugoslavia (Serbia and Montenegro) as the continuation of the old Yugoslavia.[8]

Frozen conflicts

Several states on former Soviet territory are currently confronted with 'frozen conflicts' on their territory. The cases are well known: Nagorno-Karabakh in Azerbaijan, South Ossetia and Abkhazia in Georgia and Transnistria in Moldova.[9] These unresolved *de facto* situations – regarding the 'state' question – create tensions not only within each country but also in the country's relations with Russia and the European and international communities.

Frozen conflicts come into existence when a relatively recent violent conflict over secession creates a situation of secessionist parties who effectively take control of specific territories and set up *de facto* state institutions. Such a process may threaten the break up of an internationally recognized state, a situation that is particularly disturbing at a time when the former Soviet Union republics are in a process of state and nation building. The latter phenomenon is well known from the nineteenth and twentieth century history of Europe. Such a period was, however, followed by a gradual erosion of the absolute character of state sovereignty in Europe. Although state sovereignty remains an important principle in international relations, the existence of European supranational law and (international and European) human rights protection have eroded the sanctity of national sovereignty. Moreover, from recent experiences with EU integration, one can learn that a third level of governance (the EU supranational level) may increase the number of options available in the search for a settlement of conflicts between a state and its secessionist territories or peoples. 'Secessionist conflicts which lie at the intersection of domestic and international politics can be more easily resolved if the principle of national self-determination is not confined to domestic affairs'.[10]

However, achieving agreement between international actors on the maintenance of state integrity does not necessarily constitute a solution, as international actors in some cases have a particular interest in keeping the conflict 'frozen'. As the European Union, for example, is ill disposed towards incorporating CIS countries, it can instrumentalize the existence of unresolved conflicts in the FSU States to cool down their European ambitions.

Russia has a completely different stance on this matter. As an internationally recognized 'core state successor', it sees opportunities for new geopolitical positioning. In this sense Russia avoided limiting itself to its new state identity, while at the same time it became a third tier of authority, providing space for negotiating a wide range of variables and possible schemes: for federal, accession, association and broader neighbourhood solutions. Without a doubt, the non-Russian republics, as a consequence of the Soviet implosion, legally became Russia's equals as independent states; they did not become provinces of the new Russia. However, as sovereign states, they can decide their own fate by transferring part or the whole of their state sovereignty to a third tier of authority.

The paradigm of sovereignty underlying the construction of the CIS is somewhat misleading. Although Russia stresses the sovereignty of the Newly Independent States as the leading principle underlying international relations in the territory of the former Soviet Union, precisely that sovereignty is utilized to test the chances of reintegration in the territory of the former Soviet Union. Without much care for consistency in international relations or in constitutional principles, Russia seems to be playing with possible scenarios that can lead to reintegration. As we will elaborate further, all possible options for multilevel and multi-speed integration come to the fore. Integrative movements in the CIS territory can lead to federations, confederations or supranational institutions. Framed as an open-ended strategy, this integration can take place while maintaining the international legal subjectivity of the integrated states. In other cases, unification can lead to the creation of a unitary state, a federal state or another form of constitutional order: trial and error as a way of proceeding is not perceived as a problem. However, this does not imply that states remain unchanged. The unification or disintegration of states can lead to territorial changes and changes in the sovereignty of states. Through integration their international legal subjectivity or their state identity as described in the constitution can be transformed in a substantial manner.

Izvestiia wrote in a recent article:

> Deliberations about the possible reunification of Russia and Ukraine shock many people today, because the historical and public memory

regards this possibility as a variant of Moscow domination. But things can change if the capital in the reunited state is moved to Kiev, the Mother of all Russian cities. In fact, Ukraine moved ahead of Russia democratically ... Moscow would remain the economic and media capital of the reunited state, which it actually is for all post-Soviet states now. This would be an ideal structure for a democratic state.[11]

The CIS indeed immediately provided itself with some legal and political 'entrances' to challenge the sovereignty of the FSU states. One of them is the inevitability of interference in ethnic conflicts on the territories of CIS member states. Art. 3 of the Minsk Agreement foresees this kind of 'overruling of state sovereignty' in the case of discrimination based on ethnic, cultural, linguistic or religious considerations:

The high contracting parties, desiring to promote the expression, preservation and development of the ethnic, cultural, linguistic and religious individuality of the national minorities resident on their territories, and that of the unique ethno-cultural regions that have come into being, take them under their protection.[12]

The idea of territorial revision based on ethnic considerations obtained legitimacy as early as 26 August 1991, when the Russian parliament placed the question of the Crimea high on the agenda, although Yeltsin and his government disowned that claim.[13]

In this way, similar to 'Europeanization', modern 'Russification' might refer to changes in the external territorial borders of Russia, to the development of the state's exceeding institutions of governance at the Russian level, to the central penetration of national and sub-national systems of governance, to the export of forms of distinctively Russian political organization and governance beyond the territory of the Russian state and to a political project aiming at a unified and politically stronger Russia.[14]

The rearrangement of states

Recent experiences with the disintegration and integration of states at the end of the twentieth to the beginning of the twenty-first century are quite paradoxical and even surprising, but they do not necessarily go against international law. The re-arrangement of states is well known in today's Europe: the 'velvet divorce' in Czechoslovakia, the uniting of Germany, the disintegration of the USSR, the UN project on the confederal state of Cyprus, including Greek and Turkish entities.

The current situation on the CIS territory, with its 12 member states, is variable and unsettled. New integration tendencies encompass both inter- and intra-state processes. In principle, nothing goes against the voluntary re-arrangement of states in new integrative structures. Painful experiences with empires and dominant state power positions should be avoided, however. The central question of this article is whether the hypothesis of absorption should be avoided in the newly defined international relations between the former Union republics, after their experience of the tsarist regime and the Soviet Union. The concept of absorption, as a well-known notion in international law, assumes that an existing state swallows another state or part of it. This process includes the disappearance of the swallowed state or the change of the absorbed state's national belonging: it becomes part of a new state and takes over its citizenship and its national legislation. Historical experiences between states can lead to a fear of absorption and the wish to avoid such a process. An interesting example from history is what happened to Austria on 15 May 1955. The allies signed a treaty according to which Austria was re-established as a sovereign, independent and democratic state. A future political and economic union between Austria and Germany was forbidden by the so-called 'ban of *Anschluss*'. In order to avoid such a union, Austria was forbidden to conclude any treaty or to take any measures that could directly or indirectly facilitate its political or economic union with Germany or harm its territorial integrity or economic independence.[15] However, as we discussed above, in the case of Russia and the other Newly Independent States within the CIS there was no talk about a possible 'ban of *Anschluss*'. On the contrary, the confusion with the empire continued: Russia was recognized as the successor to the Soviet Union.

By all this, Russia as a polity that hardly can content itself with its status as a 'mere state' is surely tempted to take on a multi-tier identity, and to follow an integration model, mirroring the unique supranational structure of the European Union with its blend of federal, confederal and intergovernmental elements. This integration model would not only modernize the Russian constitutional structure, but it would also be attractive for the FSU states, who at least want to preserve their territorial integrity if and when Russian pressure on their individual state sovereignty increases.

The Law of 17 December 2001

This chapter discusses only one aspect of the rapidly changing situation in the territory of the Commonwealth of Independent States. The Russian Federation on 17 December 2001 introduced into its domestic law the possibility of accepting states or parts of states as new subjects of the Russian Federation. The federal constitutional law 'On the procedure for the admittance (or acceptance: *priniatie*) to the Russian Federation and the Founding (*obrazovanie*) within its Framework of a New Subject of the Russian Federation' (with its amendments of 31 october 2005) foresees this kind of scenario.[16] The title of the law is rather confusing, but from its further wording it becomes clear that 'admittance' to the Russian Federation, on the one hand, and the founding of a new subject, on the other, are seen as distinctive processes. 'Admittance' points to the acceptance of a foreign state or part of it by the Russian Federation. This process should be initiated by the foreign partner and confirmed by an international agreement, as well as by Russian federal constitutional law. The reason for this last requirement is that the federal structure of the Russian Federation would be changed by this process.

'Admittance' is probably a euphemism as it concerns incorporation of new entities (subjects) into the Russian federal structure; this can be qualified as absorption, including the disappearance of the 'swallowed' state or the change of the absorbed state's national belonging: it would become part of a new state and take over its citizenship and national legislation.

We will not exclude the possibility that the law, as discussed below, was clearly intended. One can easily find an example of what this could imply: Russia could 'accept' Belarus as a new subject of the Federation or, after an open (de-frozen) conflict in South Ossetia or Abkhazia in Georgia or Transnistria in Moldova, Russia decides to 'admit' these conflict zones within its own borders as a 'peacekeeping' or 'peacemaking' measure.

The law 'On the Admittance' was enacted following Art. 65, Para. 2 of the 1993 Constitution of the Russian Federation, which states that the procedure for incorporation in the Russian Federation and the founding of a new subject is established by a federal constitutional law. The Russian law foresees in detail the conditions for admitting a new subject to the Russian Federation: the admittance should take place on a voluntary basis; the state's interests and the principles of federal state building, including human rights and freedoms, should be respected; the relevant economic and cultural relations between the subjects of the Russian Federation should be taken into account, as well as their socio-economic potential (Art. 3 of the law).

The 'founding' (creation) of a new subject within the Russian Federation, on the other hand, can be realized by two different processes: as the result of a merger of two or more bordering subjects of the Russian Federation, or as the result of the admitting a foreign state or part of it. The law (Art. 11) subjects the question of founding a new subject to a referendum within the interested state of the Russian Federation and to a consultation with the president of the Russian Federation (see the amendments of October 2005). The merger of two bordering subjects already has several precedents. The Perm province (*oblast*) and the Komi-Permiatskii autonomous district (*avtonomnyi okrug*) were the first to bring up the question of their uniting. On 7 December 2003, a referendum was organized on the merger of the Perm *oblast* and *okrug* with the consequent creation of a new administrative formation: the Perm *krai*.[17] On 30 June 2006, the Russian State Duma voted to create the Kamchatka *krai* as a result of the voter approved merger of Kamchatka province (*oblast*) and Koryak autonomous district (*okrug*) in 2005. The entity will officially come into being on 1 July 2007. These unification projects are part of a broader initiative to create larger administrative regions, which could presumably be more easily controlled. In any case, they contrast sharply with the admonition to the regions of former president Boris Yeltsin in the early 1990s to 'take as much sovereignty as you can swallow'.

On the other hand, the law defines admittance (*priniatie*) to the Russian Federation as adhesion (*prisoedinenie*) to the Russian Federation of a foreign state or a part of it (Art. 65, Para. 2 of the Russian Constitution does not mention a subject of such origin). Here again, the law foresees two hypotheses. If a foreign state is admitted to the Russian Federation as a new subject, this subject receives the status of republic. In case that part of the foreign state is accepted, the subject receives the status of republic, *krai, oblast*, autonomous *oblast* or autonomous *krai*. This implies that, in the case of secession of part of its territory a foreign state and its incorporation in the Russian Federation, the whole spectre of administrative-territorial divisions qualifies for a legal denomination of the incorporated territory.

We will focus on the problem of adhesion of a foreign state or part of a foreign state (*prisoedinenie*), (in other words, incorporation (*inkorporatsiia*).[18] This process is presented by the law 'On the Admittance' as a voluntary agreement on territorial changes between two states.

The way in which the change in sovereign authority over a particular territory is exactly processed, however, will depend upon the circumstances of the particular case.[19] When part of a state leaves without the consent of that state, we have a case of secession. On the other hand, partial changes to a state's territory based on the mutual agreement between states are possible. The latter type of change is only possible in the case of mutual consensus by states. From the point of view of international law this implies the transfer of state sovereignty on a part of the territory from one state to another.[20]

Therefore, it is interesting to look at the specific procedure that is prescribed by the law 'On the Admittance'. A mutual agreement (treaty) between the Russian Federation and the foreign state is necessary in both cases: in the case of admittance of a foreign state as such or of part of that foreign state (Art. 4). This treaty would regulate the relations between the states concerning territorial changes. It would be difficult to imagine a situation where the Russian Federation would conclude an agreement with only part of a foreign state (with Transniestria, for example). The Law of the Russian Federation: 'On International Agreements of the Russian Federation' of 1995 does not foresee such a possibility.[21] According to this law an international agreement of the Russian Federation refers to an agreement concluded by the Russian Federation with foreign states or with international organizations, but not with regions within a state (Art. 2).

According to the federal law of 4 January 1999 'On the Coordination of International External Economic Relations of the Subjects of the Russian Federation',[22] subjects have the right to establish international and external economic relations with subjects of foreign federal states and with administrative territories of foreign states. The consent of the Russian Federation's government and of the foreign state's organs is, however, required.

It is not clear, currently, what are the real powers of the subjects of the Russian Federation in the field of international relations. In the law 'On International Agreements of the Russian Federation' one can find two kinds of international agreements of the Federation that concern the subjects' powers: (1) international treaties of the Russian Federation relating to the exclusive jurisdiction of the subject; (2) international treaties of the Russian Federation relating to fields of joint (shared) jurisdiction of the Russian Federation and the subjects (Art. 4). Art. 72, Part O,1 of the Constitution of the Russian Federation relates to the joint jurisdiction of the Russian Federation and its subjects: 'the coordination of international and external economic relations of the subjects of the Russian Federation'. According to the same law ('On International Agreements of the Russian Federation'), the basic principles or the draft of an international agreement that relates to a subject's situation and concerns powers of the Russian Federation's joint jurisdiction with the subjects, must go through a consultation procedure. They are sent by the federal governmental organs to the interested subject's state organs. The amendments resulting from this consultation are studied during the preparation of the agreement.

The admittance of a new subject is based not only on norms of international law but also on the legislation of the Russian Federation, its Constitution and the federal constitutional laws.

The law 'On the Admittance' foresees the concrete procedure for accepting a state as a new subject of the Russian Federation: (1) the initiator of such a proposal must be a foreign state; (2) after possible conciliatory procedures an international treaty is concluded by which questions are regulated such as: (a) the name and the status of the new subject of the Russian Federation; (b) the way in which citizenship can be obtained; (c) legal successorship relating to the membership of the foreign state to international organizations, its assets and liabilities; (d) the validity of the legislation of the Russian Federation on the territory of the new subject; (e) the functioning of the organs of state power and organs of local self-government on the territory of the new subject.

A special feature of such an international agreement is that, after the signing, the Russian president makes an inquiry (*zapros*) to the Constitutional Court of the Federation to check the compliance with the constitution of the international treaty, before the agreement may come into force. If the Constitutional Court decides that the treaty is in accordance with the constitution, this treaty can be ratified. Ratification is also required for the special protocols related to special questions on the adhesion of a foreign state or part of it as a new subject (Art. 8).

From that moment on, the 'national' phase of the procedure can start. At the same time as the above mentioned international treaty, a initiative for a federal constitutional law 'On the Admittance of a New Subject in the Russian Federation' is introduced in the State Duma. This law does not apply prior to the international treaty's entry into force. Accordingly, amendments are introduced into Part 1 of Art. 65 of the Constitution of the Russian Federation which defines the number of Russian Federation subjects.

The Russian law 'On the Admittance' reminds us of the 1990 accession of the Länder of the German Democratic Republic (GDR) to the Federal Republic of Germany (FRG), a clear case in which one state was absorbed by another. The Treaty of 31 August 1990, which provided for unification of the two Germanies on 3 October 1990, refers to the 'accession' of the GDR to the FRG in accordance with Art. 23 of the basic law. This implies that the unification of Germany came about by a process of absorption of the constituent provinces of the former GDR into the existing FRG by way of extending the latter's constitution, federal legislation and, among others, its financial system. The international community accepted this process of unification, which can equally be considered 'absorption' into the FRG; it should be qualified as the continuation of the FRG and the disappearance or extinction of the GDR.[23]

The situation on the territory of the former Soviet Union

On the territory of the former Soviet Union, the situation related to the state question is much more complex: several variants of multilevel and multi-speed integration develop simultaneously, which makes the process rather chaotic and obscure. Clearly the situation has not yet stabilized; further changes are to be expected. The most impressive developments can be noticed in the integrative process between the Russian Federation and Belarus. This process has already been through several stages. On 21 February 1995, both states signed a Treaty 'On Friendship, Good Neighbourhood and Cooperation' for a period of 10 years.[24] On 2 April 1996 a treaty was concluded in Moscow 'On the Founding of a Community (*Soobshchestvo*) of Belarus and Russia'.[25] On 2 April 1997, the presidents signed a treaty on the Union (*Soiuz*) between Belarus and Russia.[26]

On 23 May 1997, an agreement was reached on the Charter of the Union.[27] In this way the Community became a Union. At the occasion of the registration of these acts in 1997 at the United Nations, the Union of Belarus and Russia was recognized as an 'international intergovernmental organization'. In principle, both the Community and the Union were qualified as international-legal regional associations. On 25 December 1998, the leaders of the Russian Federation and Belarus signed a 'Declaration on the Further Unification of Belarus and Russia'. In this declaration, both states agreed 'to continue the step by step development to the voluntary association in a Union State keeping the national sovereignty of the state-members of the Union'.[28] Together with the Declaration, a treaty was signed 'On Equal Rights of Citizens within the Union State' and an agreement 'On the Creation of Equal Conditions for Economic Subjects, Performing Activities on the Territory of the Union State'. On 8 December 1999, the presidents of Russia and Belarus signed a Treaty on the Founding of a Union State.[29]

From the point of view of constitutional and international law, a Union State can no longer be qualified as an international intergovernmental organization. This implies that the 1999 treaty 'On the Creation of a Union State' is to be considered an international treaty regulating the unification of two sovereign states but it is also the founding act for a new state.

In the case of frozen conflicts, the approach from international law is different. When part of the territory of one state becomes part of the territory of another state on a voluntary basis, one refers to 'secession' of a territory from one state to join another. Art. 15 of the Vienna Convention on Succession of State Treaties deals with this case. This case differs from the 'secession' of a territory from an existing state to form a newly created state or states (for example, when Belgium seceded from the Netherlands in 1830).

Abkhazia, a constituent part of Georgia, aims at independence and currently builds its relations with Georgia on an intergovernmental basis. In 1873, the 'Georgian Treaty' was signed (*Georgievskii traktat*), according to which seven independent state formations (including Georgia) entered the Russian empire. Abkhazia entered in 1810 as an independent state. In 1922, the Caucasian Federation was founded (Georgia, Armenia, Azerbaijan and Abkhazia, still as an independent state). In 1931, Abkhazia was included in Georgia. In an interview with *Izvestiia*, the head of the Ministry of Foreign Affairs of Abkhazia, S. Shamba, said: 'If before the war or immediately after we could speak of confederal or federal relations, then at this moment, after the referendum, the people of Abkhazia only sustain intergovernmental relations. We are an independent state *de facto* and *de jure*. To change something in this, one has to change the constitution, but the population does not allow this.'[30]

The Transnistrian conflict with(in) Moldova also intensified with the dissolution of the Soviet Union. The so-called creeping *putsch*, organized by the Transnistrian Republican Guard aided by Cossack volunteers, of gradually taking control over public institutions such as municipal and local administrative buildings, police stations, schools, newspapers and radio stations in towns and villages at the left bank, was stepped up towards the end of 1991. The Russian forces of the 14th Soviet army, stationed in Moldova, played a decisive role in the brief military conflict in Moldova. In July 1992, a set of principles for the peaceful settlement of the dispute was announced, including respect for the sovereignty and territorial integrity of Moldova, the need for a special status for Transnistria and the right of its inhabitants to determine their future in case Moldova were to unite with Romania. Various versions of multi-entity federations have been suggested in the subsequent years: a unitary state with regional autonomies or a symmetric two-state federation, with Serbia-Montenegro as the favoured model. Smaller minority groups have been advocating more radical solutions such as secession and internationally recognized independence. However, the situation remains undecided: *de facto* secession and non-recognized independence for Transnistria describes the *status quo*.[31]

Will Russia absorb these territories with frozen conflicts? It is not easy to make prognoses on the possible application of the law 'On the

Admittance'. The law has already been in force for more than five years, and there have been no noted cases of this law's application. If we look at the political map of 'Russia and the surrounding states', we see that 46 subjects of the Russian Federation border foreign states. Until now we have had a situation of non-regulation of the regional conflicts at the Russian borders. As an exercise, one can ask which state or part of it could change the composition of the subjects of the Russian Federation. First, it could be one of the former USSR republics and, in order of likelihood, the Slavic republics of Belarus and Ukraine. Second, it could be the semi-enclave of the Kaliningrad *oblast*, which is almost completely surrounded by foreign states that are now members of the European Union. And why not fantasize and remember Alaska that was sold by the Russian government in 1867 to the USA for 7.2 million dollars? Well known from the past are cases of annexation (incorporation) to the Soviet Union of foreign states or parts of them: Lithuania, Latvia and Estonia in 1940 and Southern Belarus in 1939 (the reintegration in the Belarusian SSR). The western part of Ukraine became part of the Soviet Union as late as 1939–49.

Integration within a CIS–framework?

The Foreign Policy Concept of the Russian Federation, accepted in July 2000, clearly voices Russia's priorities within the Commonwealth of Independent States:

> Starting from the concept of multi-speed and multilevel integration within the framework of the CIS, Russia will define the parameters and the character of its interaction with state members of the CIS as well as with the CIS as a whole, and also in more narrow associations, in the first place the Treaty on Collective Security. The first task is the strengthening of the Union between Russia and Belarus as the highest form in the current stage of the integration of two sovereign states.[32]

The above-analysed Russian law, 'On the Admittance', clearly opts for a unitary and federal form of state building. The confederal form, – that is, a union of equal states created by an international treaty – is not envisaged by this law. Already in 1997, in the Russian National Security Concept, the idea was brought forward that in the Russian Federation's development it was not acceptable to change federal relations into confederal ones.[33]

However, in the current stage of multi-speed and multilevel integration, the creation of associations, and even a Union State, represent a complex and contradictory process with ambiguous political and legal consequences. As a result of integration processes, different forms of state building can develop. For example, the Treaty 'On the Creation of a Union State of Russia–Belarus' did not define the form of state building: a federation, a confederation or a regional community. The analysis of the signed documents does not give an unequivocal answer to the form of the political-territorial building.

The president of the Parliamentary Union of the Union of Russia–Belarus, G.N. Seleznev, remarked that the commission elaborating the proposed constitutional act for the Union of Russia–Belarus saw it as inefficient to define exactly the kind of state to be built: 'Is the Union State a new type of state or a state for a transitory period? The future will show this'.[34]

The academic world raised a discussion on the constitutional character of the Russia–Belarus Union State. Some authors see the Union State as a confederation. According to Iu.A. Tikhomirov, the confederal model would much more effectively approach the political, economic and legal systems of the states concerned while fully conserving the sovereignty of the state participants in the association.[35] S.N. Baburin claims that it is possible to create a new state-type union, through the step by step creation of a federal association: the Russian Union. He sees this new formation as the result of the entrance of sovereign republics (former republics of the USSR), who find their place as self-governing territories within the Russian Federation or by a contractual reuniting with Russia, in which case rights and obligations of the centre and the subjects would be determined by an agreement. The subjects of this Russian Union are – according to Baburin – not in need of sovereign rights; they do not need the right to secession.[36] N.A. Mikhaleva thinks that the creation of a Union State based on the treaty of 8 December 1999 can be considered as 'a new stage in the process of the unification of Russia and Belarus in one democratic state, a higher form of integration of two sovereign states'.[37]

On the official level, the dialogue continues. When President Putin proposed, on 14 August 2002, to organize a referendum in May 2003 on the question of the final unification of the two states (the plan was to elect a unified parliament in December 2003 and a president in March 2004), he made clear that the unified institutions of state power would be constructed according to the Constitution of Russia, not Belarus. President Lukashenka of Belarus answered that this 'variant' of unification was not acceptable for him.[38]

This would imply that the scenario, designed by the law 'On the Admittance', according to which Belarus would become a subject or, more concretely, a republic of the Russian Federation, was not acceptable for Belarus. One can refer once more to the recent experience with German unification. In the case of the German unification both states signed the German-German agreement, created a currency union, and it was announced that after the unification with the new German *Länder*, the constitution of the FRG would come into force in the new *Länder* so that for all Germans, without exception, equal rights and freedoms became applicable.[39] In this case of 'absorption', the German Democratic Republic indeed became extinct, whereas the Federal Republic of Germany simply continued, albeit in an enlarged form. The Union Treaty foresaw the FRG's extension of its constitution, federal legislation and financial system. International practice accepted this approach, which was essentially assimilation and absorption.[40]

On 4 September 2002, the President of Russia corresponded to the President of Belarus about some conceptual issues of building a unitary state. Putin proposed several basic variants of an integration model for the further association of Russia and Belarus: the full integration into one unified state; a supranational construction of the type like the European Union; an association on the basis of stipulations in the treaty on the creation of a Union State.[41]

From the regions, some cautious suggestions on a possible integration with Russia have been formulated as well. The Prime Minister of the republic Abkhazia, A. Dzhargeniia, mentioned the possibility of establishing associative relations with Russia. 'It does not hinder the republican sovereignty and does not contradict the Abkhazian constitution'. However, the Prime Minister concluded, 'the question of establishing associated relations with Russia can only be officially introduced after a referendum, on which the parliament of the republic has to take a decision'.[42]

In relation to the Transnistrian republic in Moldova, several scenarios for new state constructions have also been proposed. On 19 December 1995, a referendum was organized on the independence of the republic and its independent entrance into the CIS. On 16 January 2002, the Supreme Council ('Soviet') of the Transnistrian republic took a decision on the creation of a confederation of Transnistria and Moldova. But the climax came on 18 November 2003, when the Russian ambassador in Moldova handed to the president of Moldova a memorandum from Moscow, 'On the Basic Principles of State Construction of a Union State'.[43] The memorandum was also given to Transnistria and Gagauzia and to the mediators: the OSCE and Ukraine. In the memorandum, a future federal configuration of Moldova is proposed with a unified customs as well as united financial and defence spaces. The proposal is that Moldova becomes a demilitarized and neutral state (the status of neutral state is written in the constitution of Moldova). The memorandum specifies which decisions Kishinev can take autonomously – the administration of state property, currency relations, foreign policy – and which powers it has to share with Tiraspol – the regulation of customs, rivers, the federal budget, the energy system, electoral law and the judicial system. Russia in this way claimed a role as the main guarantor of all processes of unification in Moldova.

Conclusion

The law of the Russian Federation 'On the Admission' is an interesting document with important normative content. To a certain degree, it answers the contemporary requirements and the conceptual tools prescribed by international law. The future will show how politically relevant this law will be. Soon it will be clear whether it is a real option to bring a foreign state or part of it within the Russian Federation, or whether it is just a piece of creative thinking.

Returning to the challenge of different integration processes in the territory of the former Soviet Union, one can conclude that integration by absorption became a realistic scenario after the Russian law of 2001, although it has never been used to this point. States such as Belarus or regions with frozen conflicts such as Transnistria or Abchasia or South Ossetia can be absorbed by Russia if international and national procedures for this kind of rearrangement of states are respected. These procedures can find a precedent in the German state, where the former GDR was absorbed by the FRG. In any case, the multi-tiered cooperation within the CIS space is enriched by one more option, albeit a rather radical one.

Notes

1 Declaration by the Heads of State of the Republic of Belarus, the Russian Soviet Federative Socialist Republic and Republic of Ukraine, and the Agreement Establishing the Commonwealth of Independent States. The negotiations took place in the forest reserve of *Belovezhskaia Pushcha*. The agreement was signed by the three Heads of State and the three Prime Ministers of the participant states: Russia, Belarus and Ukraine. The first official publication was in *Izvestiia*, 8 December 1991. Translation in *International Legal Materials (ILM)*, (Washington, DC: American Society of International Law) 31 (1992): 138.

2 Text of Protocol and Declaration in *Izvestiia*, 21 December 1991.

3   CIS Charter of 1993: 'Ustav Sodruzhestva Nezavisimykh Gosudarstv ot 22.01.93g', *Biulleten' Mezhdunarodnykh Dogovorov* (1994): 4–14.

4   F.J.M. Feldbrugge, 'The Commonwealth of Independent States: the Legal and Political Re-Integration of Eastern Europe', in W.J.M. van Genugten *et al.* (eds), *Realism and Moralism in International Relations* (Den Haag: Martinus Nijhoff, 1999) 25.

5   Y. Blum,'Russia Takes over the Soviet Union's Seat at the United Nations', *European Journal of International Law*, 3 (1992): 354.

6   Guidelines on the Recognition of New States in Eastern Europe and the Soviet Union, adopted by the European Community on 16 December 1991; I. Brownie, *Principles of Public International Law* (Oxford: Oxford University Press, 2003): 82–3; R. Mullerson, 'The Continuity and Succession of States by Reference to the former USSR and Yugoslavia', *International and Comparative Law Quarterly*, (1993): 473.

7   G. Hosking, 'The State and Identity Formation in Russia: a Historical Account', in K. Malfliet and F. Scharpé, *The Concept of Russia. Patterns for Political Development in the Russian Federation* (Leuven: University Press, 2003): 21–34.

8   Security Council Resolution 757, 1992 and General Assembly Resolution 47/1. See also the Genocide Convention case, *International Court of Justice Reports* (1993): 13–14.

9   For an in-depth analysis of frozen conflicts in the CIS: B. Coppieters *et al.*, *Europeanization and Conflict Resolution: Case Studies from the European Periphery* (Ghent: Academia Press, 2004).

10   *Ibid.*: 19–20.

11   *Izvestiia*, 9 February 2005.

12   Minsk Agreement of 8 December 1991: 138, *supra* note 1.

13   *Izvestiia*, 29 August 1991.

14   In this way, Europeanization was qualified by Johan P. Olsen in 'The many faces of Europeanization', ARENA Working Papers, 01/2 (2002), http://www.arena.uio.no/publications/wp02_2.htm

15   *Deistvuiushchee mezhdunarodnoe pravo* (*Current International Law*) Part 1 (Moscow: MNIP, 1996): 143.

16   'O poriadke priniatiia v Rossiiskuiu federatsiu i obrazovaniia v ee sostave novogo sub'ekta Rossiiskoi Federatsii' ('On the Procedure for Admittance to the Russian Federation and the Founding within its Borders of a New Subject of the Russian Federation'), *Rossiiskaia Gazeta*, 20 December 2001; *Sobranie Zakonov RF* (*SZ RF*), 52 (2001): item 4916; 52, 45 (2005: item 4581 (amendments)).

17   http://www.krai.perm.ru

18   'Inkorporatsiia (lat.)- vkliutchenie v svoi sostav, prisoedinenie' ('Incorporation (lat.)- inclusion in its structure, adhesion'), *Sovremennyi Slovar' Inostrannykh Slov* (1999): 237. We avoid the term 'annexation' because of its negative connotation. The term 'incorporation' is not generally accepted in international terminology. In the Vienna Convention on State Succession Related to Treaties (1978) and the Vienna Convention on State Succession Related to State Property, State Archives and State Debts (1983), some possible territorial changes are mentioned: legal succession relating to a part of the territory; the situation where the state continues to exist after the de-membering of part of its territory, the transfer of part of the territory; the separation (*otdelenie*) of a part or several parts of the territory; the division (*razdelenie*) of states.

19 M. Shaw, *International Law* (2000): 676–7.
20 B.M. Klimenko and N.A. Ushakov, *Nerushimost granits – uslovie mezhdunaro-dnogo mira* (*The Inviolability of Borders – a Condition in the International World*) (Moscow: Iuridicheskaia Literatura, 1975): 60; B.M. Klimenko, *Gosudarstvennye territorii. Voprosy teorii i praktiki mezhdunarodnogo prava* (*State Territories. Theoretical and Practical Questions of International Law*) (Moscow: Iuridicheskaia Literatura, 1974): 87.
21 *SZ RF*, 29 (1995): item 2757.
22 *SZ RF*, 2 (1999): item 231.
23 'The model provided by the German unification appears to be fully consistent with international law and of value as a precedent': M.N. Shaw, *ibid.*: 687.
24 *Biulleten' mezhdunarodnykh dogovorov*, 7 (1996): item 47.
25 *SZ RF*, (1996): item 5300.
26 *Rossiiskaia Gazeta*, 3 April 1997.
27 *SZ RF*, 30 (1997): item 3596.
28 *Rossiiskaia Gazeta*, 26 December 1998.
29 *SZ RF*, 7 (2000): item 786.
30 *Izvestiia*, 2 March 2002.
31 M. Vahl and M. Emerson, 'Moldova and the Transnistrian Conflict', in *Europeanisation and Conflict Resolution* (Ghent: Academic Press, 2004): 174–75.
32 'Foreign Policy Concept of the Russian Federation', *Rossiiskaia Gazeta* (*RG*), 11 July 2000; http://www.mid.ru
33 'National Security Concept of the RF', version 1997: *RG*, 26 December 1997; version 2000: *RG*, 18 January 2000.
34 *RG*, 27 February 2003.
35 Iu.A. Tikhomirov, *Kurs sravnitel'nogo pravovedeniia* (*Course on Comparative Jurisprudence*) (Moscow: Zertsalo, 1996): 154.
36 S.N. Baburin, *Territoriia gosudarstva. Pravovye i politicheskie problemy* (*Territory of the State. Legal and Political Problems*) (Moscow: Iurinformtsentr, 1997): 470, 474.
37 N.A. Mikhaleva, 'Pravovye problemy sozdaniia suverennogo gosudarstva Rossii i Belarusi' ('Legal Problems on the Creation of a Sovereign State of Russia and Belarus'), *Gosudarstvo i Pravo*, 6 (2002): 14.
38 *Rossiiskaia Gazeta*, 16 August 2002; *Izvestiia*, 15 August 2002.
39 On 31 August 1990, a treaty was signed between the FRG and the GDR 'On the Confirmation of the Unity of Germany (on the Unification)'. This treaty is considered as an international treaty between two subjects of international law. As a consequence, a unification of the states took place on 23 August 1990. The Volkskammer of the GDR took the decision to reunify the GDR with the FRG, according to Art. 23.2 of the fundamental law of the FRG, which came into force in their territory on 3 October 1990. In this way the so-called domestic aspect of the unification of Germany was realized. The external aspect of the unification of Germany was regulated by the victorious powers. In this framework, talks were organized under the form '2+4' on the level of the ministries of foreign affairs of the USSR, the US, Great Britain, France, the GDR and the DRG, and on 12 September 1990 they signed a treaty 'On the Final Regulation of the Relations with Germany' or the treaty '2+4'.
40 J. Frowein, 'Germany Reunited', 51 *Zeitschrift für ausländishces öffentliches Recht and Völkerrecht*, Max-Planck-Insitut für ausländisches öffentliches Recht

und Völkerrecht, Verlag W. Kohlhammer, Stuttgart (1991): 333. A series of treaties dealing primarily with NATO matters were excluded from the extension of treaties of the Federal Republic of Germany to the territory of the former GDR (Art. 11 coupled with Annex I of the Unification Treaty of 1990).

41 *Rossiiskaia Gazeta,* 5 September 2002.
42 *Rossiiskaia Gazeta,* 2 March 2002.
43 *Rossiiskaia Gazeta,* 18 November 2003.

10
The EU–Russia Common Economic Space and the Policy-Taker Problem

Evgeny Vinokurov

Introduction

This chapter delineates the phases and main activities of the negotiation process relating to the Common Economic Space (CES) between the EU and Russia. The Concept and the Road Map of the CES contain an original model in itself, combining elements of the EEA and the 'Swiss' models, and uniting horizontal and sectoral approaches. It is questionable whether the model envisaged by these documents would be capable of providing a satisfactory solution to the policy-taker challenge for Russia; that is, fulfilling the obligation to converge unilaterally on EU legislation and to follow the changes in EU legislation while possessing only limited leverage on the EU's internal affairs. The policy-taker problem may represent a major hurdle to EU–Russian economic integration in view of Russian multilateral foreign policy and its official goals.

The Concept of the EU–Russia Common Economic Space (CES) was adopted at the EU–Russia Summit in Rome (5–6 November 2003). It states that Russia and the EU are geographically close, have complementary economic structures and assets, and have strong mutual interest in further economic integration. As the existing potential for economic cooperation is not being fully utilized (Art. 8), there is a need to bring partners closer together on the road to economic integration. The next document agreed on by the EU and Russia concerning their economic integration was the CES Road Map adopted at the EU–Russia Summit in Moscow (9–10 May 2005). A significant spread is now being observed between the high flight of politics and the day-to-day bottlenecks. It is argued that there is a worrisome discrepancy between the discussions envisaging EU–Russia Common Spaces aimed at deeper integration in the medium- and long-term, and the difficult negotiations on such down-to-earth matters as the extension of the Partnership and Co-operation Agreement (PCA), Kaliningrad cargo transit, or import quotas.[1]

In the 2000s, Russia has found itself on the outskirts of the European integration process. There is a growing danger that Russia will be further marginalized. The EU has already started recoupling the economic issues of the EU–Russian dialogue with the political issues of democracy, human rights and the war in Chechnya. Furthermore, Russia's striving to preserve its influence in the CIS states and build on CIS economic and political integration may potentially lead to a clash with the EU on the issue of the compatibility of Russian, EU and CIS integration.

Against this background, the CES Concept and the Road Map contain the line of the official conceptual thinking, which is aimed at bringing the European Union and Russia closer together on the economic side, with various linkages to other fields of cooperation. The analysis of the Concept and the Road Map themselves and of the way they have evolved may be instrumental for our understanding of the nature and prospects of EU–Russia relations. Furthermore, there are important issues linked to the conceptual framework of the EU–Russia Common Economic Space that are crucial for its eventual success. The definition of the CES is provided in the text of the Concept Paper: 'the CES means an open and integrated market between the EU and Russia, based on the implementation of common or compatible rules and regulations, including compatible administrative practices, as a basis for synergies and economies of scale associated with a higher degree of competition in bigger markets. It shall ultimately cover substantially all sectors of the economy' (CES Concept, Art. 12). The task of the Concept was to create an appropriate model for this project dealing with EU–Russian economic integration. This model should combine the issues of potential economic efficiency with existing political possibilities and constraints on both sides. The basic choice is between horizontal and vertical approaches. Under the horizontal approach, the sides choose to integrate 'across-the-board', incorporating the principle of the four freedoms enshrined in the Single Market. As the movement of labour has never been an issue in EU–Russian relations, three freedoms remain: (1) free movement of goods and services; (2) free movement of capital; and (3) free movement of persons. Meanwhile, the vertical approach would mean the decision to draft a number of sector-specific agreements. We analyse the approach incorporated in the CES Concept and argue that the Concept contains an original model that combines horizontal and vertical approaches.

Furthermore, there is another issue that needs to be resolved on the conceptual level. The experiences of both the European Economic Area and the EU–Swiss agreements have shown that economic integration with the EU can cause a severe policy-taker problem for the integrating party. The EU insists that free access to the Single Market should be coupled with the corresponding obligation not to create unfair advantages for the non-EU producers. Under the existing agreements, the EU counterparts are obliged to follow changes in the EU *acquis* to a certain extent, adopting new directives in their own legislation as they come up. If this also turns out to be the case with the CES, then Russia will be exposed to the policy-taker problem; that is, it will have to follow the developments of EU legislation. In this chapter, we analyse the CES Concept from this point of view as well.

Concentrating on the Russian approaches to the economic integration with the EU, the chapter has the following structure. It starts with a description of the process leading to the CES Concept and the Road Map, delineating its phases, main activities and working mode. It is argued further that the CES Concept and the Road Map represent an original model in itself, combining elements of the EEA and the 'Swiss' models; that is, it unites both horizontal and sectoral approaches. On this basis, drawing on the experience of the EEA and EU–Swiss agreements, we go on to discuss the potential policy-taker problem that may arise for Russia.

Phases of the development of the CES

We start by delineating the major steps and phases of the negotiations leading to the CES Concept Paper and the CES Road Map. Phase 1 started during the EU–Russia Summit in May 2001, when the idea of a Common European Economic Space was introduced by Romano Prodi in discussions with Vladimir Putin. The latter responded positively, indicating Russia's interest in closer economic cooperation. A High-Level Group (HLG) was created under an appropriate mandate in Phase 2. It took a year to set up an HLG to lead the work on the concept. During the Summit in October 2001, the parties agreed to establish a joint HLG to elaborate the Concept. The designated co-chairs were Russian Deputy Prime Minister Khristenko and Commissioner Chris Patten. In March 2002, the HLG was provided with a mandate to elaborate the CES Concept by the Cooperation Council of the Partnership and Cooperation Agreement. In Phase 3, the concept was negotiated by the parties. The deadline set by the mandate was October 2003; that is, in one and a half years, or three summits away. In fact, the first Khristenko–Patten meeting had already taken place in the second half of 2001. At its second meeting in March 2002, the HLG adopted a work plan for the next eighteen months. To fulfil the task of assessing the potential impact of a CES, a number of economic assessment studies were commissioned separately by Russia and the EU. The negotiations resulted in the CES Concept, which was agreed upon by the parties as Annex I, 'The Common European Economic Space (CEES) Concept Paper' ('CES Concept,' 2003) to the Joint Statement of the Twelfth EU–Russia Summit in Rome on 5–6 November 2003 ('Joint Statement', 2003).

The work and negotiations on the CES have continued, with the adoption of the CES Road Map by the Fifteenth EU–Russia Summit in Moscow (10–11 May 2005) marking the end of Phase 4. As Russia's WTO accession is widely perceived to be a prerequisite for the CES talks to continue, waiting for the WTO accession is one of the reasons why the CES Concept was knowingly formulated rather broadly. Besides, it was also the reason for mentioning the term 'free trade' so as not to create additional difficulties in Russia's negotiations with non-EU members of the WTO. In principle, the CES development process proceeds along three tracks. Art. 19 names (1) market opening, (2) regulatory convergence, and (3) trade facilitation. The work on the concrete contents along the first track of market opening depends directly on Russia's membership in the WTO. Many of the issues of trade facilitation are also linked to the adoption of the WTO regulations (for example, customs and customs procedures). However, the work on the regulatory convergence and infrastructure can be continued in the absence of Russia's WTO membership.

In late April 2004, the European Commission submitted to its Russian counterparts a proposal for an Action Plan. Based along the lines of the Concept, this document aims at specifying more concrete objectives and measures to achieve them. The proposal concerns not only the CES but all four Common Spaces. In this way, the Commission is endeavouring to couple the Spaces together, linking, for example, the progress on the market opening with the progress on the visa-free regime. There are two reasons for adopting this approach. First, it is along the lines of the Commission's Communication on relations with Russia, which emphasizes that the EU–Russia partnership must be based on shared values and common interests.[2] It thus couples economic cooperation with the issues of human rights, democratic rule and the war in Chechnya. Second, the Commission wants to see a coherent approach so as not to create a considerable discontinuity of advancements in economic and

JHA matters that are linked to each other. Russia disagreed with the approach and insisted on decoupling these and other issues. Thus, Russia insisted on having four separate Road Maps (a separate one for each space) instead of an overarching Action Plan. Separate Road Maps would serve the purpose of decoupling various issues. Technically, the Commission would not mind four separate Road Maps, but nevertheless it would like to advance the coherency.

The four Road Maps were agreed on by the parties during the May 2005 Summit in Moscow. The Road Map for the Common Economic Space is the longest one, comprising 19 pages out of a total of 52. It reiterates the Concept in the preamble in stating that the goal of the CES is to create an 'open and integrated market between the EU and Russia'.[3] Further, it proceeds with the standard EU accession agenda, including regulatory convergence in various sectors (telecom, financial services, automotive, medical devices, textiles and pharmaceuticals), public procurement, intellectual and industrial property rights, trade facilitation and customs and so on. Telecommunication and transport networks are covered in a separate sub-section stating the objective of the creation of the EU–Russian information society area. Separate sub-sections are devoted also to cooperative efforts relating to space, environment and energy within the Energy Dialogue. Free trade is not mentioned once: the overall framework and context imply that a free trade area is not on the agenda. The words dominating the document are 'dialogue', 'cooperation', 'harmonization' and 'convergence'. While the former two are vague and often used to cover the emptiness of contents, the latter two terms avoid mentioning the vector of convergence; that is, the question as to who ought to converge on whom. In the meantime, this very issue may turn out to be the major problem standing in the way of eventual EU–Russian regulatory integration. The vagueness and ambiguity of the Road Map prompted Emerson to characterize the current state of affairs as the 'proliferation of the fuzzy'.[4] In fact, a standard road map provides not only the objectives and actions but also time schedules for realizing them. The latter element is completely lacking in the CES Road Map, as well as in the other three Road Maps forming the package of the Fifteenth Summit.

The CES is perceived as a central element in the EU–Russian integration process. In other words, there is a widely shared understanding, both implicit and explicit, that the CES is the central common space of the four envisaged Common Spaces.[5] Despite the fact that processes and negotiations run on their separate tracks, other spaces are connected to the economic issues raised in the CES and would benefit from the advances in the economic sphere. For example, the Common Space of Freedom, Security and Justice would directly benefit from any advances made in the related aspects of the movement of people (Art. 18 of the CES Concept). The issue of the free movement of persons, naturally falling within the scope of the JHA common space, was prioritized in 2003–04. However, even this issue is closely linked to the successfully facilitated economic cooperation. The external security represents an exception, as there are no direct links between the CES and the external security matters.

Top-down approach, the role of bureaucracies and the Russian business community

When analysing Russian foreign policy, it is important to account for a major formal and informal role of the president in the hierarchic governmental structure. From the viewpoint of the bureaucratic politics model, even in the system of decision making dominated by one person, he/she does not make decisions alone, but collectively, surrounded by other high-level actors, aides and consultants. The individuals and organizations who act as agents are active participants in the process. Thus, they are also 'players' who do not just represent a mechanical device but affect the outcome in a variety of ways.[6]

So far, the CES process has been based on a strong top-down approach, with the dominant role being played by the governmental bureaucracies. It was initiated from the very top during the EU–Russia Summit in May 2001. Further, the Concept was written and negotiated exclusively by the governmental officials (of MEDT and MFA), with almost no participation of the business community and with limited interest from the general public. The only economic field of Russian–EU cooperation where the bottom-up approach has been quite strong is the energy dialogue, where big business players have been willing and able to exert influence at the decision-making level in the presidential administration and in the government. The Energy Dialogue, however, is excluded from the CES at present, although Art. 17 of the Concept declares an intention to integrate its results into the CES in due course.

The survey made by *Eurochambres* in cooperation with the Russian Chamber of Commerce reveals that the CES has not been on the agenda of the Russian business community.[7] Their counterparts in the EU have acknowledged that they had some idea of the concept of CES and the ongoing discussions. The general reaction has been supportive of the idea and optimistic about the impact this initiative could have on the potential lowering of the barriers to trade between the EU and Russia. The EU business representatives cited such benefits as general improvement of the economic relations between the EU and Russia, convergence in the regulatory areas, removal of non-tariff barriers to trade, and faster economic development in Russia. Harmonized and simplified customs procedures, as well as more transparent and less bureaucratic administration, are mentioned among the specific benefits by the EU business representatives. The security of the supply of natural resources and the enhanced possibilities for investment in Russia were also mentioned as potential benefits of the CES. Some respondents emphasized that the idea was still vague and highly political, therefore significant progress was required to turn the idea into a workable action plan. At the same time, the Russian respondents were almost unanimous in stating that they had no information on the initiative from either side in the EU–Russia dialogue. Among those who did provide comments, some businessmen believed that the CES concept could become feasible only after Russia's accession to the WTO. An opinion was also expressed that the CES would result in an even stronger shock than the WTO accession.[8]

The lobbying activities of the Russian business community are concentrated on the WTO negotiations. Russia's large businesses have been lobbying hard not only to keep higher levels of tariff protection but also to retain regulatory restrictions for foreign presence in the financial services. In the bilateral relations with the EU, most attention has been devoted to the specific down-to-earth issues such as the EU import quotas on steel, chemical products and the like. By contrast, the CES negotiations did not attract as much attention from the Russian business community. The sceptical position taken by larger companies in metallurgy and chemicals channelled through the Union of Industrialists and Entrepreneurs was the only known major case of involvement. Their position is consistent with the pressures that these sectors exert within the framework of the WTO accession.

There could be two explanations for the non-involvement of the Russian business community. Firstly, the businesses did not assign significant importance to the negotiations on the CES Concept because of its conceptual and preliminary character. Secondly, the CES development remained an internal governmental affair. The public discussion on the issue was very modest, and the business community remained largely uninformed. This situation is worrisome. The CES discourse on the Russian side seems to run detached from the grass-roots level of firms and households. As an essentially governmental undertaking, the

CES might ultimately find itself in a situation where it has insufficient support – or even persistent opposition – from the business side just when the concrete contents of the CES are being discussed.

A model for the CES and the policy-taker problem

The Concept states that the CES means 'an open and integrated market' which 'shall ultimately cover substantially all sectors of the economy' (Art. 12). The Road Map reiterates the same idea.[9] The CES is understood as an objective rather than a process. In other words, 'integration' is seen as a certain degree of movement along the three freedoms (movement of goods and services, of capital, and of people); however, the degree of integration is ambiguously defined. The list of individual priority sectors and the degree of the possible depth of the integration within them are also left open-ended. In fact, the term 'free trade' does not come up in the Concept explicitly. However, there is an implicit understanding that the CES would not – in the foreseeable future and in the current framework – move further than an FTA supplemented by a deeper degree of integration in individual sectors. The Russian President confirmed this view in one of his speeches shortly after the CES Concept was agreed upon in Rome. In his words, 'we consider that the main guideline is to create a zone of free trade with increased cooperation in individual priority sectors. This primarily concerns energy and transport, science and education, ecology and telecommunications'.[10] Nevertheless, the wording of the Road Map implies that the free trade area is off the agenda and that Russia prefers to concentrate on the sectoral issues and trade facilitation.

At the present time, there are two cases of deep and comprehensive integration agreements of the EU with non-EU states: the European Economic Area (EEA) and Switzerland. Vahl mentions that the EEA and the Swiss agreements represent two conceptually different approaches to achieving the goal of ensuring access to the EU market for companies and their products across a wide range of sectors; that is, their inclusion in the Single Market.[11] The EEA is based on a comprehensive horizontal approach incorporating the principle of the four freedoms enshrined in the Single Market, whereas the EU–Swiss arrangement is in fact a bundle of sector-specific agreements. These alternative approaches have also been considered for the CES. According to Vahl,[12] 'whereas the EU initially preferred a "horizontal" approach focusing on harmonization "across-the-board", Russia favoured a "sectoral" (or "Swiss") approach, with sector-by-sector harmonization, depending on the different effects of liberalization on competitiveness in specific sectors'.

The CES is expected to cover both horizontal and sectoral targets. A number of areas have been considered for prioritized action: standardization, technical regulation and conformity assessment, customs, audit and accounting, public procurement, competition, financial services, telecommunications, cooperation in space launching, and other sectors/issues (Art. 15). Thus, the CES Concept, followed by the Road Map, effectively employs a combined approach uniting both the horizontal base (with the reference to the overarching freedoms) and sectoral issues. The horizontal approach lays the foundation for the Concept, although it is defined broadly and restricted to the relevant fields of economic activity. It is incorporated in the Concept in a specific broad way. Art. 18 of the Concept suggests that the CES should focus on four main areas of economic activity: (1) cross-border trade in goods; (2) cross-border trade in services; (3) the establishment and operation of companies (including issues related to the movement of capital); and (4) related aspects of the movement of persons. The horizontal approach is combined with the sectoral, as the Concept assigns priority to an open list of individual sectors and issues. Thus, the Concept of CES represents an original model in itself, combining the elements of the EEA and 'Swiss' approaches.

Russia does not intend to apply for EU membership, even in a long-term perspective. If Russia's foreign policy is to be conducted in compliance with this objective, it becomes a necessity to create such a model of EU–Russian relations that would allow for an economic integration of the European Union with Russia as a non-member. While Russia is willing to adjust its legislation in accordance with its pragmatic commercial interests,[13] it will try by all means to avoid the situation of being dictated from Brussels. There are several reasons for this, among which are both the subjective national pride and the objective presence of the vital interests in the Pacific region and in Central Asia. The key term in this discussion is 'the policy-taker problem'. Essentially, the problem arises when states are obliged to follow the changes in the EU legislation while possessing only limited leverage on the EU's internal affairs. As such, it has been encountered both by Switzerland and (especially) by the non-EU members of the European Economic Area (EEA). In the meantime, it has become a more serious issue for Switzerland, too.

The question arises whether the model envisaged in the CES Concept can help avoid the policy-taker problem on the Russian side. The authors of the White Book on EU–Russia Common Spaces argue that the

CES would be better defined as a codevelopment path, 'something much more sophisticated than a traditional free-trade area, although the latter dimension is very important, and it is something radically new, which cannot be reduced to a customs union or recognition of the EU *acquis communautaire*'.[14] The codevelopment path can however take various conceptual forms. Besides, it depends on both partners in the process; in other words, there are certain limits, guidelines and reference points set both by Russia and the EU.

The EEA implies a comprehensive adoption of the EU *acquis* in exchange for good market access and the right to participate in the EU decision-shaping up to a certain extent. At the same time, it makes the non-EU members of the EEA follow changes in the EU *acquis*, adopting new directives in their own legislation as they come up ('backlog implementation'). Thus, Norway and EEA members are exposed to the policy-taker problem. The sectoral model employed in EU–Swiss agreements after Switzerland left the EEA in 1992 is aimed at enabling the state to choose those areas and *acquis* chapters that it is willing to adapt while leaving aside those that it does not want to take on board ('cherry-picking'). The EU, however, has not been willing to let the non-EU countries enjoy the advantages of such partial integration into the Internal Market without taking the costs of other chapters. This led to the specific arrangements of the EU–Swiss agreements. Comparing the various options, the EEA and the EU–Swiss agreements in particular, Emerson, Vahl and Woolcock[15] came to the conclusion that the latter provide for no substantially better regime with regard to the policy-taker dilemma. On the contrary, while exposing Switzerland to much of the EU internal legislation, this model provides substantially less access to decision shaping. For example, the EU–Swiss model requires a high degree of harmonization before mutual recognition takes place; in addition, it potentially exposes Switzerland to the EU competition policy. On the other hand, while Norway and other EEA states can participate in the Commission working groups and expert groups, Switzerland has no access to the EU internal decision-shaping process except via some multilevel channels. The short answer to the question whether the type of arrangement as with the Swiss model can provide a sufficient degree of market access while retaining more policy autonomy appears to be negative.[16] The EU market access for Swiss producers is guaranteed only when Switzerland adopts the EU *acquis*. Mutual recognition only applies in the so-called harmonized sectors in which Switzerland has fully adopted the EU regulations.

Mau and Novikov[17] argue that Norway (that is, the EEA option) may serve as the model for Russia in its relations with the EU, albeit with qualifications. At the same time, Mau and Novikov go through the chapters of the EU *acquis* trying to figure out which chapters could be beneficial for Russia (and therefore should be adopted) and which chapters could be detrimental to the Russian economy (and therefore should not become an object of the EU-Russian integration). This approach is questionable. First, as already mentioned above, the EEA model would expose the country to the policy-taker problem. The latest internal political developments in Norway show growing dissatisfaction with the EEA and growing support for EU membership. This indicates that the policy-taker problem might become a trap forcing Norway to become an EU member to be able to exert some influence on the Union's policy making and, thus, to prevent policy making from being a one-way street. Russia would also want to avoid this, unless there were an intention to move Russia gradually and imperceptibly in the direction of EU membership. Second, the divisibility of the Internal Market *acquis* may be questioned. To what extent can the Internal Market *acquis* be 'sliced up', and to what extent can the horizontal approach be eroded by the exclusion of certain areas? The experience of both the EEA and the EU–Swiss agreements shows that this is hardly possible. The EU pursues the policy of linking the advantages of access to the Internal Market to the relevant costs. For example, the EU would demand the adoption of the environmental directives so as not to allow for unjust advantages for non-EU producers. So, Russia would be pressed by the EU to balance 'advantageous' and 'disadvantageous' chapters.

In view of this discussion, it is worth mentioning that the EU–Chile trade agreement rather than the EEA or the EU–Swiss bundle of sectoral agreements served as an informal technical reference point (though not as a model) for the CES Concept negotiators. It took ten years for Chile and the EU to negotiate this very comprehensive trade agreement. The negotiators in the CES case shared the perception that a prospective EU–Russia CES agreement should be more compact.

This informal reference to the EU–Chile agreement is interesting because Chile in fact manages to cooperate successfully with both the EU and NAFTA at the same time. This is close to what Russia wants; that is, to be able to pursue independent policies in the post-Soviet space and in the Pacific region. In fact, the EU–Chile Association Agreement contains not only a comprehensive FTA for goods that goes far beyond the respective WTO commitments but also goes far in the direction of free trade in services and free movement of capital. In addition, it contains elements of cooperation on customs procedures, sanitary and phytosanitary issues, standards, technical regulations and conformity assessment, as well as intellectual property rights. There are a number of priority sectors, such as wines and spirits, for which a separate agreement is included. The agreement guarantees a non-discriminatory access to telecommunication networks. It also opens up the public procurement markets. Thus, in some respects it goes beyond the envisaged scope of the CES. At the same time, the EU–Chile relationship does not imply a direct implementation of the EU directives in the national legislation so as to sustain conformity with the European *acquis*.

So, could the EU–Chile Association Agreement serve as a model for the EU–Russia CES? The EU Commission would argue that this is not the case because of the completely different structure of EU–Russian relations, the geographic proximity, and the corresponding sets of interests. The direct neighbourhood is a crucial factor, as it defines the scope and vectors of cooperation. Unlike in the Chile case, the contents of the EU–Russia CES should prioritize such vitally important issues as energy, transport and integration of infrastructure. On all of these issues, the regulatory convergence that would assure a certain degree of legislative homogeneity is essential for successful cooperation. An integration of infrastructure, in particular, calls for a relatively horizontal approach. The need for a regulatory homogeneity on the potential common electricity market can serve as a vivid example. What Chile has with the EU is an FTA, albeit a comprehensive one, and not a common economic space, which implies an integration of neighbours.

Is the original model of the CES Concept, which combines elements of the EEA and the 'Swiss' approaches, capable of providing a satisfactory solution to the policy-taker challenge? The broad and vague definitions of the CES Concept and the Road Map do not enable us to answer this question with confidence at the present time. The situation with the policy-taker problem will depend on the more concrete contents of the CES, which are still to be elaborated. The CES Concept and the Road Map in its present form provide for a large degree of flexibility, which can be interpreted both as strength and as weakness at the same time. On the one hand, it allows Russia to be sensitive about the policy-taker dilemma; on the other hand, the Concept is defined too broadly, balancing on the verge of being devoid of substance. As the Chilean experience seems to be inapplicable to the neighbourly complexity of the EU–Russian relationship, the analysis of the EU's external economic integration agreements with the EEA and Switzerland suggests that the policy-taker problem is extremely hard to avoid if Russia is striving for a comprehensive integration with the EU. Moreover, the scope of the policy-taker problem is likely to be reinforced in the case of Russia. The EEA states and Switzerland are small countries and, as such, they naturally gravitate to the EU, both politically and economically. Russia, on the other hand, is much larger. While economically gravitating to the EU, it is bound to pursue a multifaceted foreign policy due to its geographical location. Furthermore, Russia's current efforts to reassert itself as at least a dominant regional power and to pursue the (re-)integration on the post-Soviet space may condition a negative attitude toward harmonization on the EU legislation. In such conditions, the policy-taker problem is likely to become a major hurdle on the way to EU–Russian regulatory convergence and integration.

Conclusion

So far, the CES process has been based on a strong top-down approach with the dominant role being played by the governmental bureaucracies. After being initiated at the very top, the Concept was written and negotiated on the Russian side exclusively by government officials, with very limited participation of the business community and little interest from the general public. This has created a situation in which the discourse is concentrated on a detached governmental level, with the business communities and general public uninformed, not participating, and therefore indifferent to the process and its outcome. This problem is yet to be overcome for the EU–Russian CES to be successful in the future.

The Concept specifies that the CES should move along the lines of the three freedoms (goods, services and capital), supplemented by a higher degree of integration in individual priority sectors. The CES Concept of 2003 and the Road Map of 2005 represent an original model in itself, combining elements of the EE and 'Swiss' models; that is, it unites both horizontal and sectoral approaches. The question remains open whether this model is capable of providing a satisfactory solution. The policy-taker problem represents an important challenge. As the Chilean experience seems to be inapplicable to the complexity of the EU–Russian relationship, the experience of the EEA and EU–Swiss agreements shows that the policy-taker problem will be hard to avoid if Russia strives for comprehensive integration with the EU. Moreover, its scope is likely to be larger for Russia than for the EEA states. The policy-taker problem might represent a serious hurdle to EU–Russian convergence and integration in the years to come.

Notes

1 C.B. Hamilton, 'Russia's European Economic Integration. Escapism and Realities', CEPR Discussion Paper 3840 (2003).
2 EU Commission, 'Communication to the Council and the European Parliament on relations with Russia', COM (2004) 106, 9 February 2004: 7.
3 *Road Map for the Common Economic Space*, Annex I to the Joint Statement of the Fifteenth EU–Russia Summit, Moscow, 10–11 May 2005: 1.
4 M. Emerson, 'EU–Russia Four Common Spaces and the Proliferation of the Fuzzy', CEPS Policy Brief, 71, May 2005: 1.
5 Other Common Spaces envisaged in the Joint Statement of the Twelfth EU–Russia Summit in November 2003 are the Common Space of Freedom, Security and Justice; the Common Space of External Security; and the Common Space of Research and Education.
6 G.T. Allison and P. Zelikow, *Essence of Decision* (New York: Longman, 1999): 272–3.
7 Eurochambres and the Russian Chamber of Commerce, Survey 'EU–Russia Trade and Investment: Practical Barriers', October 2003, sect. 7. www.eurochambres.be
8 Eurochambres and the Russian Chamber of Commerce, *ibid.*: 15–17.
9 Road Map (2005): 1.
10 V.V. Putin, 'Speech of the President of the Russian Federation, Mr. Vladimir Putin, at a meeting with representatives of the European Round Table of Industrialists and the Round Table of Industrialists of Russia and the EU Mission of the Russian Federation to the European communities', Press Release 38/03, 2 December 2003, www.russiaeu.org
11 M. Vahl, 'Whither the Common European Economic Space? Political and Institutional Aspects of Closer Economic Integration between the EU and Russia', in T. de Wilde d'Estmael and L. Spetschinsky, (eds). *La politique étrangère de la Russie et l'Europe* (Bruxelles: Peter Lang, 2004): 167–201.
12 *Ibid.*: 17.
13 V. Mau and V. Novikov, 'Otnosheniia ES i Rossii: prostranstvo vybora ili vybor prostranstva?', *Voprosy Ekonomiki*, 6 (2002): 133–43.
14 I. Samson and X. Greffe, *The White Book 'Common Economic Space: Prospects of Russia–EU Relations'* (Moscow: Russian-European Centre for Economic Policy, 2002): 17.
15 M. Emerson, M. Vahl and S. Woolcock, *Navigating by the Stars. Norway, the European Economic Area and the European Union* (CEPS Paperback, 2002).
16 *Ibid.*: 44–6.
17 Mau and Novikov, *ibid.*: 142.

Conclusion: Challenges of Integration – the EU, the CIS and Russia

Katlijn Malfliet, Lien Verpoest and Evgeny Vinokurov

Today, we are confronted with an enormous ambivalence in the understanding of European integration politics. Some observers stick to the 'widening versus deepening' concept and advocate a continuation of the enlargement process, be it at a slower pace. Others prefer a shift to the intergovernmental option or plead for a core Europe with a largely differentiated policy towards the various peripheries. Less often do observers look at the pan-European perspective, which includes a view on Russian foreign policy and CIS integration processes.

Instead of traditionally studying developments in EU integration and their implications for the rest of Europe, this book started with an analysis of the CIS as an integration mechanism. In Part I, Irina Kobrinskaya and Evgeny Vinokurov looked at a process that we ambitiously called 'In Pursuit of Integration within the Post-Soviet Space'. Notwithstanding the difficulties of finding the right conceptual approaches for the developments in the post-Soviet space, both authors observe a field of changing national and international priorities that do not eliminate this loose construction of CIS international cooperation, although member states are reluctantly and selectively entering into hard law obligations. The EU is playing an important role in the integration design of the post-Soviet space. It is being mirrored both in the strategies and the design of the regional integration constructed by Moscow. The Russian Medium Term Strategy 'makes a provision for the utilization of successful experiences of the EU in the development of integration processes in the CIS area'. The original idea for CIS cooperation promoted by Russia relied on integration along the lines of the four freedoms, which had to be accompanied by concerted monetary, budgetary, tax, customs and currency politics as well as the harmonization of economic legislation. The Russian presidential decree of 14 September 1995 was an early announcement of this approach: the position of CIS states was considered by Russia as dependent on its relations with Russia, thus conditioning the scope of economic, political and military assistance that Russia would be willing to render to its CIS neighbours. The recent integration designs are characterized by the same approach. Although the CIS is supposed to move in stages toward a full-scale EU type of common market, this ambition has – in a kind of intermediate stage – moved towards sub-regional integration processes, such as the Single Economic Space. The latter is strongly supported by Russia, but Belarus, Ukraine and Kazakhstan have also joined.

Although the CIS has not lived up to its hopes of creating an EU-type identity, it did not collapse either. Some sub-regional entities (the Single Economic Space, the Eurasian Economic Community and the Collective Security Treaty Organization) possess remarkable 'development enhancing' or catalyzing features. The approach of the CIS as a multi-speed and multilevel integration mechanism with embedded flexibility is one of them. Another is the weighted voting on common decisions, which will automatically lead to the dominance of Russia.

Perhaps we have grown tired of the continuous failures within the CIS (treaties were not signed, ratified or implemented by the parties, summits did not come to final decisions and so on). The Kazan summit in summer 2005 admitted that the CIS found itself on a threshold: either it would achieve significant advances or it would be washed away completely. Contrary to the previous period, Russia is now willing to accept the costs in order to push other CIS states towards integration.

Also in the first part, John Willerton and Mikhail Beznosov carefully weighed the CIS alternative bilateral–multilateral arrangements in order to analyse Russia's pursuit of its Eurasian Security interests. Using the analysis results of an extensive database of CIS security agreements, they concluded that we are confronted with a multi-tiered approach that has a logic permitting engagement with unilateral discretion. Nearly a decade and a half of extensive negotiation has yielded a complex set of arrangements representing varying levels of collective security for different groups of FSU–CIS states. With no state surrendering its sovereignty and a resurgent Russia continuing to assert its 'natural' regional leadership role, any region-wide collective security arrangement will have to be sufficiently flexible to maintain all states' active engagement. The multi-tiered approach that Russia and other FSU states have taken permits engagement with unilateral discretion. For the CIS security space, the operational word is 'potential'. The CIS emerges as a multi-tiered approach to regional security and a combined approach of multilateralism and bilateralism. Willerton and Beznosov saw this security cooperation as having evolved from 'narrow' multilateralism in the early 1990s to multi-tiered cooperation combining multilateralism with 'expansive' bilateralism.

In this regard, the CIS's past achievements and future promise should not be discounted. A complex set of arrangements that represents varying levels of security for different groups of FSU–CIS states has been established, with none of the states ceding its sovereignty. This approach guarantees sufficient flexibility for maintaining all states' active engagement while Russia continues to assert its 'natural' regional leadership role. In this way, the authors came to the conclusion that – looking at the multilateral security architecture that has been built in the period of 1992–2004 – a workable foundation of understandings and arrangements was laid.

In summary of the book's first part, we can say that notwithstanding all doubts about a possible future for CIS integration (and by this we mean not only the CIS agreements *per se* but the whole ensemble of integration agreements and mechanisms), its authors agree on two things. First, although the integration in the post-Soviet space cannot be characterized as a success, it cannot be judged as a failure either. Second, a difficult balance still has to be reached between the reluctance of the member states to cede (part of) their sovereignty, the need for Russia to assert its 'natural' leadership and the idea of a multilateral economic and security architecture. Various factors suggest that the integration in the post-Soviet space has certain prospects, as it continues to reinvent and to reidentify itself. Third, the evolution of Russian foreign policy is central to the process. Russia is now ready to pay the price for reasserting its influence in the post-Soviet space (by asserting its leading role and by increasing its global weight), hoping that integration will pay off threefold – economically, in terms of security and geopolitically.

In the second part of this book, we looked at the developing relations between the EU and the post-Soviet space. This relation developed, until recently, in the framework of EU foreign policy. One of the most important trademarks of EU foreign policy is its structural character, starting from a soft security concept and trying to develop relations with neighbouring countries and regions by exporting its magnificent idea of peace through democracy and the market. Marius Vahl and Holger Moroff carefully analysed this policy. The Common Foreign and Security Policy of the European Union, a rather recent and ambitious move, envisioned the relations with Russia and the former Soviet republics as a priority. The Common Strategy towards Russia was, however, one of the admitted failures of this CFSP in its difficult fight with the national interests of EU member states. Relations with CIS countries have been least developed, but in the course of the 1990s the EU was forced to review its relations with Russia and the CIS countries. EU enlargement entailed new ideas on the 'strategic partnership' with Russia. It became clear that Russia understood quite differently the 'strategic partnership' than the EU. On the other hand, we must recognize that during the first years of PCA implementation, Russia somehow strengthened the EU through the idea that it could behave as a normative power. After enlargement to the eight post-communist countries and as a consequence of Russia's assertive nation-building strategy, the Russian discourse changed to a more selective approach, taking the concept of partnership more seriously as a mutually beneficiary bilateral relation between two international subjects.

The Eastern Enlargement induced the European Union to rethink its integration policy in more cautious terms. The European Neighbourhood Policy is clearly an alternative for the option of enlargement by membership applications. In this perspective, Tom Casier introduced constructivist concepts and looked for the limitations of declared ideas in foreign policy. The EU presented the ENP as mainly a security policy aiming at stability for the enlarged EU by creating privileged and differentiated relations with the states surrounding the European Union. The EU presented this as an advantage to the new neighbours because it provides the opportunity of sharing the benefits of European integration without having the prospect of membership. The question is of course whether the logic of 'appropriateness', which included conditionality in accession (Schimmelfennig), can work if the crucial incentive is absent: the neighbours lack the prospect of membership, although they benefit from some of the fruits of integration.

The third part of this book looked at various patterns of integration within the CIS space. Lien Verpoest discussed how isomorphism plays its role in the institutional adaptation of Ukraine and Belarus. The institutional parallels between the structures of the organizational fields of the CIS and EU are of particular interest. Mechanisms of CIS integration in general and other sub-regional initiatives in particular (EEP, EEC) reveal interesting similarities with EU integration efforts. In particular, the institutionalization of the Belarus–Russia state, as well as Putin's repeated statements that Belarus–Russia integration should evolve on the lines of EU integration appears to be an explicit case of institutional mirroring between organizational fields.

Rilka Dragneva and Antoaneta Dimitrova chose the case of Ukraine between the CIS and the EU to discuss patterns of integration and regime compatibility. Ukraine surely has recognized its interest in participating in the CIS but, as many other former USSR republics, it has been ambivalent in its CIS policies and has been reluctant to legally underwrite commitments within a Russia-led organization. Possible incompatibility between membership in the EU and in the CIS is an important drive for this hesitating attitude. The authors make an important distinction between legal obstacles to the relation with EU and CIS regimes and the perception of their incompatibility.

Another pattern of integration is the so-called absorption hypothesis, according to which the Russian Federation provides prospects for admitting states or parts of states as new subjects for the Russian Federation. Katlijn Malfliet and Gennadi Kurdiukov explored this troubling and important, though under-researched, subject. Belarus could be thought of as a case of full integration into the Russian Federation. Those who would reject the idea of an independent state being absorbed by another state will be confronted with the precedent of the former GDR, which was absorbed by West Germany. Breakaway regions of the post-Soviet states represent another facet of this issue. Frozen conflicts, creating tension within the former Soviet republics, but also in the relations to Russia and to the European and international communities, trigger the image of Russia as a peacekeeper and possible homeland for regions as Transnistria, Abkhasia and South Ossetia. This option, as a possible path for integration, lost its purely hypothetical character as a Russian federal constitutional law regulated the possible absorption of former Soviet Union republics or parts of them, thus giving Russia a capacity to profile itself as a multi-tier governance structure and as an actor of 'modernized Russification'.

Finally, Evgeny Vinokurov discussed the EU–Russia Common Economic Space as an essential component of the EU–Russian potential integration framework. The four Common Spaces provide an interesting integration path, as they allow Russia to distance itself from the ENP while providing an original model combining elements of the EEA and 'Swiss' models, uniting horizontal and sectoral approaches. But notwithstanding the potential of the EU–Russian bilateral integration, the road to EU–Russian integration will be bumpy. One of the reasons to think so is that, as Vinokurov argued, the Common Spaces model is not necessarily capable of providing a satisfactory solution to the policy-taker problem; that is, the obligation to converge unilaterally on the EU legislation and to follow the changes in the EU legislation while possessing only limited leverage over EU internal affairs. As the policy-taker problem is likely to be very sensitive for Russia, it can become one of the major hurdles. All in all, however, the EU–Russia Common Spaces outline a comprehensive integration, which is capable of having a major impact on the European continent and the post-Soviet space.

We regard two major powers in the post-Soviet space: on the one hand, the enlarged European Union and, on the other, Russia, who now possesses not only the ambition to become a self-conscious nation with great power but who also has the means to do so. Russia, as repeated throughout the book, is willing to invest in further integration with its neighbours. The perception of the impact and role of these two powers on the European theatre becomes increasingly important.

The former Soviet Union republics are reluctant to come under Russia's shadow again. But the in-built flexibility with exit options and reliance on soft law makes it possible for Russia to hold all former USSR republics. Nevertheless, the CIS is coming to a critical point in its development: either it steps up its integration or it will lose all attractiveness. In this process, we see that the multilateral level is being abandoned for a more consistent approach, which represents a combination of restrictive mul-tilateralism and bilateralism. Ukraine is a good example in this perspec-tive. Ukraine has great economic interests in the CIS, especially in the Single Economic Space, but it does not want to get stuck in a corner as its major foreign policy aim is EU membership. The question remains whether the two memberships will still be compatible after the creation and implementation of a CIS customs union. The EU has always behaved as a cool lover towards Ukraine, and the New Neighbourhood Policy made this even more obvious: the EU is not eager to take in Ukraine. If the EU were to accept Ukraine, Georgia, Moldova or other CIS members, the EU would have 35 plus members. Look at the picture through the scope of Russian minorities: around 10 million Russians would the reside in the European Union. Quietly, the scenario of FSU countries (excepting the Baltic states) joining the EU has become hypothetical.

What about another scenario, a real 'divorce' picture, where all CIS members take their own foreign policy decisions whether to leave or to stay? That scenario is launched by Georgia, Moldova and Ukraine, coun-tries where overtly anti-Russian political elites hold power and spread the news that they are prepared to quit the CIS. The alternatives are uncertain, however, as EU membership is hardly an option. Perhaps they could remain together in an anti-Russian coalition, sustained by the West, including the USA. But in this case they would be cut off from their primary energy provider and the largest market nearby. Perhaps they could really go for an intensive cooperation with the USA, as Azerbaijan could envisage.

These scenarios are weak against the possibility that Russia will continue its quest for influence in the CIS through its multi-speed and multilevel integration. Economic imperialism is a very important reason to do so. The psychological factor of post-Soviet shock is another. Russia is continuously striving to be *the* regional power. Nevertheless, we observe that despite certain recoil in the second Putin presidency, Russian foreign policy in the 2000s has, on the whole, become more discernible and predictable in a pragmatic way.

All parties and states willingly or inadvertently involved in the processes of integration in the post-Soviet space face their own challenges of integration. Let us conclude by outlining the challenges ahead.

Russia faces the challenge of defining, sustaining, and advancing its integration with neighbouring countries. This challenge is enormous, taking into account that the FSU states are often reluctant to integrate with the dominant neighbour. Consequently, Russia's striving for influence/dominance in the post-Soviet space has a bumpy road ahead. One should also take into account the strong link between Russian domestic and foreign politics. Russian domestic developments are crucial for the whole integration process in the sense that a more democratic and market-oriented Russia is likely to pursue different paths and utilize different means to achieve its integration goals. It is also very likely to be more attractive to its neighbours. In contrast, a more authoritarian Russia is likely to be more willing to emphasize geopolitics to the detriment of its economic welfare.

A separate line of consideration is the Russia–Belarus Union. Both sides face the challenge of upgrading the Union to have a properly functioning customs union, a common currency or even a common state; these are potential goals.

Very importantly, in its relations with the EU, Russia faces the task of putting substance into its integration pursuits within the four Common Spaces. It is likely to go down multiple paths: a horizontal approach (freedom of movement of goods and services, capital and people) and a sectoral approach wherein sector-specific agreements are concluded. The EU–Russian integration in the fields of economics and security may have enormous implications for the whole post-Soviet space. The potential effects of Russia strengthening its European choice and becoming an integral and inherent part of Europe are huge. A comprehensive EU–Russia integration (falling short of EU membership but perhaps eventually reaching the scope of the European Economic Area or the EU–Swiss agreements) would become a major anchor of stability and prosperity in the region.

For the EU, the challenge is twofold. First, it has to advance the ENP, making it a workable and attractive instrument of integration given the mounting unwillingness to enlarge indefinitely. Second, the European Union has to define and advance its integration with the largest post-Soviet state, Russia. Progress in EU–Russia relations has been slower than anticipated in the early to mid-1990s. We observe a worrisome divide between words and deeds. The challenge of EU–Russian integration is complicated by the intricate links with the ENP and by the necessity to design and implement an efficient *Ostpolitik*. Although Russia is not part of the ENP, the two EU policies are thoroughly interdependent.

For Ukraine, the challenges of integration are vital. The country faces the delicate and increasingly difficult task of defining and pursuing national interests while balancing Russia and the EU. The compatibility of simultaneous integration with the EU and Russia is under question but, as is often the case in real life, the possibility of choosing just one side is wishful thinking. Ukraine will have to maintain and develop relations with both the EU and Russia. This is a task of enormous complexity.

Similar challenges are faced by Georgia, Moldova and other post-Soviet states on the European continent. It might also become the challenge for Belarus, should it become a more democratic and open state. GUAM is one means used by the states of the western CIS to escape the dominance of Russia and cooperate in the fields of security, economy and energy supplies.

Lastly, although we did not touch explicitly the five Central Asian states of the former Soviet Union, their challenges are at least as complicated as those of the states in the western CIS. Kazakhstan, Uzbekistan, and their smaller neighbours face the challenge of balancing between Russia, the USA (which has vast interests in Central Asia) and the rising power, China. They are eager not to be attached exclusively to Russia through such integration frameworks as the SES and EurAsEC but to develop closer links in the Asian direction; for example, through the Shanghai cooperation or through a web of bilateral links. In doing this, the keywords are 'security' and 'infrastructure'. The latest Russian–Kazakh initiative, the Eurasian Development Bank, is a move in this direction, as the Bank will focus on supporting joint infrastructural projects in the region.

Going back to the European continent, the major question is how the overlapping near abroads of the EU and the CIS will be perceived. Will Europe have its *in-between countries* again? To avoid this outcome is probably the most important challenge of European integration. An optimal scenario is connected to Russia pursuing comprehensive integration with the EU. That would probably make it possible for the two major powers, Russia and the EU, to reconcile their interests and to cooperate in making the post-Soviet space a stable and prosperous area through a network of comprehensive integration agreements.

Index